CL16

...rkov

• Stavropol

PERSIA

• Odessa

B L A C K

S E A

Constanza

Wallachia

SYRIA

• Bucharest

ANIA

• Constantinople

BULGARIA

CYPRUS

OTTOMAN
EMPIRE

• Sophia

SERBIA

R E D
S E A

M E D I T E R R A N E A N

ALBANIA   GREECE

S E A

Key	
——	Borders
- - - -	Front line 1914
◇	*Battles/Events*

THE EASTERN FRONT
1914–1920

THE HISTORY OF WORLD WAR I

THE EASTERN FRONT
1914–1920

FROM TANNENBERG TO THE RUSSO-POLISH WAR

MICHAEL S. NEIBERG & DAVID JORDAN

FOREWORD BY PROFESSOR GARY SHEFFIELD

amber
BOOKS

This edition first published in 2008

Published by
Amber Books Ltd
Bradley's Close
74–77 White Lion Street
London N1 9PF
United Kingdom
www.amberbooks.co.uk

ISBN: 978-1-906626-00-6

Series Commissioning Editor: Charles Catton
Editorial: Ilios Publishing, Oxford, UK
Picture Research: Terry Forshaw and Susannah Jayes
Design: Jerry Williams
Cartography: Patrick Mulrey
Indexer: David Worthington

For editorial or picture enquiries please contact editorial@amberbooks.co.uk

Printed in Dubai

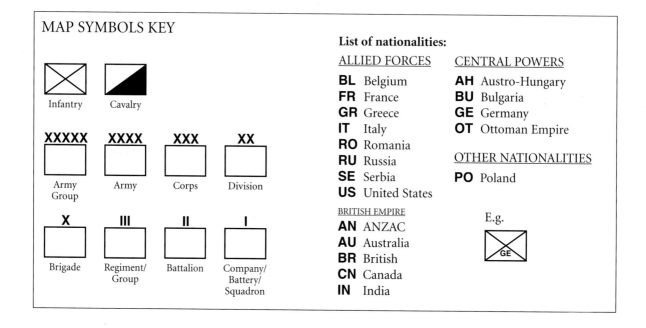

MAP SYMBOLS KEY

Infantry	Infantry
Cavalry	Cavalry
XXXXX	Army Group
XXXX	Army
XXX	Corps
XX	Division
X	Brigade
III	Regiment/Group
II	Battalion
I	Company/Battery/Squadron

List of nationalities:

ALLIED FORCES

BL Belgium
FR France
GR Greece
IT Italy
RO Romania
RU Russia
SE Serbia
US United States

BRITISH EMPIRE
AN ANZAC
AU Australia
BR British
CN Canada
IN India

CENTRAL POWERS

AH Austro-Hungary
BU Bulgaria
GE Germany
OT Ottoman Empire

OTHER NATIONALITIES

PO Poland

E.g.
GE

Contents

Foreword

When the Berlin Wall came down in 1989, it triggered the beginning of the end of a period of history that began with the assassination of Archduke Franz Ferdinand in Sarajevo 75 years earlier. The death of the heir to the thrones of Austria-Hungary fanned the smouldering embers of international rivalry into life, and within six weeks most of Europe was at war. World War I destroyed the existing international balance; brought down mighty empires; created the conditions that led to the rise of fascism and communism; made a second global conflagration likely, if not inevitable; and even sowed the seeds of the Cold War. When, after the collapse of the Soviet Union in 1991, historians looked back, they readily identified 1914, the outbreak of World War I, as the beginning of the 'Short Twentieth Century', the bloodiest period in history.

Such a critical era demands to be properly understood, and I am delighted that such a distinguished Anglo-American team of historians – all of them acknowledged experts in their fields – have written a series of admirably accessible books on the war. As it happens, all of them are colleagues, past or present. They have succeeded magnificently in presenting accounts of the key campaigns that skilfully interweave narrative with some incisive analysis incorporating up-to-date research. This is grown-up history for the 21st century.

Gary Sheffield
Professor of War Studies
Centre for First World War Studies
University of Birmingham

A Russian soldier on the Eastern Front.

INTRODUCTION

The Balance in the East

Russia's defeat at Japan's hands in the Russo-Japanese War (1904–05) left her humbled and beaten. The determination of her leaders to return their nation to the ranks of great powers ran counter to massive internal structural problems. Austria-Hungary's threats to Serbia in 1914 gave those leaders the chance they sought to once again play the role of great power.

There is an old Russian adage that proclaims that Russia is never as strong as she looks, but Russia is never as weak as she looks. In 1914 it was hard for anyone, including the Russians themselves, to know exactly how weak or strong Russia was. Politically the country seemed to have recovered from the revolution of 1905, and the regime of Tsar Nicholas II seemed to most observers to be as solidly in place as ever. Economically, the country remained overwhelmingly agricultural, but it had made some important strides in industrial production in the first years of the twentieth century and was now capable of producing much more of what it needed.

The violence and upheaval of the 1905 Revolution soon passed, leaving the Tsarist system in full control of Russian politics. It was, however, a haunting reminder to many Russians of what might happen if Russia lost another war.

Diplomatically, Russia had alliances in place with France and Britain, although the former was both more secure and more important in terms of Russian foreign policy.

RUSSIA'S ALLIANCES

Russia's immense size and human resources made it an ideal ally, especially for France. Sitting on the eastern edge of Germany, Russia provided a massive counterweight, distracting German attention away from France. Over the years, the French had repeatedly urged the Russians to agree to aggressive, offensive strategies in the event of war designed to place the maximum amount of pressure on the Germans from two directions at once. To sweeten the deal and to improve Russia's internal lines of communications, the French had invested heavily in Russian railway networks in order to allow the Russians to move supplies to the front much more quickly than had ever been possible before.

The British alliance was, for both sides, much more a matter of convenience. The Anglo-Russian understandings had been designed to eliminate the threat that war might break out between the two powers over the issue of Afghanistan, and with it the western approaches to India. With the threat of war in Central Asia removed, Russia and Britain were free to devote their energies to other pursuits. Russia's decision to extend its influence east into Manchuria had met with disaster at the hands of the Japanese, making the British alliance all the more important in giving the Russians time to recover.

Nevertheless, although the Russian alliance made good strategic sense for both Britain and France, neither country was totally happy with the association. Both France and Britain were democratic societies with representative governments and active socialist movements. The Russians, by contrast, stood for all of the worst aspects of reaction and

Bulgarian troops during the Balkan Wars. Still reeling from defeat to the Japanese in 1904–05, Russian leaders stayed out of the Balkan Wars of 1912 and 1913. They were determined not to risk irrelevance in the region by staying out of the Balkan Crisis in 1914.

repression, offering their subjects virtually none of the freedoms that Frenchmen and Britons had come to take for granted.

The left in both countries disliked having their foreign policies tied to that of the Tsar and his regime while the right in both countries tended to remain suspicious of Russian expansionist designs. Especially in Britain, diplomats were very careful not to commit themselves to do too much to help the Russians in the event of a crisis. Nothing in the Anglo-Russian agreements signed in this period bound Britain to go to war for Russia's sake.

The Franco-Russian agreement, by contrast, did contain measures for collective security. France needed Russia much more than Britain did and as a result had come to live with the distasteful aspects of a

The 7.62mm Russian Mosin-Nagant rifle dated to 1891. Designed by a Russian and manufactured in Belgium, it was an adequate rifle for veterans, but was inaccurate in the hands of inexperienced soldiers. The Mauser rifle used by the Germans was a better weapon.

Russian alliance. The French had named a beautiful bridge (the Pont Alexandre III, ironically located just a few hundred metres from where Napoleon is entombed) for Nicholas II's father. In 1896, after Nicholas himself laid the first foundation stone. The flattery of the bridge was part of a much larger series of contacts between the two nations that went far beyond the diplomatic. French investment in Russia increased dramatically and cultural contacts increased as well. In 1909 the Ballets Russes made their first appearance in France to rave reviews. Strategic necessity had indeed made for strange bedfellows.

For the Russians, the alliances with Britain and France helped to secure a diplomatic situation that posed a number of challenges. After 1905 the Russians had largely given up on extending their influence in the East, and had decided to re-engage in the West. They hoped to increase their influence in the Balkans and improve their image significantly among the great powers of Europe. All three of the great Eastern European empires, however, stood in their way.

Their most intractable foe was the Austro-Hungarian Empire, which deeply resented Russian meddling in the Balkans and Russian support for Serbia, whose bellicose leaders dreamed of creating a powerful, pro-Russian pan-Slavic state. Russian interest in the Balkans also unnerved Ottoman Turkey, which had lost two recent wars against Serbia and its Balkan allies.

Nor, despite their diplomatic connections, were the French and British entirely pleased with Russian expansionism. Virtually all Europeans suspected that the ultimate Russian goal was control of the warm-

Nicholas II (1868–1918)

Assuming the throne in 1894 at the age of 26, Nicholas and his wife were firm advocates of the absolutist principle that gave the Tsar the right to rule Russia by the will of God. In 1905 he had to agree to reforms in the face of revolution, but in 1911 he appointed a conservative prime minister who helped him to roll back many of the changes. Insecure and sensitive, he distrusted most of his close advisers and came to rely on the advice of his wife. She proved as insensitive to the suffering of the Russian people as he did, resulting in the slow royal reaction to the misery of the Russian people in wartime.

Republican France and autocratic Russia formed an unexpected yet durable alliance. The two powers had agreed to conduct major offensives as quickly as possible in the event of war to keep Germany off balance.

water ports in Ottoman Turkey, with Constantinople as the biggest prize of all.

A Russian acquisition of Constantinople represented a much greater leap in Russian power than either France or Britain (to say nothing of Germany and Austria-Hungary) envisioned. After all, the French and British had united just 50 years earlier to fight the Crimean War specifically to prevent such an occurrence. Allies they may have been, but no one in Paris or London wanted to see the Russians gain such a powerful foothold on the eastern Mediterranean. Moreover, most officials in Europe presumed that if Russia did gain Constantinople, it could well lead to the dissolution of the Ottoman Empire, an event that neither the French nor the British advocated in 1914.

The situation with the Ottoman Empire presented Russia with one of its major foreign policy and military problems. The gradual weakening of the Ottomans had led observers to call it the 'sick man of Europe', and most Russians concluded that the collapse of the Ottoman Empire should provide some important opportunities for Russia to fill the power vacuum. Perhaps more importantly, the Russians were loath to see their Austro-Hungarian rivals gain at the Ottomans' expense instead.

The Ottomans, moreover, presented an unusual problem for the Russians because of their religious and ethnic affinity with the millions of Muslims the Russians had forcibly annexed in the Caucasus region. Russian fears that the Ottomans might issue a call for jihad that would set their southern territories ablaze both gave them cause to seek a more pliable regime in Constantinople and sufficient anxieties about the prospects of war with the Turks.

THE PROBLEM OF SERBIA

But Turkey was just one of several fronts the Russians had to defend. From a social and domestic political standpoint the Austro-Hungarian front was the most important. For almost a decade, the Austrians had been locked in a struggle with a resurgent Serbia for influence in the Balkans. This conflict affected Russia through the development of a pan-Slavic ideology used by the Russians to justify their position as a guarantor of freedom to Slavs in southeastern Europe. Focusing on a shared culture and adherence to Orthodox Christianity, the Tsar and his advisers had styled themselves the protectors of the Slavs of

Russia suffered crippling losses in the Russo-Japanese War, forcing a major rearmament effort after the war, much of it funded by France. The Russians hoped to complete their rearmament plan in 1917.

overall Serbian exports grew dramatically as a result of the crisis, underscoring the failure of the Austrian policy and boosting Serbian revenue. Frustrated, the Austro-Hungarians annexed the province of Bosnia-Herzegovina in 1908 partly to close off that market to the Serbs.

Serbia read the annexation as a threat to their security and a not very cleverly veiled warning from Vienna to fall in line or face a similar fate. The Serbs responded by increasing their calls for the formation of a greater Slavic state in the Balkans that would unite peoples from around the region. As those in Vienna understood all too well, hundreds of thousands of those people lived inside the Austro-Hungarian Empire. The Austro-Hungarians therefore heard Serbian calls as a threat to the very unity and sanctity of the empire itself. As tensions between the two states increased, the Serbs naturally called on their Russian 'protectors' to put some action into their frequent and extravagant statements of pan-Slavic harmony.

Even without much Russian support, the Slavs themselves handled the Turks through the formation of a Balkan League that humiliated Ottoman armies in the Balkan Wars of 1912 and 1913. As a result of these victories, Serbia doubled in size and more than doubled in confidence and hubris. Still reeling from its debacle in 1904 and 1905, and unwilling to fight the Ottomans over a third-party conflict, the Russians had done little to help the Balkan League in its fight. Some

the Balkans against either Turkish or Austro-Hungarian pressure.

Austro-Hungarian relations with Serbia grew increasingly shrill and tense. In 1903, a bloody coup in Serbia had violently replaced a generally pro-Austrian regime with an openly pro-Russian one. Three years later, the Austrians responded with a trade embargo against Serbia's most important export product, thus giving the controversy the name 'the pig war'. The embargo backfired, as Serbia quickly found new Bulgarian, French, Russian and even German markets for its pork. With the help of Russian financing,

Russians feared that their failure to help the Serbs in the war might undermine their role as Slavic protector, but the Serbian victory left both the Serbs and the Russians in a jubilant mood. Serbia had achieved at least regional power status and, consequently, Russia's closest Balkan ally had become a real asset. The situation in the Balkans, however, was a tinderbox waiting for a spark.

Ironically, given the blood that flowed between the Germans and the Russians in the twentieth century, many Russians in 1914 saw Germany as the least of their problems. A significant number of ethnic Germans (the so-called Baltic Germans) held key

Siberian troops defend Port Arthur against a Japanese assault during the Russo-Japanese War of 1905. One of the features of the war was the extensive use of entrenchments on the battlefield, a fact that was not picked up by the major European powers.

positions in the Russian administrative, professional, business and even military elite. Tsar Nicholas II enjoyed much more cordial relations with his cousin Kaiser Wilhelm II than he did with his other cousin, Britain's King George V. The Tsar's wife was known to be openly pro-German and even among many Slavophile Russians there was admiration for the efficiency, wealth and modernization of the Germans. There was also an undeniable similarity in the way both the Russian and German political elites mistrusted and feared the spread of democracy and constitutionalism.

But if there was much in common between Russia and Germany, there was much pulling them apart as well. As we will explore below, the Germans did not reciprocate any admiration of Russia. More importantly, the Germans had come to see the Russians as part of the great 'encirclement' of

Germany along with France and Britain. Thus while the Kaiser and the Tsar might enjoy one another's company, Wilhelm was angry at Nicholas's continued alliances with Britain and France. Conflict between the two seemed inevitable, even if much of that conflict owed its origin to problems between the two powers' allies as much as any problems between the powers themselves.

GERMANY

The Germans, for their part, saw nothing worth admiring in Russia. Much of this attitude came from centuries-old German racism against Slavs. The Germans saw in the Russians, and Slavs more generally, everything that they despised. The Russians were the polar opposites of Germans: unruly, filthy, and backward in almost every sense. They had failed to take advantage of the massive natural resources of the Russian hinterland and had been badly humbled by an Asian power in war, both inexcusable failings in the eyes of early twentieth-century Germans. If anything, the Slavs were seen as impediments to the modernization and development of Eastern Europe and its incorporation into the European system.

German disregard for the Russians had serious consequences. The Germans expected that the Russians would be slow to mobilize and inefficient in their use of their military power. German officers were aware of some of the strengths of the Russians, especially the size of their army and the expanse of their territories, but the Germans were not afraid. They presumed that the natural German advantages of efficiency, leadership and industry would allow them to win a war against a gigantic, but clumsy Russia. Most German senior officers, moreover, believed that an offensive war against Russia was preferable to defensive holding operations because a major offensive would put unbearable strains on the Russian state, as the war against Japan had done in 1904 and 1905.

Germany's Count Alfred von Schlieffen counted on a slow Russian mobilization in designing Germany's war plans. He expected that the size of Russia and its presumed inefficiency would buy Germany six weeks to defeat France.

In part because the Germans disregarded both the ability and agility of the Russians, German war planners decided to execute an attack on France first. German planners presumed that the Russians would take at least six weeks to mobilize their forces and begin to move west. The now famous Schlieffen Plan thus gambled everything on a lightning strike through Belgium and France that would isolate Paris and force the surrender of the French Government at the end of those six weeks. Then the Germans could move their forces east by train and be ready to defend against any Russian offensive that might materialize. If, as some suspected, the Russians had still not mobilized fully within six weeks, then the Germans could conduct an attack of their own into Russia.

The astonishing confidence of the plan would not have been possible without the equally astonishing manner in which the Germans dismissed the Russians out of hand. Simply put, virtually no one in the German leadership could image a scenario whereby

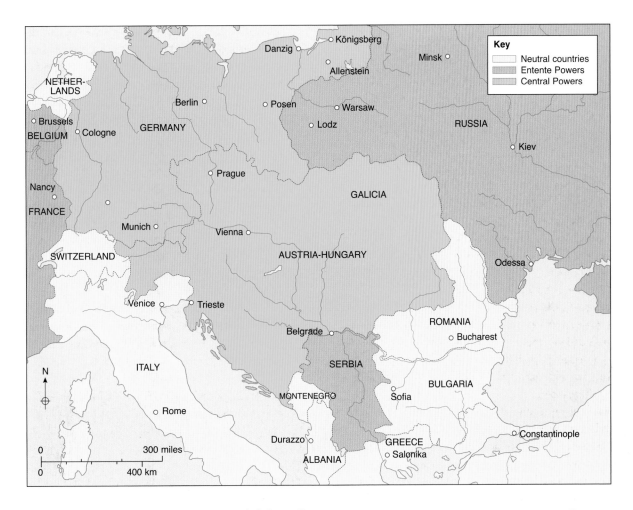

Key
- Neutral countries
- Entente Powers
- Central Powers

the Russians could mobilize, deploy and fight well enough in the war's opening weeks and months to influence German strategy and operations in Western Europe. Only a few officers understood enough of the Schlieffen Plan to see how much of a gamble it really was. If even one of its guiding assumptions proved false, then the entire eastern part of Germany would lay dangerously exposed to a Russian advance. East Prussia, the part of Germany most directly in the path of any likely Russian advance, was also home to the estates of many members of the German elite.

The fear and dread of what a Slavic occupation of Germany might mean kept at least one member of that elite awake at night. Paul von Hindenburg had retired from a distinguished German military career to his East Prussian estate. He spent much of his

The massive size of the Eastern Front made it virtually impossible for armies to construct the kinds of trench systems that characterized the Western Front. Geographic features like forests, swamps and mountains also played larger roles in the east.

retirement walking around East Prussia examining the possible avenues of approach the Russians might take around the region's forests and lakes, and then envisioning the most effective German counter-measures. According to one anecdote, he was not entirely happy with what he saw. His wife had asked him his opinion of planting apple trees on the estate and he is supposed to have responded that there was no point, as the only people who would eat the apples would be Russians. Little did he know both that he would soon have the chance to defend East Prussia

two countries shared a long border that opened up many opportunities to develop shared transportation and military infrastructures. Friendly relations allowed each country to save the tremendous expense of fortifying the border. Economic links were also strong, helping to convince the Hungarian part of the empire of the value of closer links to Germany.

Still, trust between the Catholic Austrians and the Protestant Prussians had never run too deep. Most of the senior Austrian officers had forgiven, but not forgotten the Prussian humbling of Austria in the war of 1866. To their eyes, the Germans appeared arrogant and generally condescending. The Germans, for their part, shared Napoleon's famous view of the Habsburgs as being always one army, one idea and one year too late. The largely agricultural Austro-Hungarian Empire lacked the funds to modernize its army to German expectations and, much to Germany's chagrin, the Austrians played far too many games in the Balkan backwater rather than focusing on the Russians.

Relations grew even worse when Germany broke off general staff talks with the Austrians in 1911 because of their suspicions that the Russians had a

Alfred Redl was an Austrian officer who spied for Russia. His unmasking led to his suicide and a German presumption that the Austro-Hungarian military could not be trusted. As a result the two allies shared very little strategic information, hampering the Central Powers' war effort.

and that one day, after another war with the Russians, the estate would indeed transfer to a Slavic state, but that it would be Poland, not Russia.

Hindenburg's worries were a minority viewpoint. Few other German officials would have delayed planting fruit trees out of fear of the Russians. Oddly enough, most Germans spent more time worrying about their two allies than they did their largest potential enemy. Connections with Austria-Hungary should have been excellent. Military elites in both countries spoke German and both saw Russia as a likely future enemy. The Austro–German alliance was one of the oldest and most solid in Europe, and the

Kaiser Wilhelm II (1859–1941)

Assuming the throne in 1888, the young Kaiser Wilhelm II took control of German affairs by dismissing the legendary Otto von Bismarck in 1890. He possessed a petty jealousy of his English cousins, once calling King Edward VII 'Satan'. Anxious to improve Germany's global position, he advocated the construction of an expensive navy and pressed for Germany to challenge the British and French for colonial holdings worldwide. He widely admired the military and revelled in his role as supreme commander of the German armed forces. He understood the military much less than his demeanour suggested, however. His bellicosity played a major role in the increasingly hostile European environment of the pre-war years.

spy in the highest ranks of the Austro-Hungarian Army. They were right. The spy's name was Alfred Redl, a highly respected intelligence officer who was credited with many innovative techniques. In 1907, Redl had been named head of Austrian intelligence and was one of the highest-ranking officers in the army. He was also homosexual and deeply in debt, two facts that the Russians discovered. They began alternately to bribe and blackmail him into giving them Austro-Hungarian military secrets. German intelligence officials picked up on the betrayal before the Austrians did as a result of an envelope filled with cash that had been sent from Berlin to a post office in Vienna, presumably by Russian agents. The letter, addressed to a pseudonym that Redl used, was returned to Berlin where its contents were discovered and, when combined with the discovery of another letter sent to that address that contained the addresses of spy centres in France and Switzerland, raised the alarm.

The Germans informed the Austrians of their discovery of a spy. The Austrians staked out the post office hoping to find out the real identity of the man using the pseudonym. Ironically enough, intelligence officers Redl had personally trained found him out and confronted him in May 1913. Under questioning by his own methods, Redl admitted that he had been a spy but it remains unclear if he gave the Austrians much other information of use. His examiners left the room after placing a loaded revolver on the table. They had given Redl the chance to avoid the humiliation of a trial by shooting himself, which he dutifully did. With Redl dead, the Austro-Hungarian political establishment

began a cover-up to try to hide the embarrassment of one of their brightest officers having spied for Russia, but the Germans knew that their suspicions had been right all along and that the Austro-Hungarians had had a high-level spy operating in plain view for years without discovery.

The Redl affair emptied whatever credit of faith and trust the Germans had had in their main ally. Although Redl himself was dead, the incident seemed

Field Marshal Paul von Hindenburg (left) and Crown Prince Wilhelm (centre), the Kaiser's son. Both men were deeply steeped in Prussian military traditions and both rose to high ranks during the war itself.

to show that the Germans had been right to suspect the military competence of the Austrians. As a result of this suspicion, the Germans became even less confident of an ally that they felt they could nevertheless not afford to lose. The result of this seeming paradox was an increase in the German arrogance that the Austrians so disliked. Perhaps more importantly, neither side was privy to the war plans of the other. Consequently, neither side understood that no plan existed to deal with the Russians if they should mobilize faster than anticipated.

Germany had one other ally, Italy. In 1881 when they joined the Triple Alliance, the Italians were concerned about the expansion of France at a young Italy's expense and saw a German alliance as protection against such expansion. Over time, however, the French Third Republic showed little

The Kaiser is shown here during a state visit to Turkey. He styled himself the protector of the Muslims in the hopes of undermining the Muslim parts of the British Empire, but found most Muslims unreceptive.

A fanciful image of a united Triple Alliance against France. In reality the three powers had deep mutual suspicions. Neither the Germans nor the Austrians were surprised when Italy left the alliance in 1914. The bubbles each carry the name of a French colony.

interest in territorial expansion in Europe and as a result Franco-Italian relations warmed considerably. Relations between Italy and Austria-Hungary, however, had grown steadily worse. Italian nationalists demanded that Italy annex parts of the Adriatic coastline, including the port city of Fiume, on the ostensible basis that these were historically Italian territories. The Italians also grew shriller in their demands for parts of the Dalmatian coastline and the south Tyrol region in the Alps. To be sure, these regions contained many Italians, but only in parts of the south Tyrol could one plausibly claim that Italian majorities existed. More importantly, all of these territories belonged to Austria-Hungary, placing Italy in the odd diplomatic position of demanding territorial concessions from an ally.

Austro-Hungarian Emperor Franz Joseph had been on the throne since 1848. He had the respect of most of Europe's leaders, but his age (he was 84 in 1914) made the issue of his successor an important one.

away from the German front. Losing Italy meant not just losing the threat to France, but the sizeable Italian fleet in the Mediterranean as a way to interdict British and French commerce.

Dissatisfaction with both Italy and Austria-Hungary helps to explain German fascination with an alliance with the Ottoman Empire. Both nations shared an historical mistrust of the Russians and the Kaiser hoped to use the Ottoman Empire's religious authority to undermine British control of Muslim India. The Kaiser had even made an appearance in Constantinople in a fez proclaiming Germany the protector of the world's Muslims, a statement that mystified and confused most who heard it. As a more believable sign of his desire for growing contacts, the Kaiser had sent a high-level military mission to Turkey to help modernize the Ottoman Army and its coastal defences, and had also vastly increased German investments in Turkey, especially in supporting the construction of the so-called Berlin to Baghdad railway.

For the Germans, dissension between their two main allies was an unusual, but nevertheless serious problem. Germany felt that it needed both allies and sought to find ways to compromise. German suggestions over the years that the Austrians might cede a few territories with large Italian populations in the interest of alliance harmony only served to infuriate the Austrians further and make them dig their heels in even deeper. Tensions grew so bad by 1914 that Germany had grave doubts (correct, as it turned out) that Italy would honour any of its alliance commitments in the event of war. Those commitments had included sending Italian troops to help defend Alsace and at least a show of force on France's southeastern border to draw French forces

As tensions rose in the weeks leading up to war, the Germans staked more and more on the Ottoman connection. Just days before the onset of fighting a stroke of good fortune helped them. As war between Britain and Germany loomed, the British cancelled shipment of two recently completed modern battleships to the Turkish Navy on the grounds of national security. The ships had been paid for in part by public subscription, and most Turks saw the cancellation as a slap in the face. The Germans had two battleships in the Mediterranean at the time and they knew that the British would never let those ships get back to German waters. Therefore, at almost the same time that war was declared in Europe, the Germans made the smart decision to transfer the two ships to Ottoman control, knowing that the British would not fire on a ship from a still neutral nation. The two ships would thus be saved and would cement the links to Turkey by making good the British insult to Turkish pride. After daringly avoiding the British ships sent to track them, the *Goeben* and the *Breslau* arrived in Constantinople on 10 August where they entered the Turkish Navy as the *Yavuz Sultan Selim* and the *Midili*. The German commander of the ships,

The assassination of Franz Ferdinand put more than succession to the Austro-Hungarian throne in doubt. It threatened the peace of the Continent when German and Austro-Hungarian leaders decided to use it as a pretext for a Europe-wide war.

the most powerful vessels in the Ottoman fleet, was soon named commander-in-chief of the Ottoman Navy. By then the Germans and the Ottomans had already signed an alliance and the Italians had announced their intention to remain neutral.

AUSTRIA-HUNGARY

Austria-Hungary's position was in many ways the most complicated of the Eastern European powers. A multi-ethnic empire dominated by Germans and Magyars (Hungarians), the empire was itself a defiance to the logic of nationalism that had been so forceful in carving out modern Europe. The empire contained members of almost all of Eastern Europe's minorities, along with the all the complexities that such a mix of languages, cultures and religions

implied. The empire tried to hold this conglomeration together through a generally high level of official tolerance (Austria-Hungary, for example, had the Continent's only Jewish generals) and shared allegiance to the central institutions of the empire, the monarchy and the army. Both of those institutions, however, were too closely identified with the German elite to be seen as representative.

Ever since its collapse, the weaknesses of the Austro-Hungarian state have become its most dominant features among historians. This picture is not far from the truth. Based on the outdated principle of multi-ethnic nationalities, it was seen by many at the time as being 'on the wrong side of history'. The emperor, the ageing Franz Joseph, had been on the throne since 1848, making him the oldest monarch in Europe. He neither inspired much confidence nor proved particularly well adapted to meet the changes of the twentieth century. Economically, the country was largely agricultural, although it did possess several important industrial centres. Politically, the empire worked through an antiquated system of two separate bureaucracies, one based in Vienna and one in Budapest, which worked with different systems and different languages.

Nevertheless, the empire was counted by all of its contemporaries as a great

power, even if it was one on the decline. It controlled a massive amount of territory, much of it strategically placed, and if its bureaucracy was cumbersome, it still managed to function most of the time. The empire also had a large population and an officer corps that

> ### 'It will be a hopeless struggle, but nevertheless it must be, for such an ancient monarchy and such an ancient army cannot perish ingloriously.'
>
> Franz Conrad von Hötzendorf

thought itself the inheritors of a proud tradition worth defending. Although Austria-Hungary was not a wealthy state, the army was able to get from it most of what it wanted and, in several areas, it was highly respected. Even the Germans sought out the excellent artillery pieces that emerged from the Skoda Works.

Despite outward manifestations of confidence, a deep sense of anxiety pervaded Austria-Hungary's leadership. The state's elite felt that it had no dependable allies and a host of potential enemies. In fact, one of its allies (Italy) was also one of its most likely future enemies. The assassination of the Archduke Franz Ferdinand in June 1914 seemed to make clear what Austria-Hungary ought to do next. Most members of the state's elite wanted to fight a punitive war against the Serbian state that it held directly responsible for the assassination. Such a war would also eliminate the Serbian threat once and for all and leave Austria-Hungary as the dominant force in the Balkans.

The chief of the Austro-Hungarian general staff, Franz Conrad von

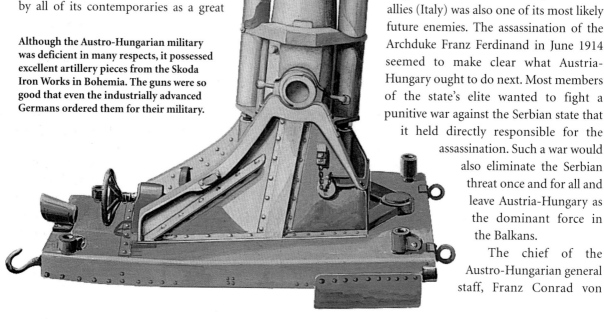

Although the Austro-Hungarian military was deficient in many respects, it possessed excellent artillery pieces from the Skoda Iron Works in Bohemia. The guns were so good that even the industrially advanced Germans ordered them for their military.

Hötzendorf, had been arguing for such a war for years. Known in Austrian circles as a hothead who repeatedly argued for pre-emptive wars both in the Balkans and against Italy, Conrad saw several other important advantages in a war with Serbia. The victory that he fully expected would result would reverse the empire's decline and confirm Austria-Hungary's placement among the ranks of the great powers. Conrad believed strongly that the government had made an unforgivable mistake by not striking the Serbs while they were occupied with their war against the Ottoman Empire in 1912. Now with the heir to the Austro-Hungarian throne and his wife dead at the hands of a Serbian terrorist group with ties to the government, the time had come, he believed, to right

Conrad von Hötzendorf (right) had been arguing for war against Serbia for years. As chief of the Austrian general staff, he seized upon the assassination of Franz Ferdinand as a proper and useful justification for war. He wished to return Austro-Hungary to its former status as a leading great power.

the wrong and deal with Serbia in the most violent manner possible. The assassination had given him the perfect opportunity to fight an offensive war while at the same time playing the international role of victim.

The problem, Conrad knew, was that war with Serbia might also mean war with Russia. That problem, he hoped, had been solved by the German 'blank cheque' offer of support. German officials had decided that the assassination of a member of the royal family had to be answered and therefore that Austria-Hungary would be entirely within its rights to invade Serbia.

The Germans had also concluded that the Russians would in all likelihood enter the war as a result. Having noted the massive improvements and investments the Russians and French were making to their militaries, the Germans determined that the odds were more in their favour in 1914 than they were likely to be in the future. They therefore told their ally to do what was necessary against Serbia and count on full German support to deal with the consequences.

What Conrad failed to realize, however, was that German mobilization for war meant that Germany would execute and implement a war plan that sent seven-eighths of its forces against France in the west. There they would be of little help to the Austro-Hungarian forces that would mostly head south to crush Serbia. As a result of the failure to coordinate their war plans, the two powers had inadvertently left themselves with grossly inadequate coverage against the Russians. Even before this amazing oversight was understood, Conrad knew that the Austro-Hungarian Empire, with its many weaknesses, was headed into a dangerous future. 'It will be a hopeless struggle,' he wrote just before the fighting began, 'but nevertheless it must be, for such an ancient monarchy and such an ancient army cannot perish ingloriously.' Ingloriously or not, the Austro-Hungarians were indeed on their way to perishing.

CHAPTER 1

The First Battles

Russian leaders supported their country's entry into World War I, hoping to recover their nation's power and prestige in the Balkans. The first battles went much better than many Russians expected, especially against the Austro-Hungarians. But the Russian Army soon suffered massive twin defeats that underscored the fundamental weaknesses of the Russian system.

When war broke out in the first days of August, seven of Germany's eight field armies headed west on their ill-fated attempt to knock France out of the war in six weeks. While the Germans moved through Belgium and into France as part of the Schlieffen Plan, the forces of Austria-Hungary began mobilization aimed at meeting the wide variety of threats the war presented to them. Conrad had designed a war plan that divided his army into three components: one to deal with Serbia, one to move into southern Poland to hold off the Russians and one in reserve that could go north or south depending on the events in the war's opening

Russian infantrymen form a skirmish line early in the war. Russian officers were generally unimpressed with the quality of Russian soldiers, most of whom had little enthusiasm for the war and little identification with pan-Slavism.

27

phases. While the plan looked good on paper, it overloaded the Austro-Hungarian transportation and communications systems, and soon proved to be an unmanageable tangle. Many units had to march for days to get to their assigned train stations only to find that there were no available trains to take them to the front. Conrad also wanted to be careful about which ethnic groups he sent where. Thus many of the forces to fight the Serbs came from far-flung (but not Slavic) parts of the empire like Bohemia.

All of Germany and Austria-Hungary's planning counted on the Russians mobilizing very slowly. Only

The large Polish Salient offered both opportunities and challenges to the Russians. They feared a joint German and Austro-Hungarian pincer attack on the salient, but also understood the advantages of assembling forces inside it.

a presumption of Russian ineptitude would have dared to allow Conrad to send the majority of his forces elsewhere. As the Germans, under Helmuth von Moltke, gambled on a quick defeat of France, so, too, did Conrad gamble on being able to eliminate Serbia quickly without significant Russian interference. Only 20 Austrian divisions went into Poland to guard against Russian movements. Both Moltke and Conrad had assumed that capturing the enemy capital would give them the victory they sought, thus enabling forces to be redirected in plenty of time to meet the Russians. Both men were to be seriously disappointed.

Russia threw a giant spanner into all of the planning by Germany and Austria-Hungary, now known collectively with the Ottoman Empire as the Central Powers. In the first place, the Russian people

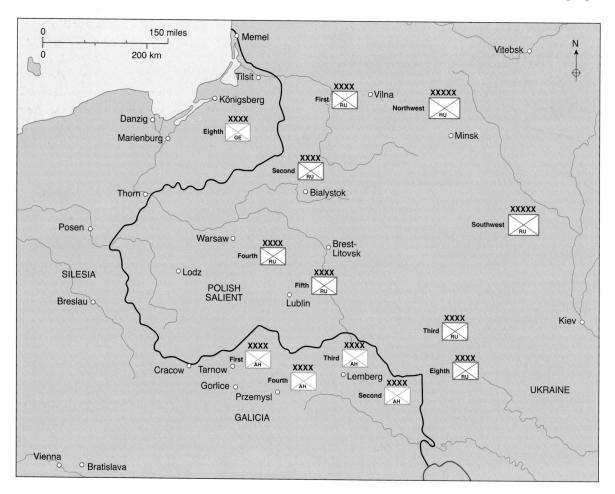

Grand Duke Nikolai, the Tsar's uncle, did not want the job of commander-in-chief. He believed he was ill suited to the task, despite a generally high reputation among Russian officers. He only accepted the position out of loyalty to his nephew the Tsar.

Russian planners had concluded that the immensity of their army and the size of Russia itself made it unwise to mobilize all resources first then deploy to the field. Doing so would simply overwhelm the rail network and the training camps at mobilization centres. Under the new plan, units would deploy into the field as soon as they were ready to do so. In a small country, such a plan would have risked placing too few men in the field to resist a determined enemy invasion. For the Russians, however, it meant that tens of thousands of men came into the field every week. The first divisions to be ready could go onto the offensive, while the second and third waves stood by to reinforce success, or, in a worst-case scenario, provide the required troops for a defence of the Russian homeland.

If the Central Powers had indeed coordinated their strategy and launched a joint invasion of Russia, it is unlikely that this mobilization scheme would have been equal to the task of defending Russia. The Russians had a badly exposed bump in their line

met the Tsar's call for mobilization on 30 July with an enthusiasm that few expected. This enthusiasm was mostly limited to young men in the growing Russian cities, but even so, thousands of young men joined the army and urban reservists reported to their units without much trouble. The Tsar made impassioned speeches to his people calling on all Russians to unite in a time of national crisis. Even in the countryside, peasants seemed to accept the necessity of the war, although they exhibited much less enthusiasm than the urbanites of Moscow and St Petersburg. The new Russian railways also came into play, as men and supplies moved from the hinterland of Russia to its mobilization centres with reasonable speed and efficiency. The Russians were still far behind the speed and efficiency of the Germans or the French, but all observers noted how much better the mobilization went than many Russians had feared.

The key to the Russian mobilization plan lay in the central idea of a staged mobilization. Essentially,

> 'The three Governments agree that when terms of peace come to be discussed, no one of the Allies will demand terms of peace without the previous agreement of each of the other Allies.'
>
> Triple Entente declaration, 4 September 1914

known as the Polish Salient that the Germans and Austro-Hungarians could have hit simultaneously from the north and the south. But no such operation materialized as the Germans headed west and the Austro-Hungarians headed south, giving the Russians some much-needed space and time in which to

Austro-Hungarian soldiers, like these men, spoke a dizzying array of languages and came from dozens of often mutually antagonistic ethnic groups. This diversity imposed a special burden on the Austro-Hungarian mobilization process.

mobilize and deploy. It is entirely possible that the Russians knew the general outline of Central Powers planning: the Austro-Hungarian plans were likely slipped to them by Colonel Redl, their spy in the General Staff, and German intentions might well have been known from their French ally, who had divined the general outline of the Schlieffen Plan.

RUSSIAN WAR PLANS

What to do with the men that the Russians mobilized posed a different problem. The Russians had long assumed the need to fight both Germany and Austria-Hungary in the event of war, but the distances involved created tremendous challenges for Russian

planners. The distance from Moscow to Berlin was 1860km (1156 miles) and the distance between Berlin and Vienna was 678km (421 miles), much too far away for a single campaign to encompass both enemy capitals. The terrain of Eastern Europe also posed challenges, as it possessed few railways and was generally lacking in the kinds of supplies an army needed on the march. Supply and logistics would present insurmountable challenges for a Russian general staff not well known for such skills.

In 1910, General Yuri Danilov proposed a solution to this dilemma. He discarded previous Russian war planning that had been based on the Napoleonic experience of withdrawing deep into Russian territory, sacrificing men and land and forcing the enemy to advance over poor terrain. Trading space for time had worked a century earlier, but Danilov thought the 1812 experience not worth repeating. Perhaps more importantly, he understood that times had changed and that a massive withdrawal into the Russian interior might have catastrophic consequences for Russian morale and the security of the Tsarist regime. He also knew that Russian and French generals had based their planning around coordinated offensive action against Germany to place pressure on the Germans from both the west and the east simultaneously. Russia would therefore need to throw away outmoded ways of thinking and develop an offensive war plan.

His solution became known as Plan 19, after the 19 army corps that he hoped to have ready to lead the first wave. Danilov had assumed that the Germans would attack France first, thus leaving East Prussia vulnerable. Two Russian armies would thus advance into East Prussia, a highly developed province that could provide food and fuel to an invading army. One of the Russian armies would then head toward Berlin while the other moved into mineral-rich Silesia. In the early phases of the war, the remaining Russian units would stay on the defensive around Russia's outdated but still useful fortifications to repel any Austro-Hungarian attacks from the southwest. Once a sufficient number of units had mobilized in Ukraine, the Russian Army could also begin an offensive against Austria-Hungary along the Carpathian Mountains.

Residents in St Petersburg demonstrate in favour of the war during a brief display of national unity. The notoriously anti-Semitic Tsar even reached out to Russia's Jews in 1914, but the mood of cooperation did not last.

The Balkan Wars

The first Balkan War saw Serbia and its allies, Bulgaria, Greece and Montenegro, capture the Ottoman provinces of Novibazar and Macedonia in 1912. The war pushed the Ottomans in Europe back to the Gallipoli Peninsula and a small bridgehead protecting the western approaches of Constantinople itself. The Russians looked on favourably and offered the Balkan League its support, but did not engage directly. In 1912–13 the Second Balkan War broke out among the members of the Balkan League for their share of the spoils. The wars were a complete humiliation for the Ottoman Empire and a moment of great triumph for a resurgent Serbia.

The unexpectedly rapid Russian mobilization gave Russian commanders the resources to launch two attacks at the same time. Within 15 days after the declaration of mobilization on 30 July, the Russians had 27 divisions ready for combat. A week later, another 25 divisions were ready for combat. In all there were 90 Russian divisions in Europe and 20 more divisions in the Caucasus theatre by 1 September. The Russian high command thus decided to launch the attack on East Prussia, but abandon the essentially defensive part of the plan in favour of immediate operations against Austria-Hungary's belt of Carpathian fortifications that guarded the mountain passes into the agricultural heartland of the empire in northern Hungary.

As a result, Russia was prepared to send enormous forces against Germany and Austria-Hungary simultaneously while the Germans and Austro-Hungarians were looking the other way. If these forces had been intelligently led they might have done some serious damage. The Russian officer corps was, however, rife with personal and professional rivalries that made efficient command and control virtually impossible. Two mutually suspicious cliques had developed, one based around modernizers in the War Ministry, the other based around more traditional ideas in the army's general staff. The rivalries had grown so intense that many senior Russian officers were barely on speaking terms with one another and many more had diametrically opposed views on the nature of war. It had become policy in Russia to deal with this rivalry by assigning officers from both cliques to the same headquarters staffs in an effort to force them to overcome their differences, but this approach had largely failed, instead reinforcing the rivalries and jealousies.

Given the factionalism and rivalries in the army, Nicholas II looked to find an overall commander who might be able to rise above the fray. Even as the armies were deploying into the field, he changed senior leadership, asking his uncle, the distinguished military veteran Grand Duke Nikolai, to assume command. Nikolai reluctantly agreed to his nephew's request. Although widely respected for championing reform in the Russian Army, Nikolai had been out of the mainstream of Russian military thinking since 1909 and had only heard faint inklings of the details of Plan 19. Thus the first task of the new Russian commander was to find out exactly what his own army's plans were. He soon discovered to his dismay that the army had made wholly inadequate preparations for communications in the field and that important logistical details had been ignored altogether. It was not an auspicious start for the new commander of the largest army in Europe.

RENNENKAMPF AND SAMSONOV

Nikolai knew that the primitive state of Russian communications would pose tremendous problems to any effort at centralized command and control. Almost all messages sent from his office to the front went first to Warsaw, where they were decoded then sent forward to army and corps commanders by messenger. This cumbersome system was designed in part to compensate for the simple codes the Russians used. Changing code books across a vast and expansive Russian empire proved to be so daunting a task that the Russians tended to rely on older codes, which greatly increased the chance of their being broken. Sending messages overland by courier was a distinctly nineteenth-century way of doing

This image of a Russian soldier disguises the poor quality of equipment that most new recruits received. The large but inefficient Russian industrial and transportation systems had difficulties keeping men supplied throughout the war.

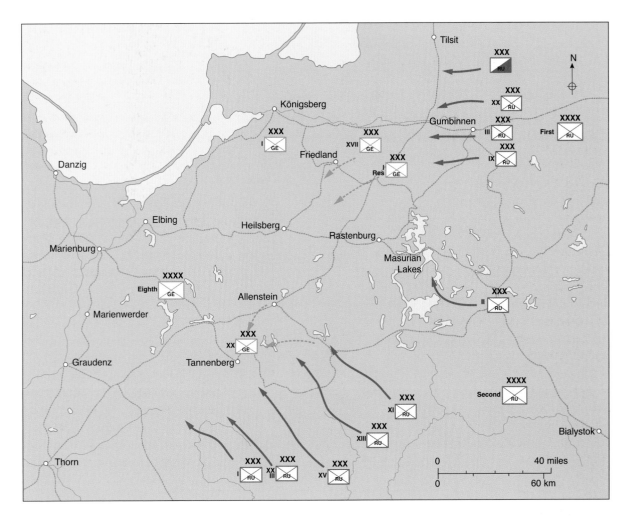

The initial Russian success in mobilizing much faster than the Germans had anticipated allowed two Russian armies to threaten East Prussia, the traditional seat of the Prussian elite. The commander of the German Eighth Army therefore decided on a massive retreat.

business, but it significantly reduced the chances that the Germans would intercept a message and either decode it or gain another clue into how to break the Russian code system.

As a result of the Russian communications problems, command and control became unusually decentralized. While Moltke tried (with mixed results) to command the German Army from a field headquarters in Luxembourg and the French commander Joseph Joffre was able to monitor events

and issue orders from his splendid headquarters in the Château de Chantilly near Paris, Nikolai could do little more than send his field commanders to the front and hope for the best. The quality of those commanders and the coordination between them would play a key role in determining the success or failure of the Russian armies in the field.

The invasion of East Prussia fell to the Russian First and Second armies, whose commanders were on opposite sides of almost every one of the rivalries and factions of the Russian Army. The First Army commander was Pavel Rennenkampf, a member of a Baltic German family who had risen quickly through the ranks of the Russian Army. Like many of his fellow Baltic Germans, Rennenkampf saw absolutely no

French President Raymond Poincaré meets King George V in a symbolic act of unity. Along with the Russians, the French and British determined not to seek a separate peace with Germany. Russia's defeats, however, gave their allies concerns.

travelled and often-repeated story of the two men getting into a fist fight on the railway station in Mukden during the war had been greatly exaggerated, but there was no exaggeration of the intense hostility between the two men. Unlike Rennenkampf, whose connections were in the general staff (called the Stavka), Samsonov's links were in the War Ministry. Samsonov had been serving as governor of the far-away province of Turkestan when he was brought west to command the Second Army. The time apart had not made the two Russian commanders any more inclined to forgive and forget.

Together the two field armies were constituted as the Northwest Front (or army group) under the command of Yakov Zhilinski. A former military governor of Warsaw and then chief of staff of the Russian Army, Zhilinksi was probably the Russian officer who was most familiar with the plans of their French allies. He believed strongly in the need to attack Germany with as much force as possible as early as possible in accordance with the general outline of the Franco-Russian strategic talks he had supervised before the war. He was extremely unpopular for his dictatorial methods but he had an intimate understanding of the Russian Army and its general strategic outlook.

The command and control system of the Russian invasion of East Prussia thus could hardly have been less suited to modern war. The commander-in-chief, Grand Duke Nikolai, the Northwest Front commander, Zhilinksi, and both army commanders were all new to their posts. The two army commanders

contradiction between his German ancestry and his loyalty to the Russian state. He had fought in the Boxer Rebellion in China and had proved to be especially ruthless in 1905 in taking back two towns on the Trans-Siberian Railway from revolutionaries. For that act, the Tsar had singled him out for future promotion despite reports that he had mishandled his forces in combat in the Russo-Japanese War.

Several of the reports criticizing Rennenkampf's conduct in the war had come from Alexander Samsonov, who commanded the Russian Second Army. Rennenkampf had never forgiven Samsonov for his intense criticism, both in the field and in reports to the Tsar and the army general staff after the war. A well

Domestic Unity

In all of the belligerent countries, the war led to an outpouring of patriotic sentiment. In Russia, the famously anti-Semitic Tsar even arranged to meet with prominent Jews as a sign of domestic unity. Political parties put aside much of their internal bickering and, in both Russia and Germany, parliaments ceded much of their authority to the executive. In Germany, the Kaiser initiated a policy of *Burgfriede*, or civil truce, between factions. He famously told his people that 'I no longer recognize parties. I only recognize Germans'. These truces lasted until 1917, when the pressures of war began to erode them.

were not on speaking terms, and the front commander was disliked by both. Orders from the Stavka went by telegraph from Moscow to Warsaw then to Zhilinski's field headquarters by courier and then to the army headquarters, if they could be located. Acknowledgement of receipt of the order had to follow the same path in reverse.

As if the personal rivalries were not serious enough, the Russians also faced immense challenges of geography. In between the First and Second armies sat the 97km-long (60-mile) Augustowo Forest and the 145km-long (90-mile) chain of lakes known as the Masurian Lakes. Any major offensive operation against East Prussia would force the First Army to go north of these barriers and the Second Army to go south of them. As a result their routes of march would become dangerously divergent and they would be in no position to offer mutual support to one another until they had advanced more than 240km (150 miles) and moved far to the west of the lakes. Given that speed and suppleness of manoeuvre were not the Russians' strong suit, and given that the two armies would for all intents and purposes not be able to maintain secure communications between them, the task was daunting in the extreme.

Still, given that the bulk of the German Army was in Belgium and France, the Russian offensive at first experienced little resistance. Knowing that he was badly outnumbered, the commander of the only

German army in the east, a friend of the Kaiser named Maximillien von Prittwitz, had decided on 20 August to move west more than 160km (100 miles) and draw the Russians into East Prussia. Once inside Germany, he knew that the Russians would be unable to use the German railway network, which used a different gauge from the Russian.

Prittwitz also knew that his subordinate commanders would be fighting on terrain they had

General Pavel Rennenkampf was descended from Baltic Germans and earned a reputation for ferocity during the 1905 Revolution. His slow-footed performance in 1914 led to dismissal from the army and a court inquiry.

trained on for years and would thus be in a much better position to round up and defeat isolated Russian units, even if those units were larger, by surrounding them and cutting them off from their lines of supply.

THE BATTLE OF GUMBINNEN

Prittwitz was just about ready to order the final phase of the withdrawal when the Russian communication problems changed the picture dramatically. German I Corps intelligence officers had picked up a local message from Rennenkampf to his division commanders that had been broadcast, *en clair* (meaning without the use of codes), over radio waves. The message ordered a halt in movement on 20

The Russian invasion of East Prussia led to a critical command change in the German Eighth Army. The cautious Max von Prittwitz was dismissed and the new team of Paul von Hindenburg and Erich Ludendorff was sent east.

August just south of the border town of Gumbinnen to give his men a rest and to allow supplies to be brought forward. The order went to I Corps commander, General Hermann von François, an aggressive officer with more than the usual German hatred of Slavs. He was already aghast at Prittwitz's proposal to withdraw and voluntarily cede parts of Germany to the Russian invaders and had subsequently disobeyed his orders and moved his units east, not west. François informed Prittwitz that he was going to attack the Russians at Gumbinnen instead of falling back. Prittwitz had his doubts, but gave his impatient subordinate permission to proceed.

To make sure that the attack had every chance of success, Prittwitz ordered two of his corps to join François at Gumbinnen, leaving his fourth corps in reserve. François recklessly pressed ahead without waiting for the other two corps to complete their preparations. He attacked the much larger Russian

General Alexander Samsonov confidently led his forces into East Prussia, unaware that the Germans were preparing to spring a trap on him. His subsequent massive defeat at Tannenberg led him to commit suicide rather than face the consequences back in Russia.

forces at 4am on 20 August, achieving surprise and pushing Russian forces back as far as eight kilometres (five miles). François thought that he had scored a major victory and urged the other two German corps to come forward and complete the annihilation of the Russian First Army.

The two corps arrived on the battlefield piecemeal, with one arriving at 8am and the other only arriving at midday. François had in fact only fought against a weak advance guard; as the Germans forced their way east they came up against the main body of First Army, including its artillery. The three German corps fought separately against powerful (if inefficiently employed) Russian forces. Seeing how badly they were outnumbered and outgunned, the German XVII Corps began a withdrawal at the end of the day. The other two corps, including François's I Corps, had

little choice but to follow suit, leaving more than 6000 German prisoners in Russian hands.

Prittwitz panicked. His units were in disarray and he expected Rennenkampf to pursue with the utmost vigour. He also had no clear idea of where Samsonov's Second Army was. He therefore feared that he might be encircled and destroyed by much larger Russian forces. He designed an even more ambitious retreat, proposing to retire behind the Vistula River to buy time, even if such a withdrawal essentially meant abandoning all of East Prussia to the Russians. Prittwitz informed Moltke of his new plan, but his commander's reaction was not what he had expected. Directing the attack on Paris from his headquarters in Luxembourg, Moltke went into a rage and ordered the withdrawal stopped immediately. He also informed Prittwitz that he and his chief of staff were being removed from command, leading to Prittwitz's retirement. The defence of East Prussia would fall to the hands of new commanders with new ideas.

THE BATTLE OF TANNENBERG

Prittwitz's replacement was Paul von Hindenburg, who quickly forgot all about his apple trees and sped to the train station at Hanover. The imposing general had been retired for three years, but he had lost none of his professional demeanour or his ability to sum up a military problem quickly. After spending his retirement thinking about a Russian invasion of East Prussia, he was now in the position to do something about it. Moltke knew that Hindenburg would bring a steady hand to the Eighth Army and that he would not panic as Prittwitz had. He also knew that Hindenburg would command respect from loose cannons like his corps commander François.

At Hanover train station, Hindenburg met his new chief of staff for the first time, General Erich Ludendorff. Ludendorff had become one of Germany's first heroes of the war by designing and executing the German capture of the powerful Belgian fortifications at Liège. Ludendorff had pounded on the door of the town's citadel with the hilt of his sword demanding the surrender, making a name for himself in Germany and earning the trust and respect of Moltke and the Kaiser.

German infantry, with their distinctive helmets covered, advance as part of the Tannenberg campaign. The swift decision making of the German Eighth Army commanders allowed German forces to encircle and cut off their Russian foes with minimal losses.

Ludendorff was unpopular and unpleasant as a colleague and a superior, but he was also a hard worker and a reliable administrator who could turn Hindenburg's strategic vision into operations.

On the train from Hanover to their new command, the two men discussed their options and the intelligence reports from the field. According to those reports, Rennenkampf had shown little desire to move his units forwards after his success at Gumbinnen despite the fact that just one German cavalry division

sat opposite him. Ludendorff concluded that although the Russian First Army had been victorious at Gumbinnen it had obviously suffered badly enough to make it cautious. He guessed that if it had not moved forwards immediately to exploit its success, then it was likely planning to stay where it was to receive reinforcements and supplies.

By the time they reached East Prussia, Hindenburg and Ludendorff had realized that the most enticing opportunity lay in concentrating against Samsonov's Second Army. With Rennenkampf paralyzed, and highly unlikely to risk his tired army by coming to the aid of his arch-nemesis, the Second Army was ripe for the picking. Thus although it had been beaten at Gumbinnen, the German Eighth Army would not retreat to the Vistula, but would instead resume the offensive by falling on both flanks of the Russian Second Army, with the ultimate goal of turning it in against itself, cutting it off from all hope of rescue and supply and forcing it to fight to its death or surrender.

On arrival at their new headquarters, Hindenburg and Ludendorff discovered that the Eighth Army operations officer, Lieutenant-Colonel Max Hoffmann, had already come to the same general conclusions. He had prepared orders for his new superiors' approval to move François's I Corps by rail to the town of Seeben, where it would be on Samsonov's left flank without the Russians' knowledge. Two more corps would move by foot, with XX Corps moving directly opposite the Russians to hold them in place while XVII Corps would close the trap from the north and fall on Samsonov's right wing. The one solitary cavalry division would remain opposite Rennenkampf's First Army to screen it and keep a close eye on its movements.

The German commanders did not see their plan as a gamble, nor did they worry about the setback at Gumbinnen. They were in very comfortable intellectual territory in designing what the Germans called a *Kesselschlacht*, or killing cauldron. Such a daring manoeuvre had been taught to generations of German officers as the best way for a smaller army to defeat a larger one by more rapid movement, the attainment of surprise, and attacks on two flanks simultaneously. The model was the great Battle of Cannae in 216 BC where Hannibal had encircled and annihilated a much more powerful force of Roman legions. Indeed, the idea was so familiar to officers trained in the German staff system that three officers who had never worked together before, independently saw it as the obvious solution to the problem in front of them.

Their beliefs were confirmed by two more *en clair* Russian messages that the Germans intercepted. The first was from Rennenkampf's staff to Samsonov's informing them that the Russian First Army would

In the more open spaces of the Eastern Front cavalry could still play its traditional reconnaissance role. It could also still be used to pursue retreating enemy soldiers and cut off lines of retreat.

move slowly towards the northwest. The message confirmed that the two Russian armies would continue to march in diverging directions and that Rennenkampf would be in no position to come to Samsonov's assistance even if he felt inclined to do so. The second message was in response to the first, with Samsonov's staff giving Rennenkampf's staff (and, unwittingly, the Germans as well) their anticipated lines of march for the next two days. An elated Hoffmann rushed both messages to Hindenburg and Ludendorff. The latter was so amazed at the Russian

sloppiness that he dismissed the messages as a crude Russian deception operation. Hoffmann told him of similar messages the Germans had already intercepted and convinced Ludendorff of their authenticity. Messages found on a dead Russian officer provided more evidence to overcome Ludendorff's scepticism.

Samsonov never saw what hit him on 27 August, just a week after the Russian victory at Gumbinnen. Zhilinski had informed him of the First Army's triumph and advised him not to expect significant German forces to be in his sector, as they would likely begin a retreat. He therefore told Samsonov that he could advance in a leisurely manner. Unworried about any German resistance, Samsonov moved his centre corps forward, leaving its flanks dangerously exposed to any possible assault.

The Germans used just one cavalry division to screen the Russian First Army while the remainder of the German Eighth Army moved south to surround the Russian Second Army. German forces were therefore able to encircle the Russians and destroy them.

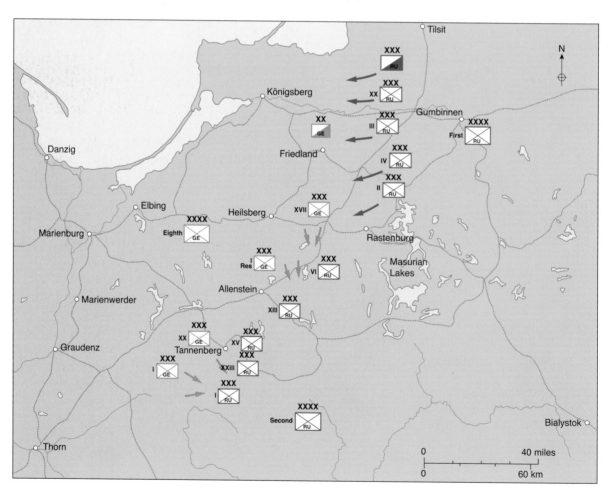

German field artillery crossing a river in full flow on the Eastern Front. The German 77mm field gun was designed to advance with the infantry and provide fire support on the move. It was the German equivalent of the famous French 75mm field gun.

Taking advantage of the Russian slackness, the Germans responded with rapid movements aimed at encircling the Russian Second Army before Samsonov could even divine the size of the German forces opposite them. François, humbled just a bit after his bloody error of judgement at Gumbinnen, argued with Ludendorff for more time to properly prepare his artillery. Afraid of losing the critical element of surprise, Ludendorff urged action, and François finally complied. On 27 August, he stretched his I Corps to the south of the Russian left flank, and reached Soldau just inside the Russian border on Samsonov's main route of supply. He then moved north and east, seizing key roads and making any Russian retreat from the battlefield all but impossible.

The Future of Pavel Rennenkampf

Rennenkampf faced charges of incompetence after his handling of the opening moves of the war. Although he had fought better than Samsonov, the latter was dead by his own hand and Rennenkampf became the easiest scapegoat. His German last name led to additional charges of treason, although these charges were unfounded. He faced a trial for mismanagement of public funds and only avoided prison through the grace of some of his well connected friends. He retired to a *dacha* on the Black Sea and in 1918 was approached by the Bolsheviks as a possible commander for the Red Army on the assumption of his hatred for the regime that had humiliated him. He refused the offer, whereupon the Bolsheviks accused him of treason and had him executed.

A German defensive position on the Eastern Front. German infantry were on the whole better trained, better equipped and better led than their Russian counterparts. After Tannenberg and the Masurian Lakes, German officers grew confident in their ability to beat the Russians.

Nervous and tense hours followed as the rest of the trap was sprung. By the morning hours of 28 August, the Germans had control of almost all of the main roads leading to Samsonov's forces. Combat began in the north when a Russian corps, advancing without support, ran into a German corps. The Germans, who were fully aware of the Russian presence and were lying in wait for them, smashed the Russians and sent them reeling back in panic. Surprised at the unanticipated presence of German forces in the area, Samsonov ordered a general withdrawal that night. The full severity of the situation came slowly to him as he realized that he was completely cut off. His men began to panic, throwing down weapons and running east as fast they could, only to end up trapped by

strong German forces already sitting on their lines of retreat.

Confusion and panic reigned in Russian lines. Without supplies and without communications, panic spread quickly. Rennenkampf's forces were more than 113km (70 miles) away and would obviously not provide any help at all. On 29 August, Samsonov himself gave into the panic. He told a staff officer, 'The Tsar trusted me. How can I face him after such a disaster?' He then headed off into the woods, where he committed suicide rather than face capture by the Germans. He was one of the lucky ones. Samsonov's powerful army of 150,000 men had suffered one of the most lopsided defeats in military history. More than 30,000 Russians were killed and almost 100,000 entered prisoner of war camps where they faced a dismal future of forced labour and appallingly bad conditions. The Germans needed 60 trains to move all of the Russian equipment they captured. German casualties were less than 20,000.

It was probably Max Hoffmann who first suggested calling the victory Tannenberg, in revenge for a nearby 1410 battle at which the Slavs had defeated the Teutonic Knights. He, Ludendorff and Hindenburg shared in the glory of the victory and later competed for their share, with Hoffmann especially claiming that the plan had been his all along. Zhilinksi soon lost his job as the man most responsible for the destruction of four Russian corps. To be sure, Russia still had 33 more corps in the field or ready to deploy, but Tannenberg had destroyed any hope that they might see an easy march to Berlin. It had also seemingly confirmed the superiority of German efficiency and methods over those of their hopelessly antiquated Russian foes.

THE BATTLE OF THE MASURIAN LAKES

With the Russian Second Army decisively defeated and German confidence soaring, the Eighth Army decided not to sit on its laurels. Even before Tannenberg,

Moltke had decided to reinforce it, although initially the reinforcements were intended to provide extra men to defend East Prussia. These reinforcements included two corps that Moltke controversially removed from the right wing of the German First Army in Belgium, later leading to charges (most of them not supported by evidence) that if he had not removed them, the Germans might have been able to complete their victory in the west. After Tannenberg, Moltke continued to send new drafts of men to the east. By September, the Eighth Army had 18 infantry and three cavalry divisions. Plans were already in the works to add two new field armies in the east.

The Germans again tried to take advantage of poor Russian communications and slow Russian deployment. On news of the disaster at Tannenberg,

Russian cavalry had a long and proud tradition. Several of the Russian Army's top commanders had been cavalrymen. The Russians used cavalry to screen and reconnoitre in the vast distances of the Eastern Front.

Rennenkampf had sent part of his army south as a precaution, but the movement had been designed poorly. As a result, part of the Russian First Army was separated from the main force and therefore dangerously exposed to any rapid German concentrations. Once again, Russian headquarters contributed to the problem by misunderstanding German intentions. Stavka informed Rennenkampf that he had nothing immediate to worry about as the Germans were expected to head to the Warsaw area.

Instead, the Germans hurried north to try to do to Rennenkampf what they had just done to Samsonov.

The culmination of the Battle of Tannenberg. The Russian Second Army, now encircled by the corps of the German Eighth Army, was largely destroyed, with losses of 130,000 out of its strength of 150,000 men.

François marched his corps more than 113km (70 miles) in just four days, placing it on the southern flank of the detached part of Rennenkampf's forces. François attacked the Russians on 7 September, forcing the detachment to retreat north to the presumed safety of the rest of the Russian First Army, and compelling Rennenkampf to change his deployment and route of march from the west to the south. Rennenkampf acted cautiously and methodically, and was understandably anxious to avoid putting himself in the kind of trap that had ensnared Samsonov. Still, he could not move too far to the north without running into the strong German forces at the fortress of Königsberg.

Rennenkampf therefore decided to play it safe. He sent two divisions south to form a rearguard that

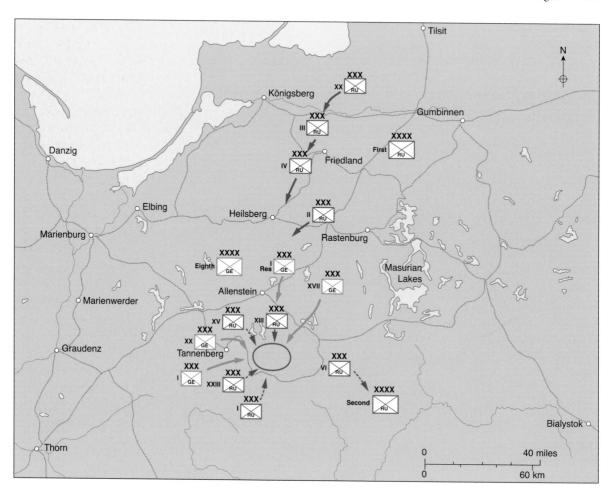

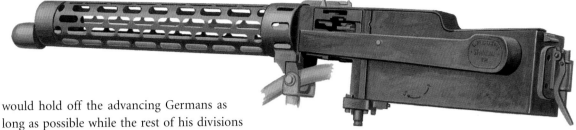

would hold off the advancing Germans as long as possible while the rest of his divisions slipped the noose and headed east to the safety of the Russian border. On 9 September, the rearguard began its furious defence, trapping advancing German units in the forests and narrow lanes between lakes. At the same time, the Russians badly exposed themselves to German machine-gun and artillery fire by conducting furious and haphazard charges. Rennenkampf's decision allowed most of the First Army to escape, but in three days of fighting, the Russians still lost an amazing 150,000 men and 150 artillery pieces. Most of the men in the two rearguard divisions ended up dead or prisoners of war.

Rennenkampf took few chances even with his withdrawal. He moved his men 80km (50 miles) to the east, evacuating East Prussia and giving it back to the Germans. Returning to Russia meant at least temporary safety because the Germans could not move men or supplies by rail until they had accumulated enough rolling stock on the Russian gauge. Finally, a piece of good luck helped the Russians when heavy rains started to fall in mid-September, turning the dirt roads into mud and slowing any German pursuit. The Russians needed time to regroup, replace their losses, and reassess their strategic approach to the war.

For their part, the Germans were disappointed at the lost chance to eliminate another Russian army, but they had done very well for themselves. Their losses had been much smaller than those of the Russians, but they came from much smaller armies and thus the Germans, too, needed to reinforce and resupply.

Nicknamed 'The Devil's Paint Brush', the German Spandau machine gun, introduced in 1908, could fire 500 7.92mm rounds per minute. This model dates from 1915 when the cumbersome water jacket was replaced by this perforated air-cooled barrel.

Especially in light of German setbacks in the west at the Battle of the Marne, the victories in the east were welcome news for the Germans and suggested to many officers that the Germans might be better served to stay in trenches on the Western Front and repel French and British attacks while seeking to repeat the formula of Tannenberg in the east, thus knocking the Russians out of the war.

Thus began a grand strategic argument in German circles between 'westerners' and 'easterners'. The former argued that deep operations into Russia were risky and extremely taxing on German logistical lines. They understood how deftly and efficiently the Germans had beaten the Russians not once, but twice. Still, they knew that the Russians had enormous reserves of manpower upon which they could call and looked aghast at repeating Napoleon's mistake of chasing the Russians deep within their own territory. Instead, they called for a full effort to defeat France and Britain on the Western Front following the theory that the Russians would not be able to stay in the war without their allies. Victory in the west would give Germany most of what it had fought the war for, especially favourable trade terms and colonial concessions. The Germans would also be likely to be

> 'I beg most humbly to report to Your Majesty that the ring round the larger part of the Russian Army was closed yesterday.'
>
> Hindenburg's message to the Kaiser on the Battle of Tannenberg

The Russian Army relied on the M1902 light field gun. It fired a 76.2mm shell at a maximum range of 6420m (7020 yards). Although the gun was adequate, Russian artillery techniques were not as advanced or as sophisticated as those in the German Army.

able to hold on to whatever lands in Poland and the Baltic region that they had taken.

Easterners argued that the hopes for victory on the Western Front were slim. The German drive on Paris having failed, the two sides had begun to entrench and the war in France showed every sign of reaching a stalemate. In the east, on the other hand, the distances were too great for a system of entrenchments to be effective and the Germans had already shown a remarkable superiority to the Russian. Easterners called for strengthening the defensive lines in the west and attacking the Russians with full force. Once the Russians had been beaten, they argued, Germany could redirect troops to the west and have sufficient striking power to break the deadlock in France.

These discussions animated German officers in the autumn of 1914 and for a long time afterwards. The real question involved not just strategy, but logistics. German officials had to determine whether new

troops and new weapons would go west to France or east to Russia. No German officer, whether a westerner or an easterner, wanted to see Germany become mired in a perpetual two-front war that most felt the Germans would eventually lose. Some way still had to be found to win the war quickly, although the debate continued as to where German resources might best be employed for years to come.

Safe for the time being behind their borders, the Russians soon recovered from their panic and took stock of their resources. They knew that they could replace the manpower losses of Tannenberg and the Masurian Lakes, and they also knew that the French and British would help them replenish their lost artillery pieces. Reorganization of their forces was the first priority, with the Russians especially concerned about German intentions against the centre of the Polish Salient. They also hoped to use the units of the Southwest Front, which had not been involved in the battles of Tannenberg and the Masurian Lakes, in a drive into Galicia against the Austro-Hungarian Empire's armies.

Thus, while Tannenberg and the Masurian Lakes might go down in the annals of German military history as unusually successful battles, they had not achieved the aim of taking one of Germany's foes out of the war. On the contrary, the Russians were preparing an offensive of their own. The Russian reorganization removed many incompetent commanders and forced a fundamental rethinking of Russian strategy that promised to pay dividends. France and Britain, although stressed on their own front, extended financial credits to the Russians to help them pay for needed equipment and to give them the flexibility to call more men to the colours. Russia still showed signs of both great weakness and, despite its losses, great strength.

AUSTRIA-HUNGARY'S GALICIAN OFFENSIVE

While Germany's war against the Russians had been a surprising success, Austria-Hungary had experienced calamitous failure almost from the start. Conrad's elegant plans fell apart owing to the fragility of the Austro-Hungarian railway network and his astonishingly blithe dismissal of the threat posed by the Russians in his war planning. On the outbreak of hostilities, Conrad sent 200,000 men to invade Serbia.

The much different 'force-to-space' ratio on the Eastern Front made the digging of extensive trench systems much less efficient. War in the east was therefore more fluid than war in the west.

War without Trenches

Although some parts of the Eastern Front featured intricate trench systems, the distances involved forbade the kinds of solid trench networks common in France and Belgium. War in the east therefore centred around communications hubs like highway crossings, forts and railway stations. As at Tannenberg, the side that moved faster and more deftly usually held the advantage. The much more effective German staff system gave Germany that advantage in almost all of its engagements with the Russians.

Constituted as Minimalgruppe Balkan, they were led, ominously enough, by the man who had been in charge of security for Franz Ferdinand's fateful visit to Sarajevo. They were to enter Serbia simultaneously from the west and northwest and capture the Serbian capital of Belgrade.

But the Serbs proved to be a much tougher opponent than most Austro-Hungarians had supposed. Most of the soldiers in the Serbian Army were veterans of the two Balkan Wars of 1912 and 1913. They were therefore experienced and battle hardened. They also had the advantage of fighting to defend their homeland, whose rough terrain featured numerous mountains and rivers to which the Serbs had added an impressive ring of field fortifications. In mid-August, the Serbs drove the Austrians back even though they possessed few modern weapons and almost no heavy artillery. Convinced that they had proven their invincibility, the Serbs boldly invaded Austria-Hungary, hoping to be seen as liberating the Slavs of the hated empire and fomenting a pan-Slavic rebellion.

The Austro-Hungarian setbacks in Serbia produced important ripple effects throughout Eastern Europe. At the same time that his invasion of Serbia was falling apart, Conrad became aware of the full implications of Germany's commitment to win the war in the west before turning east in force. He recognized the gravity of the situation immediately, as no large German forces coming east to deter the Russians meant that the Russians were free to concentrate in Poland and even in Galicia. Even those German forces that were in the east, the Eighth Army, went north to defend East Prussia instead of into the Polish Salient where they might have helped the Austro-Hungarian positions nearby. Thus, not even the two titanic German victories of Tannenberg and the Masurian Lakes provided much help to Conrad, as they were too far away from his own positions to impede or threaten the Russians moving toward him.

Even with the strength of the fortresses taken into consideration, this force was insufficient if the Russians arrived in force. This fear struck Conrad and his staff as the full weight of the situation became clear. The Austro-Hungarians could expect little to no help from their German allies for several months owing to the heavy commitments to France and, to a lesser extent, East Prussia (commitments for which Conrad never forgave them). The Austrian Second Army was all that was available to provide some extra help to A-Staffel, the main force consisting of four armies. It contained 10 divisions and was called B-Staffel under the Austro-Hungarian war plan.

But B-Staffel faced problems of its own. Its units came from all over the empire and had to be concentrated and organized before Conrad could decide where they should go. The war plan called for that concentration to occur in Galicia in the north because the railway network was much more efficient there. Thus B-Staffel was organizing and forming near where it would be needed if Conrad decided that the Russians were the greater threat. When, however, the

Russian cavalry on the move early in the war. Their weapons were too light to allow them to engage large German formations, but they could be effective in limited missions such as reconnaissance.

invasion of Serbia failed and the Serbs actually invaded Austria-Hungary, Conrad instead ordered B-Staffel sent south. The chaos and confusion of war made it virtually impossible for B-Staffel to move south with any speed at all. As a result, it spent most of August organizing and trying to move first north then south then north again when the Russian threat appeared the more dangerous. It thus did not fight at all during the month.

Fortunately for the Austro-Hungarians, the Russians in the south mobilized more slowly than they had in north. They were commanded by Nikolai Ivanov, whose most compelling qualification for the job was a firm and unwavering belief in absolute monarchy as the only appropriate political system for Russia. He had brutally suppressed the Kronstadt naval mutiny in 1906 and been rewarded with command of

the Kiev military district and the patronage of Nicholas II. Upon the outbreak of war he assumed command of the Southwestern Front (army group) of four armies comprising more than 400,000 men with thousands more on the way. Unsure of himself and terrified of making a mistake that would disappoint the Tsar, Ivanov missed a series of opportunities to deploy quickly and put pressure on Austria-Hungary while it was distracted by the Serbian campaign and the confusion created by its own mobilization plan.

Three of Ivanov's four army commanders were equally as cautious as he was. General Alexei Evert, another officer with Baltic German origins, was given command of the Fourth Army at the last minute. Like Ivanov, he believed in being cautious and did not want to go on to the offensive until he knew his army better and every conceivable detail had been worked out to his satisfaction. He was so particular that many of his peers thought he was more interested in making excuses for his inaction than he was in defeating the Austro-Hungarians. To his left in

Austrian soldiers at rest in the war's early months. A confused war plan forced the Austro-Hungarian high command to move its men frenetically between fronts, creating a great deal of fatigue, especially among reservists.

command of the Fifth Army was Wenzel von Plehve, who was not a Baltic German, but a Prussian who had chosen service in the Russian Army as a young officer because he expected that he could rise faster and higher in the service of the Tsar than in the top-heavy army of the Kaiser. Serving in a foreign army for reasons of career advancement had been common before the twentieth century but ascendant nationalism had made it seem like treason. Plehve was therefore an unusual species of officer in 1914, but he remained loyal to the Tsar, although he much preferred fighting the Austro-Hungarians to his own Germans. He was reasonably competent, but was also seriously ill, probably with cancer.

The one exception to this list of mediocre Russian commanders was the Eighth Army commander, Alexei Brusilov. He was, ironically, vacationing in Germany

Austrian soldiers firing light artillery rounds near the fortress of Lemberg. The fortress guarded one of the strategic passes in the Carpathian Mountains as well as a key rail junction. It was therefore an important lynchpin in Austrian strategy.

when Archduke Franz Ferdinand was assassinated. He had originally seen no reason to hurry home, but when Austria-Hungary delivered its ultimatum to Serbia he sensed the danger and headed back to Russia. At the Berlin train station he saw crowds demanding war with Russia and knew that war was imminent. He rushed back to the Eighth Army and began to prepare it for the invasion of Galicia. He was one of the best trainers and planners to be found in any army in 1914 and had already developed innovative tactics for the new battlefield that he expected the killing power of machine guns to create.

While the Russians dithered, Conrad decided that his best defence against the Russian Army would be an offensive to clear Galicia and secure the approaches to the mountain passes. On 23 August, he ordered the First Army to advance northeast in the direction of Lublin and the Fourth Army to advance on its right. Further to the southeast, the Third Army would advance due east from Lemberg. The B-Staffel was ordered to move (again), this time north to secure the right flank of this advance. Conrad was gratified to learn that the Germans had begun to form a new army, the Ninth, in the area north of Cracow that could help secure the offensive's other flank.

At first, the operation showed signs of success. The First and Fourth armies, advancing northeast, pushed Evert's Fourth Army and Plehve's Fifth Army back, driving them almost 160km (100 miles). But the northeastward advance created a gap between the Fourth Army and the Third Army to its south, which was advancing due east. The Third Army ran into trouble when it reached a fortified Russian position known as the Gnila Lipa Line on 26 August. There, Brusilov's Eighth Army and the adjacent Third Army sprang a trap and smashed in the flanks of the Austrian advance. Conrad responded by ordering the Fourth Army to change its route of march and move south to help out the beleaguered Third Army.

The Fourth Army's commander, Moritz von Auffenberg, vigorously protested the order. With his forces driving the Russians back, he saw no reason to stop his attacks in order to reinforce the failure of the Third Army. He also argued that changing his route of march would dangerously expose his flanks to an attack from the Russian Third Army as well as creating a gap that would expose the Austro-Hungarian First Army. Conrad disagreed and reissued the orders to a furious Auffenberg.

Auffenberg's fury was soon proved valid. The gaps between the Austro-Hungarian armies left them unable to come to one another's aid. Anchoring their attacks around Brusilov's success in the south, the Russians moved into those gaps, threatening the flanks and lines of

After destroying Samsonov's Second Army at Tannenberg, the Germans turned on Rennenkampf's First Army near the Masurian Lakes. Rennenkampf managed to get part of his army out of the trap, but still suffered a massive defeat.

Alexei Evert had a long and successful military record that included service in the Russo-Turkish War of 1877. He led inconsistently in 1914 but was nevertheless given command of an army. A supporter of the Romanovs, he died under mysterious circumstances in 1918.

communications of all three Austro-Hungarian armies. Auffenberg took little comfort from Conrad's belated ability to see the situation for what it was and order a retreat. The Second and Third armies began a retreat that eventually covered more than 160km (100 miles) and put them up against the Carpathian Mountains, surrendering all of their gains and more. Auffenberg led part of his Fourth Army to the Carpathian foothills, barely escaping a Russian encirclement in the process. The rest of the Fourth Army was cut off from its intended line of retreat and had little choice but to head to the presumed safety of the fortress city of Lemberg. The city, however, was not ready to receive thousands of tired and bedraggled soldiers, creating a major drain on food, clothing and other critical supplies. The appearance of the defeated soldiers also lowered morale in the city, with disastrous consequences.

Although Auffenberg had been right to question Conrad's decision making in the campaign, Conrad succeeded in blaming him for his alleged failure to reach the Third Army in time to prevent the retreat from being necessary. Auffenberg lost his command and retired into obscurity. The Austro-Hungarian position became increasingly dire. The Russians could now advance unhindered towards the fortresses of Lemberg and Przemysl, which were the

gateways to the Carpathian Mountain passes and the keys to unfettered use of the railways of Galicia. It only remained to be seen how quickly the Russians could organize and move. The first few weeks of the war had gone terribly for Conrad and the Austro-Hungarian Army, requiring them to plead for help from their German allies. That help would soon come, but at the price of Austro-Hungarian strategic and operational independence.

The Czech Skoda works provided the Austro-Hungarian artillery corps with some excellent weapons, including this 149mm Model 14 howitzer. Its great drawback was its weight, which made it difficult to move unless broken down into two pieces.

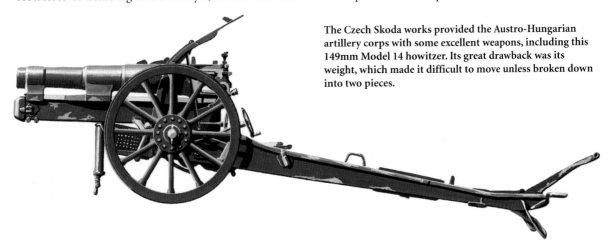

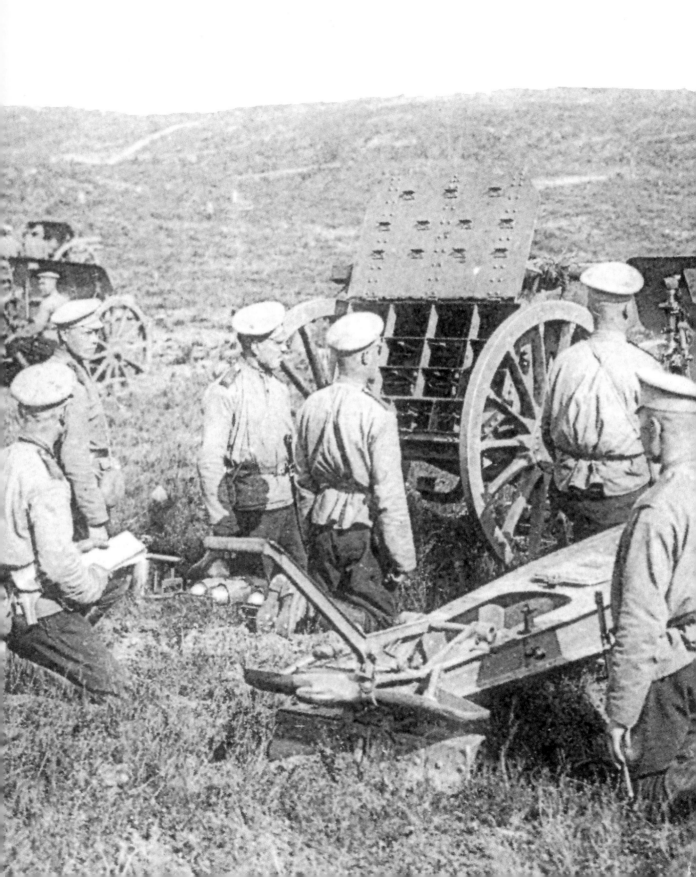

CHAPTER 2

Galicia and Poland

Although two entire Russian armies had been badly beaten by the Germans at Tannenberg and the Masurian Lakes, other Russian armies enjoyed considerable success against the Austro-Hungarians along the Carpathian Mountains. These victories helped the Russians remain in the war and gave them confidence that they could still win a great victory.

The Austro-Hungarian retreat that followed the Russian victory in Galicia soon developed into a rout. Thousands of Austro-Hungarian soldiers, most of them ethnic Slavs, simply deserted from the army. Many of them walked to Russian lines hoping to exchange information for food. Some even switched sides to fight with their fellow Slavs in the Russian Army against the hated Austro-Hungarians. In late August, the Austro-Hungarians reassembled the few men still under their control and set up a line of defence east of the fortress of Lemberg. The demoralization of the troops, however, made the line weak and the Russians had little trouble closing in on

Russian field artillerists firing over 'open sights'. The Russians were less experienced in sophisticated techniques such as indirect fire, wherein a spotter signalled the location of enemy targets to concealed artillerymen.

it from several directions. Russian Eighth Army commander General Alexei Brusilov pushed his Russian soldiers hard from 26 to 30 August, arriving at the Austro-Hungarian line near Halicz before the Austro-Hungarians had been able to finish even rudimentary defensive preparations.

On 31 August, Brusilov attacked and routed the right wing of the Austro-Hungarian line. Russian troops conducted a spirited bayonet charge, terrifying the already wavering Austro-Hungarians. Casualty estimates for World War I, especially on the Eastern Front, are notoriously inaccurate, but contemporary figures put Austro-Hungarian losses at 5000 men and 32 artillery pieces, many of which had not even been put in position to fire. As a drenching rain turned roads to mire and further demoralized the Austro-Hungarians, they retreated again, this time to a semicircle running north and east of Lemberg. As Austro-Hungarian soldiers continued to desert en masse, gaps in the defensive lines appeared that they could not fill. For more than a week, the Russians put pressure on the line, slowly and steadily driving the Austro-Hungarians out of their field defences and into the fortresses outside Lemberg itself.

As August turned to September, panic began to spread inside Lemberg. There was plenty of food and ammunition to allow the Austro-Hungarians to offer a reasonable defence of the city and its fortifications, but the scene of so many bedraggled and defeated soldiers sent the city into a paroxysm of fear of what the oncoming Russians might do. Rumours of thousands of men fleeing from the army and gross incompetence in the officer corps added to the mood of fear. The town's leaders undoubtedly knew that the main body of the Austro-Hungarian Army had moved well west, meaning that if the city did try to offer a

> ### Two Descriptions of the Carpathian Mountains
>
> *1. Troops from the side from which the Russians had to come faced the least favorable passes, and operated with the least shelter from biting winds. … Steep and craggy in their northern expanse, they fall away toward the south in broken, sloping plateaus. The passes vary in length from seven to 230 miles. Peaks rise to 8000 feet, the Gerlsdorfer, the highest, reaching 8737.*
>
> *2. The Carpathians have no formations to compare with Alpine groups or our own Rockies, but there are innumerable peaks, which vary in altitude from 5000 to 8000 feet. Because of the involved character of the passes, they have been for ages effective barriers against invaders. Prolonged siege warfare is impossible in the Carpathians. Trenches could be used for the protection of particular positions, but there could be no continuous lines of trenches.*

sustained and prolonged resistance to the Russians, it could expect little immediate help. And as the city and army's leaders must also have known, the customs of siege warfare dictated that the longer a city held out, the more vicious would be its sacking.

Amid this environment, the smashed remnants of five Austrian corps converged on a terrified Lemberg. Some Austro-Hungarian units had managed to recover and offer belated resistance, but it was far too little too late. The Russians began an artillery bombardment of the city and moved infantry around it to cut off possible avenues of retreat to the west. In the early morning hours of 2 September, Russian troops began to enter the city's suburbs. The Austro-Hungarians sent the only troops at hand to meet the

Austro-Hungarian officers survey a battlefield. Despite an official policy of encouraging diversity, the officer corps of the Austro-Hungarian Empire was disproportionately German in origin, and this bias grew more pronounced in the higher ranks.

This image of elaborate Austrian field defences rarely matched the reality. Defences in the vastness of the Eastern Front more commonly centred around river crossings, railway junctures and other strategic locations which needed protecting from the enemy's forces.

charge. They were part of one of the last remaining contingents of Slavs and the Russian commander ordered his men to fire above their heads as a signal that they could safely surrender themselves rather than be killed. The Slavs understood the message and threw down their guns and walked to Russian lines. Non-Slavic troops fled in the opposite direction. Most never made it out of the closing Russian noose.

Russia achieved the first major Allied victory on any front by capturing the city on 3 September. The defeat of the Austro-Hungarian forces outside Lemberg had been so thorough that the Russians entered the city itself without firing a shot, an event that created a scandal inside Austria-Hungary. Reports that Slavic residents had welcomed the Russians as liberators also served as a bad omen for the possible future

disintegration of the polyglot Austro-Hungarian Empire. The capture of Lemberg, which the Russians soon renamed the more Slavic-sounding Lvov, provided a critical morale boost not just to Russia, but to France and Britain as well. Estimates of the number of Austro-Hungarian prisoners of war stretch to 130,000, of whom perhaps 60,000 voluntarily deserted. Along with the prisoners came almost 700 artillery pieces, 2000 machine guns, 500,000 rifles (many of them from the city's large arsenal), mountains of ammunition, tons of food and control of the region's most important railway hub. More than eight rail lines converged at Lvov and the Russians soon took possession of captured rolling stock and the most important locomotive factory in Galicia as well.

The triumph at Lvov was soon followed by news of the important Franco-British victory on the Marne. Momentum seemed to be on Russia's side, but by September 1914 the Russian drive into Galicia had stalled. As often happened on the Eastern Front, armies advanced much further than their lines of communication could supply them, and the reorganization of Lvov for Russian purposes would take some time. Fresh Austro-Hungarian units had managed to set up a new line of defence near Grodek, roughly halfway between Lvov and the next major Austrian-Hungarian fortress complex at Przemysl, 97km (60 miles) to the west. The Austro-Hungarian left was anchored on the San River, a barrier that the Russians, acting with their customary caution, did not want to test until they had taken the time to regroup and reorganize.

The Russians did, however, begin to move against the city of Jaroslav on the San. They appear to have only wanted to stretch their forces towards the river to prepare for a future crossing. Russian forces fired shells into the city as they approached it, sending residents there into a panic like the one that had gripped Lemberg. Upon seeing the Russians approach in force, Austro-Hungarian forces voluntarily withdrew from Jaroslav, thus surrendering the entire San River. Their withdrawal also forced them to abandon the critical railroad from Cracow to Przemysl. The Russians cut the line and took command of the northern approaches to the massive Austro-Hungarian fortress complex at Przemysl, less than 48km (30 miles) away. At the same time, Brusilov moved on Grodek, the last major town on the eastern side of Przemysl, taking it with few casualties on 12 September.

The Russian position now looked much more favourable for a major autumn campaign. They controlled two of the three main rail lines leading into Przemysl and had effectively severed the Austro-Hungarian Empire from the rich agricultural and mineral resources of Galicia. Control of Przemysl would allow them to approach the Carpathian Mountain passes into Hungary and their cavalry patrols had already ridden into the Dukla Pass and found it lightly guarded. Russian generals therefore turned their focus on Przemysl, whose fall would leave the road to Cracow (and beyond Cracow, German Silesia) open. Such an operation would also remove the last barriers to an invasion of Hungary.

Przemysl, however, was a much stronger position than Lemberg had been, even with the loss of the rail

Two Russian officers near the fortress of Przemysl. The Russian officer corps was rife with rivalries that included family hatreds, professional and parochial jealousies, as well as ethnic differences. These tensions often complicated major military operations.

lines leading to Lemberg and Jaroslav. It held a more advantageous natural position and had been designed so that the outermost ring of fortifications protected bountiful fields and orchards that could keep a garrison supplied with fresh fruit and vegetables. Przemysl had also been stocked with more modern guns and had ammunition to supply those guns for months, if necessary. The Austro-Hungarian command had faith in the units it had stationed there and Przemysl was expected to be able to withstand a siege for eight months or more.

ASSAULT ON PRZEMYSL

The fall of Lemberg had also led the Austro-Hungarians to take more precautions with Przemysl. They evacuated the city's civilian population, both to avoid the spread of panic and to ease food and supply requirements. Mostly Poles and Ruthenians, the residents of Przemysl were believed to have distinct pro-Russian sympathies; thus the Austro-Hungarian generals in charge of the region also saw a military value in their removal. More than 80,000 new Austro-Hungarian soldiers came into the region to bolster the original 40,000 men who held the outer defences, and they brought with them vast stores of all kinds. The local commanders boasted that Przemysl could easily withstand a siege until May 1915 without reinforcement or resupply.

The Russians completed their initial approaches toward Przemysl by 26 September. Rumours had reached Russian lines that the garrison of Przemysl was demoralized and suffering badly from cholera. The Russian commander sent a message by radio to the Austro-Hungarian commander of the fortress asking him what terms he would accept for a surrender. The general replied that all talk of surrender was impossible until he had exhausted all of his supplies and means of defence. Believing that the Austro-Hungarians were bluffing, the Russians decided to storm the outer fortifications, but they met with surprising resistance. Lacking siege guns and now unsure about just how strong the garrison of Przemysl was, the Russians decided to settle in for a prolonged siege.

October brought predictably deteriorating weather, greatly complicating Russian attempts to bring large siege guns forward. The guns did not arrive at Przemysl until March 1915. Without those guns, the Russians could not hope to inflict enough damage on the fortresses to compel their surrender. They therefore decided to bypass Przemysl and set up their defences on the approaches to it in order to cut it off from any Austro-Hungarian relief attempts. As Cracow, not Przemysl, was their ultimate objective, the Russians not unreasonably concluded that time was on their side, even as they received reports of large-scale concentration of German soldiers in Cracow to prevent the Russians from moving into German Silesia. They therefore decided that bypassing Przemysl in favour of pressing on with their advance on Cracow before the Germans could set up their defences was the best course of action.

The Russian decision meant little to the Austro-Hungarians in Przemysl where a cold, bitter winter wrecked havoc on the garrison's morale and its health. News of the dispatch of German units to Cracow had boosted spirits, but when the Germans failed to come to their help, the men in Przemysl came to realize that they were being abandoned, not rescued. The Germans, they soon concluded, were in Cracow as part of a forward defence of their own interests in Silesia, not as part of a joint effort to rescue an ally. The men of Przemysl had been left to fend for themselves as long as they could, then they would have to face the Russians alone. By spring, they were low on ammunition, medicine and food. In March, the heavy Russian siege artillery finally arrived and began a systematic shelling of the fortifications.

> 'The garrison of the fortress held Przemysl to the very last hour that human force could do so in the military sense of the word.'
>
> Austro-Hungarian Minister for War

A Russian Cossack in Lemberg after its capture. The Cossacks had a particular reputation for cruelty, and were feared by their German opponents. They acted as the shock troops of the Russian Army and used their horses to increase their battlefield mobility.

Realizing that they could not hold out indefinitely against a heavy artillery bombardment, the Austro-Hungarian commander ordered a series of breakouts to find a favourable route of escape for as many of his men as possible. They all failed, as the report of the Austro-Hungarian Minister for War makes clear:

'Events developed around Przemysl more quickly than was expected. The last sortie officially reported was directed towards the east, and was undertaken not with the view of effecting the relief of the fortress, but to find out if the surrounding Russian force was as strong towards Grodek and Lemberg as in the other directions, and whether the Russians had fortified their positions in the Grodek direction, as well as to the south and west of the fortress.

'It was ascertained during the sorties that this was the case. The Russians, in fact, built counter-fortifications all around the fortress, even in the direction of their own territory, preparing for all eventualities.

'In fact, the last reports coming from the fortress all confirmed the report that the Russians built a new fortress all around the besieged territory. The fortifications were so constructed as to constitute an impenetrable obstacle to inward attacks, just the counter-form of the fortifications and defensive works of the fortress itself. The Russian ring was constructed exclusively against Przemysl with unparalleled skill and rapidity, and with all available means of modern technology.

'On the west a well fortified defending line and on the south a large Russian army stood in the way of any

attempt to relieve Przemysl. In addition, the roads leading towards Russia were well fortified, as the last sortie proved.'

The garrison at Przemysl had held out for almost 200 days, finally capitulating on 22 March 1915. The Austro-Hungarians lost 100,000 men, most of them entering Russian prisoner of war camps as starving and diseased shells of the men they had once been. Most Germans and Austro-Hungarians expected the Russians to head south, over the Carpathian passes and into Hungary rather than advance on the forts of Cracow, which could offer resistance to a siege for at least as long as Przemysl had. Having shown no particular aptitude for warfare to this point, the Austro-Hungarian general staff was out of ideas and looked to their German allies for help. For their part, the Germans saw all of their worst fears about the Austro-Hungarians confirmed. They had, however, decided that they had to rescue the Austro-Hungarians, and that the way to do so was through a

August von Mackensen (left) was the first commoner to be named a Royal Adjutant. In 1899 the Kaiser ennobled him. He was a corps commander at Tannenberg in 1914 and in the following year was named to command the Ninth Army. He would often wear the uniform of the 1st Life Hussars.

series of bold offensives to relieve the pressure on Hungary and drive the Russians back. Despite their success, the Germans knew that the Russians had taken heavy losses of their own in 1914 and had placed themselves in a difficult position to supply and reinforce. As was the case near Tannenberg, the Germans looked for places to take advantage of Russian overstretch and Russian sloppiness.

THE CAMPAIGNS IN POLAND AND THE BATTLE OF LODZ

The shattering Russian successes in Galicia in 1914 and early 1915 had occurred against the weaker Austro-Hungarian forces in the southern theatre. Further to the north, the much more powerful

Germans conducted operations aimed at clearing the Polish Salient of Russian troops and capturing Warsaw. Fresh from their major successes at Tannenberg and the Masurian Lakes, they expected to make relatively quick work of the Russians and hoped to deal them a fatal blow before the onset of winter made further pursuit impossible. A strike into Poland late in the year offered enticing possibilities, as it was close enough to Germany to allow for consistent lines of supply. The Germans could then spend the winter developing Warsaw and other cities as supply depots for campaigning in 1915.

For their part, the Poles had decidedly mixed loyalties. People who identified themselves as Polish lived in parts of the Russian, German and Austro-Hungarian empires. Thus ethnically Polish soldiers fought in the armies of all sides. While some Poles had an affinity with their fellow Catholics in Austria, most of them identified themselves as Polish and had few warm feelings for any of the great European powers. Nevertheless, the Poles knew that they sat in the area most likely to be fought over in any war in Eastern Europe. Most hoped beyond hope that the war might somehow lead to the establishment of an independent Poland, but even the most ardent Polish nationalists had trouble articulating a realistic scenario that might produce such an eventuality. When the war began the Tsar issued a statement promising Poles autonomy in the Russian Empire in return for their loyalty in the war, and the Germans soon followed suit with a similar pledge. While such ideas may have sounded better than nothing, most Poles looked upon them with a healthy dose of scepticism.

The German command team of Hindenburg and Ludendorff did not concern themselves with the problems of the national identifications of the peoples of Eastern Europe. They were too busy planning their next campaign. By mid-September 1914, the Germans

Recollections of German Prisoners of War Captured on the Eastern Front

When you know that the prison camps are all in distant, cold Siberia, try and think of the lot of prisoners. Yet for the moment the Germans were content. They were allowed to sleep. This is the boon that the man fresh from the trenches asks above all things. His days and nights have been one constant strain of alertness. His brain has been racked with the roar of cannon and his nerves frayed by the irregular bursting of shell. His mind is chaos.

One thing he knows, he must fire and fire and fire. It does not matter if the gun barrel blisters his fingers with its heat, never must it stop. That is the only way to hold back the line of wicked bayonets. When the bayonets come it is death or a Siberian prison camp. But when a soldier is once captured he feels that this responsibility of holding back the enemy is no longer his. He has failed. Well, he can sleep in peace now.

The fighting for the Bzura was a desperate, endless struggle. Days of seesaw battle found the Germans pressing the major part of their military might against

Some Slavs captured from the Austro-Hungarian Army volunteered to fight in the Russian Army in order to avoid the misery of the POW camps.

the angle made by the Bzura and Rawka with the Pilitza River. Charge and counter-charge were the order of the day and night. Supermen, indeed, are these soldiers of the first line who stagger forward and back with repulse and attack.

German troops assemble during the 1914 offensive on Warsaw. The city was the historic capital of Russian Poland and therefore was an important symbol as well as a key communications centre. It thus was a primary target of German operations.

had sent enough reinforcements to Poland to form a new army, the Ninth, based around Posen. A veteran of Gumbinnen and Tannenberg named August von Mackensen soon commanded it. Mackensen wore the distinctive headdress of his original regiment, the elite 'Death's Head' Hussars. With its shako bearing an imposing skull and crossbones and Mackensen's own strict military bearing, he was the very model of a German general. Like most of his German peers, he had full confidence in himself and his men. He also held the Russians in contempt and was as convinced as anyone that the German Army could repeat the thrashing of the Russians at Tannenberg almost any time it wished to do so.

Thus Mackensen took his new German Ninth Army into the field almost as soon as it had been created despite the fact that no fewer than three Russian armies sat opposite him and badly outnumbered him. He planned to smash in the centre (or face) of the Polish Salient, hoping to drive the Russians east and take

Warsaw before the onset of winter forced a halt in operations. Hindenburg saw immediate value in the operation and hoped that as a side benefit, a German drive on Warsaw might distract Russian attention from Galicia and thereby provide the Austro-Hungarians with at least a modicum of indirect help. German engineers built roads through the forests and began converting the Polish railways to the German gauge as they advanced in order to ease supply problems.

Russian defences were in the hands of Nikolai Ruzski, a veteran if unremarkable general, who had the confidence of his friend Tsar Nicholas II. He had three armies under his command. The First Army, under Pavel Rennenkampf, had still not fully recovered from its thrashing at the Masurian Lakes and the Second, which had been mauled at Tannenberg, was still reorganizing under completely new leaders. The Russian Fifth Army came north to help bolster the line. Unable to form a solid defensive line with such disparate forces of such uneven quality, Ruzski opted to defend the major river crossings.

This strategy seemed to bear fruit in mid-October when the Russians used heavy artillery to turn back a German attempt to cross the Vistula near Novogeorgievsk and another near Ivangorod. The

Russians then attacked and pushed the Germans back away from the Vistula, inflicting huge casualties at Kozience. Frustrated, the Germans called in Zeppelins to bombard Warsaw from the air, hoping to instil panic and confusion. They dropped 14 bombs, the first attack of its kind in Eastern Europe. The Germans, however, cancelled air operations when the Russians got a major morale boost from shooting down a Zeppelin and when it became obvious that the 1914 version of shock and awe would not achieve the desired ends.

On 15 and 16 October the Germans renewed their attacks on Warsaw, almost forcing the Russians to abandon the city. However, the weight of Russian numbers and the strngth of their artillery enabled them to hold on. Reinforcements arrived from Siberia,

tough-looking men followed by ample stocks of ammunition and trainloads of food. Even erstwhile anti-Russian Polish nationalists enthusiastically cheered them as they arrived with a brass band leading the way. The Germans retreated to the northwest, torching farms and slaughtering livestock as they went, partly to prevent these resources from falling into Russian hands and partly as vengeance for the people of Warsaw's support of Russia. This policy of scorched earth probably ended any possibility of Poles joining the German side, although Russian behaviour in the Polish countryside was often little better.

The Austro-Hungarian fortress of Przemysl held out longer than the fortress at Lemberg. It surrendered in March 1915, opening the route to western Galicia and the approaches to the strategic cities of Tarnow and Cracow.

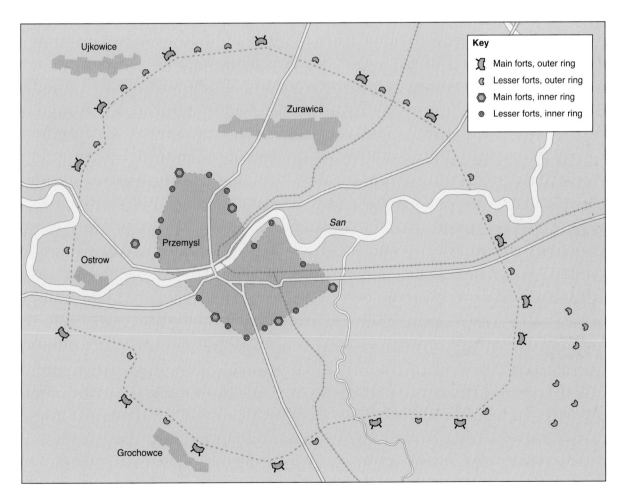

Hindenburg was angry at the lost opportunity to take Warsaw and blamed the Austro-Hungarian failure in Galicia for freeing up too many Russians. He decided to begin placing Austro-Hungarian divisions inside the German Ninth Army command structure. He presented the idea to Conrad, the Austro-Hungarian commander, as a fait accompli, not as a proposal to be discussed, on 1 November. Conrad was stung by the insult to both the sovereignty of the Austro-Hungarian Empire and his own military acumen, but, given the beating his forces had taken in Galicia, he knew he had no choice.

The German Ninth Army became the Central Powers Ninth Army and was dominated by German commanders from top to bottom.

Now with full control of all of the Central Powers forces in the Polish Salient, Hindenburg and Mackensen began another drive for Warsaw. At the

same time, the Russians misread their intelligence and mistakenly believed that the Central Powers were in full retreat from Poland and therefore exposed to an aggressive pursuit. They therefore attacked, choosing the junction of the German and Austro-Hungarian forces near Kielce. They succeeded in pushing the Austro-Hungarians back, confirming in Hindenburg's mind the wisdom of his decision to begin the amalgamation of Central Powers forces under German tutelage. Russian Cossacks chased retreating Central Powers soldiers, cutting off their lines of communication and taking no prisoners. By 10 November, the Russians had almost cleared the Polish Salient of German and Austro-Hungarian forces and stood poised to launch deep attacks of their own.

THE RUSSIAN RESPONSE

The Russians were elated. They had seemingly proved that they had recovered from the twin disasters of Tannenberg and the Masurian Lakes. More importantly, they were simultaneously putting pressure on the Germans in the Polish Salient and the Austro-Hungarians in Galicia. Russian forces were within 32km (20 miles) of Cracow and some Russian patrols had ranged 24km (15 miles) into Silesia and Prussia. Grand Duke Nikolai took considerable pride in these victories, sending a telegram to his French counterpart Joseph Joffre that boasted of 'the greatest victory since the beginning of the war'. Undoubtedly, Nikolai intended for the French to receive the subtle hint that at this point of the war the Russians had inflicted significantly more casualties and taken more land from the enemy than the French and British combined. Russia's advance guards were just 320km (200 miles) from Berlin.

Nikolai could not have known that, on 10 November 1914, the Russians probably stood at the height of their power on the Eastern Front. Despite having inflicted tremendous casualties on their enemies, the Russians, too, had bled badly and had

German soldiers near Lodz. Located near Warsaw, the city was the scene of intense fighting in late 1914. The Germans eventually took the city, but at great cost, allowing the Russians to hold Warsaw at the end of the year.

lost their most experienced officers and NCOs. Having advanced so far so fast, the fragile Russian supply system was showing signs of cracking. At the same time, the Germans were regrouping and reorganizing, promising to make any sustained advance into Silesia or on Cracow very bloody. More seriously, the Russians had advanced haphazardly, according to local conditions and the vagaries of geography. As a result, there were significant gaps between units, meaning that, as at Tannenberg, Russian armies had exposed flanks and could not easily come to one another's aid.

Thus once again the strengths of the Germans could come into play against the weaknesses of the Russians. Hindenburg, aware of his inferiority in men and artillery, issued cautious orders, hoping to manoeuvre his units into the gaps between Russian armies and compel them to withdraw without fighting a major battle. Nevertheless, he told his commanders to look for opportunities for attacks against the Russians, whom he believed were 'approaching the

The Russians used medium artillery pieces like this 15cm gun to destroy the fortifications at Lemberg and Przemysl. This gun's design dated to 1877 and had limitations, but proved adequate against the Austro-Hungarian defences.

end of their tether'. Captured Russians reported that even officers had gone days on half rations or much less. Hindenburg therefore hoped to use German dexterity to move the Russians back by finesse if possible, by force if necessary.

Within five days, the Germans had seemingly proved Hindenburg right. On 11 November, Mackensen had spotted an exposed flank in the unfortunate Russian First Army, commanded by Rennenkampf. The Germans drove into the flank and pushed Rennenkampf north, away from the Russian Second Army. Rennenkampf lost 12,000 men, most of them prisoners of war cut off from the rest of the Second Army by faster and suppler German forces. The situation looked too much like a replay of Tannenberg for Grand Duke Nikolai, who removed Rennenkampf from command on the spot and grew concerned that the Russian Second Army was about to be encircled once again. On 15 November, Nikolai ordered the Second Army to move to the supply depot of Lodz. He also sent thousands of reinforcements to the city to prevent the Germans from trapping the Second Army once again.

Hindenburg pointed to the surrender of almost 20,000 Russians in less than one week as evidence that his advance was breaking the will of the Russian soldier and at the same time securing Silesia from a Slavic invasion. The Kaiser must have agreed; on 17 November he promoted Hindenburg to field marshal, the highest rank in the German Army. Perhaps distracted by their own success, none of the senior German commanders noted that the Russian Fifth Army had covered 113km (70 miles) in two days through a snowstorm, giving the Russians a total of seven corps in and around Lodz. Even if he had been notified, it is unlikely that Hindenburg or his staff would have thought the Russians capable of such a feat. Ludendorff was mistaken enough to read Russian movements as preparations for a massive withdrawal to Warsaw and the Vistula River.

Thus, for once the Russians had surprise and the upper hand. Fighting at Lodz, moreover, put them

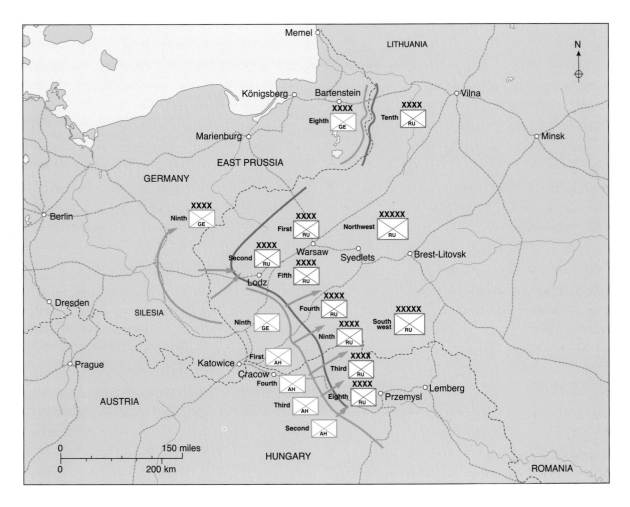

near a supply centre and compensated for their poor lines of communications. By 18 November the Russians were close to encircling the Germans, but lacked the skill to complete the manoeuvre. A German corps broke through the Russian lines, then attacked the Russians from the rear, all through another snowstorm that literally and figuratively froze the Russians in place. The German corps seized 16,000 Russian prisoners of war and 64 artillery pieces. Confused officers in the Russian First and Second armies, fearful of another calamity, began to retreat back to Warsaw. Soon the city was full of wounded men and straggling soldiers looking for their units.

The Germans would certainly have liked to have pursued, but lacked the numbers needed to do so. With

The German invasion of the Polish Salient involved intense fighting amidst poor weather conditions. The Russians had better lines of communications into the salient than the Germans had around it, but the latter still managed to capture Lodz, a significant prize.

winter approaching they settled for occupying Lodz, then the second largest city in Russian Poland. They entered the city on 6 December, having flattened the face of the Polish Salient, although not as much as they would have liked. By the end of 1914, the Germans had seized 90,650 square kilometres (35,000 square miles) of formerly Russian territory and transferred more than 10 million Poles from Russia to Germany. The first year of the war on the Eastern Front had ended with more casualties, more movement and more men engaged than its more famous counterpart in the west.

The fluidity of the Eastern Front caused tremendous hardship for civilians caught in the crossfire. Poles like these refugees were in an especially difficult position as their countrymen fought in the German, Austro-Hungarian and Russian armies.

Like the Western Front, however, no one could predict what would happen in 1915 or how much longer the killing would go on.

THE SECOND BATTLE OF THE MASURIAN LAKES

Hindenburg stayed busy throughout the winter. He and Ludendorff reorganized German lines of communication, tightened the defences of Cracow in order to secure Silesia, and increased their hold over the units of the Austro-Hungarian Army in Russian Poland and Galicia. They also designed a new offensive to take place in the region of the Masurian Lakes aimed at securing the left flank of their new possessions in Poland and forcing the Russians to

withdraw east of the Vistula River. The operation was to be two pronged. In the north the German Eighth and Tenth armies would attack the Russian Tenth Army in the narrow land corridors between the Masurian Lakes where they had achieved such a victory in 1914. In the south, Mackensen's Ninth Army would make another drive on Warsaw.

Mackensen's drive was a feint, but the Russians eagerly swallowed the bait. Hindenburg had ordered his intelligence officers to sweeten the pot by spreading the rumour that the field marshal had promised that he would capture Warsaw as a present for the Kaiser's birthday, 27 January. The ruse worked as the Russians reinforced the Warsaw sector.

Using more than 600 artillery pieces, Mackensen's artillerists opened up a furious barrage that convinced the Russians of the imminence of a major operation. On 4 February, the Germans attacked in a snowstorm, gaining an impressive eight kilometres (five miles) before deciding not to risk their gains; instead they headed back to more secure supply lines. The Russians succeeded in chasing the Germans and inflicting more casualties than Hindenburg and Mackensen had expected, but the diversion had done its job.

The main attack was to come in the north and the belated birthday present Hindenburg had in mind for the Kaiser was not Warsaw but another Tannenberg. Wilhelm had even transferred his headquarters from the west to the east to see his armies at work against the hated Slavs. Hindenburg had used the Russian concentration around Warsaw to move 300,000 men into East Prussia and had divided them into two armies. One of them had as its base Tilsit and the Niemen River, where in 1807 Napoleon and Tsar Alexander I had signed a treaty that enforced a new order for Europe. It had included French control over Warsaw and the humiliation of Prussia. In 1915

France and Russia again threatened Prussia, but this time the forces of the Kaiser were in an altogether different position.

The battle began on 7 February, as the actions around Warsaw were winding down. The Russians were taken by complete surprise and the Germans began an aggressive attack on the southern flank despite terrible cold and snow. Two days later the Germans hit the Russian northern flank, driving it in as well. In all the Germans advanced 113km (70 miles) in seven days. Another great German success seemed to be near at hand, but one Russian corps, the XXII, holed up in the Augustowo Forest and fought extremely

Russian troops fight in the Polish Salient in 1914. Winter warfare posed special challenges of supply and movement. Normally, these challenges benefit the defender, and they did so in 1914 as the Russians withstood German assaults.

One way to deal with the bad weather common during the Eastern Front winters – Russian ski troops are shown here on patrol. Several Russian units were from icy places like Siberia and knew how to deal with the cold.

well for more than a week, thus making the advance of the Germans on either side impossible. At one point a Russian cavalry charge in the forest almost brought the entire operation to a stop when it came close to grabbing the Kaiser himself.

The battle, sometimes called the Battle of Augustowo or the Second Battle of the Masurian Lakes, was another disaster for the Russians. The German claims of 100,000 Russian prisoners of war were probably inflated, but not by too much. The Russians did manage to piece together enough men to contain the offensive and, alongside the worsening weather conditions, were able to keep the Germans from turning south towards Warsaw. The Kaiser proclaimed a great victory, claiming that 'our beloved East Prussia is free from the enemy', but the Russians were still in Warsaw and far from the end of their resources.

More seriously, the Russians had maintained important pressure on the Austro-Hungarians amid better weather in Galicia. By March, they had captured three passes in the Carpathian Mountains and, with

the fall of Przemysl, the Russians were able to move thousands of men south. Any threat to Hungary had to be taken seriously because the critical grain fields there were central to German plans to compensate for food lost to the British blockade. Moreover, most Germans assumed that if Hungary looked weak, Romania would enter the war to get the spoils of Transylvania before the Russians overran it. Romania's entry into the war, combined with a British success in the recently opened Dardanelles campaign (where naval attacks began on 19 February), would have drastic consequences for the Ottoman Empire and Central Powers' fortunes in the Balkans. Thus, although about this time the Kaiser made his famous statement that the Carpathian Mountains were not worth the bones of a single Pomeranian grenadier, his generals knew better. The Austro-Hungarians would need to be saved from their own manifest incompetence in the Carpathians even if all other operations had to be put on hold.

GERMANY TAKES OVER

As a result of Austria-Hungary's abysmal performance in the Galician campaigns, German senior officers had become convinced that, in the words of a phrase that made the rounds in 1915, they were shackled to a

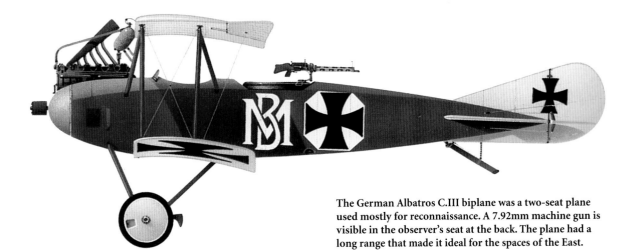

The German Albatros C.III biplane was a two-seat plane used mostly for reconnaissance. A 7.92mm machine gun is visible in the observer's seat at the back. The plane had a long range that made it ideal for the spaces of the East.

corpse. Italy's signature to the Treaty of London (whose terms were secret, but generally suspected in Berlin) in March 1915 complicated the position of an already stretched Austro-Hungarian Empire and forced its army to plan to defend another front. Italy declared war on Austria-Hungary shortly thereafter and began combat operations in the Isonzo River valley in May. At the same time, the risk of the Romanians invading Transylvania had not gone away either. Austria-Hungary was suffering badly from its wounds, and the fact that many of these wounds were

self-inflicted did little to help the Germans figure out what they should do next.

They finally concluded that, corpse though it may be, Austria-Hungary was too important to German interests to allow it to be carved up by the jackals and vultures on its borders. An Austro-Hungarian collapse would sever Germany from its ally in Turkey and any possible future allies in the Balkans. More importantly, Germany needed Austria-Hungary to tie down tens of thousands of Russian soldiers (even if they did so ineptly) and secure the southern approaches into Germany. Finally, the Germans feared that their international prestige might drop even further if it appeared that they had abandoned their most important ally.

Thus, closing the lid on the corpse's coffin was out of the question. But so was what German officers saw as the status quo of Germany defeating the

Russian ski troops used as light infantry. Of special interest are the white uniforms that allowed the troops to blend into the snow and therefore be harder to spot from the air. The Russians did not have many such troops, but they were occasionally effective.

73

Italy Enters the War

Italy entered the war in the spring of 1915 to gain territory at Austria-Hungary's expense. Italy's decision at once complicated and re-energized Austria-Hungary's military position. Italy's entry forced the Austro-Hungarians to find more men to defend yet another front, this one in the brutal conditions of the Julian Alps. On the other hand, the declaration of war from Italy, a former ally, appeared to most people in the empire as a blatant stab in the back. It thus led to a rise in morale, even among some of the ethnically Italian parts of the empire. The Italians soon became the one enemy that all peoples of the empire could agree to hate.

Italian Bersaglieri celebrate Italy's declaration of war in 1915. Italy's entry into the war forced the Austro-Hungarian Army to divert resources to another front. The Austro-Hungarians sent a Croatian general to that front with orders to hold the mountain passes along the Isonzo River.

Russians only to have the Russians compensate with massive victories over Austria-Hungary. The Germans therefore began to assume more and more dominance over Austro-Hungarian forces, with German officers taking command of more units and Austro-Hungarian forces even starting to wear German uniforms and use German equipment. German senior officers stopped consulting with or, in some cases, even informing their Austro-Hungarian counterparts on decisions regarding shared matters of strategy and operations. Austria-Hungary survived, but at the cost of becoming a virtual vassal state to their larger and more powerful ally.

THE STRATEGIC DILEMMA

From the perspective of Berlin, the survival of Austria-Hungary was important first and foremost for what it could mean for Germany. Throughout the winter of 1914/15 the Germans were locked in a heated argument about where the war might be won in the near future. 'Westerners' argued that no amount of lopsided victories in the east could knock out Russia

and eliminate the Napoleonic nightmare of a deep pursuit into the barren steppes. They wanted a full effort on the Western Front dedicated to knocking out France and Great Britain which, they argued, would in turn force the Russians to sign a peace treaty that would allow Germany to keep its eastern gains. At this point, the westerners included several influential senior officials, including chief of staff General Erich von Falkenhayn.

The easterners argued that the war in the west had devolved into a series of sieges that would do nothing but attrite German forces and wear both sides out to no eventual purpose. They did not believe that the British and French lines could be broken, nor did they believe that any major strategic goal like Paris was within the short-term reach of German forces. They argued that the Germans in the west should straighten out their defensive line, dig stronger trenches, and go

Austro-Hungarian artillery moves into action; note the planks to help movement over the muddy ground. The empire's economy was largely agricultural, and the strains of an industrial war began to show. The Germans provided help, but that help came with strings attached.

fully on to the defensive. Such a movement, they contended, could free up as many as 12 corps to be moved east for grand encircling operations against the Russians. Victories in the east, they argued, might knock the Russians out of the war, thus freeing up the full weight of the German Army to fight on the Western Front. At the very least, the Germans would add thousands of square kilometres of eastern territory to their empire, some of which they might even be able to trade back to the Russians in exchange for territorial or economic concessions elsewhere. Politically, the east held out the promise of more great victories on the scale of Tannenberg, or at the very

German Field Marshal Erich von Falkenhayn had little respect for his Austrian allies. He called them 'childish military dreamers' and the Austrian people 'wretched'. He nevertheless saw the need to support the Austrians in their hour of need.

British and to mask the movement of a limited number of troops that he would send east. The total number of troops fell far short of the 12 corps that many easterners had sought, but the transfers, as well as the arrival of new conscripts, would give the Germans enough men to launch a major offensive in the east in the spring. The western offensive became the Second Battle of Ypres, which began in late April. Lacking men because of the troop transfers to the east, Falkenhayn decided to employ poison gas for the first time on the Western Front. The gas created enormous gaps in the Allied line, but, lacking large manpower reserves, there were no troops to exploit the gaps thus created.

If the Second Battle of Ypres failed to give the Germans control of Flanders, it did meet its mission of masking the transfer of more German troops to the east. The Russians remained ecstatic over their capture of Przemysl in March and assumed that the German offensive near Ypres meant that the Germans would focus their efforts in the west in 1915. With the Germans in charge of staff work for the great eastern offensive, moreover, the Russians had a harder time divining enemy intentions than they had had with the notoriously porous Austro-Hungarian staff system.

least the possibility of the capture of major symbols like Warsaw. The west, by contrast, seemed to offer little but more inconsequential fighting.

The debate failed to reach resolution so Falkenhayn finally settled on a compromise. He would launch a small offensive in the west to distract the French and

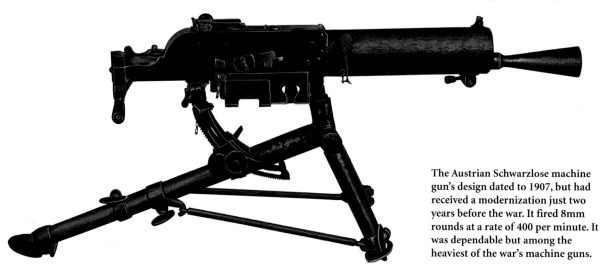

The Austrian Schwarzlose machine gun's design dated to 1907, but had received a modernization just two years before the war. It fired 8mm rounds at a rate of 400 per minute. It was dependable but among the heaviest of the war's machine guns.

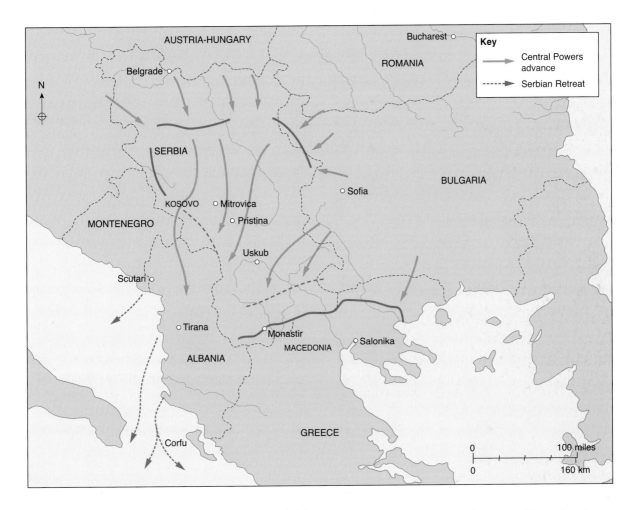

The German concentrations had placed nine field armies in the east, four of them north of Warsaw, one immediately opposite Warsaw and four south of Warsaw. The Russians were still more numerous and were fighting on their own territory. The significance of fighting in Russia lay less in some mythic attachment to Mother Russia and her sacred soil than in the fact that all railway lines in the theatre were on the Russian, not the German gauge. To compensate for their numerical inferiority, the Germans had worked carefully and deliberately to concentrate their assets in a region where they might obtain a local superiority of numbers.

The area they chose was the region between the towns of Gorlice and Tarnow in Galicia. The region sat near the Carpathian Mountains and was more than

The war in Serbia ended in a clear Austro-Hungarian victory, after German intervention. If the war had not expanded into a general European war, that victory might have ended the conflict, but instead it became just a minor sideshow to a much larger war.

240km (150 miles) away from Warsaw. The choice of Gorlice-Tarnow thus shows that the Germans were more interested in providing immediate assistance to the faltering Austro-Hungarians than they were in the final capture of Warsaw. Only if the breakthrough at Gorlice-Tarnow succeeded would an attack on Warsaw open.

All of the planning for the operation was German. Falkenhayn did not even see the need to inform his Austrian counterpart, Conrad, of the decision to attack until three weeks before the scheduled start date despite the fact that thousands of Austro-Hungarian soldiers (now commanded mostly by Germans) would take part. Perhaps the Germans were right to cut their allies out of the loop. By late April, they had concentrated 357,000 Central Powers troops in the Gorlice-Tarnow region against 219,000 Russians. They had also managed to create an advantage in artillery pieces in the sector of 1500 heavy guns to 700. The Russians never suspected either the size or the intentions of the Central Powers forces opposite them.

THE START OF THE OFFENSIVE

The German offensive began at first light on 2 May. For four hours all of the guns in the German artillery park fired along a 48km (30-mile) front. The idea of this short but intense 'hurricane' bombardment was to instil shock into the enemy, crush his barbed wire and provide the impetus for an infantry assault before reserves in the rear could be alerted and brought forward. The artillery would also clear the field of resistance in order to allow the presumably less sophisticated Austro-Hungarian units and the inexperienced recent German call-ups to fight at odds in their favour. Once the Russians began to panic and retreat out of their trenches, German shrapnel fire could decimate them in the open field, thus placing

the burden of victory on the experienced gunners rather than the green infantry.

The plan worked to perfection. It took less than 48 hours for the armies of the Central Powers to break through the lines of defence formed by the Russian Third Army. Two Russian corps alone took almost 70,000 casualties in two days. The Russians had been caught in a redeployment of forces to the Carpathians in anticipation of a crossing of the passes into Hungary as soon as the snows melted. Thus, they could offer little help to the beleaguered forces at Gorlice-Tarnow. All the Russian headquarters could think to do was issue a rather silly order forbidding Russian soldiers to retreat.

The collapse of the Russians at Gorlice-Tarnow had immediate ripple effects all over the Eastern Front. Units at Gorlice-Tarnow themselves began retreating as many as 16km (10 miles) per day despite the high command's order. As a result of their retreat, units in the Carpathians were now threatened with encirclement or being trapped against the mountains. They began their own retreat to the San River, but many never made it there as German advance guards reached the crossings and secured the bridges first. Russian units south of Warsaw were also at risk of being attacked in the flank or enveloped. The

German Report on the opening of the Gorlice-Tarnow Offensive

Reports of prisoners are unanimous in describing the effect of the artillery fire of the [Germans] as more terrible than the imagination can picture. The men, who were with difficulty recovering from the sufferings and exertions they had undergone, agreed that they could not imagine conditions worse in hell than they had been for four hours in the trenches.

Corps, divisions, brigades and regiments melted away as though in the heat of a furnace. In no direction was escape possible, for there was no spot of ground on which the 400 guns of the Teutonic allies had not exerted themselves. All the generals and staff officers of one Russian division were killed or wounded. Moreover,

insanity raged in the ranks of the Russians, and from all sides hysterical cries could be heard rising above the roar of our guns, too strong for human nerves.

Over the remnants of the Russians who crowded in terror into the remotest corners of their trenches there broke the mighty rush of our masses of infantry, before which also the Russian reserves, hurrying forward, crumbled away.

In barely 14 days the army of Mackensen carried its offensive forward from Gorlice to Jaroslav. With daily fighting, for the most part against fortified positions, it crossed the line of three rivers and gained in territory more than 100km.

breakthrough at Gorlice-Tarnow had turned into a rout on a massive scale. In the first week alone more than 140,000 Russians fell into the hands of the Central Powers, so many that the Germans stopped keeping track of them. Unknown thousands more were killed or simply deserted.

What became known as the 'Great Retreat' was underway, whatever the wishes of the Russian high command to stop it. On 3 June, German units walked back into Przemysl without firing a shot, loudly singing patriotic songs as they did so. The fortification that the Russians had spent so much time and energy besieging, and finally capturing with such fanfare, had to be given back to the enemy. The Germans quite ungraciously made boasts about how easy it had been

Austrian troops march back into Lemberg after the Russian retreat. The Germans took credit for the victory, although they did allow Austrian troops the honour of marching into the fortress. The incident further strained relations between the two Central Powers.

to take Przemysl back from the Russians and questioned how the Austro-Hungarians could possibly have lost it in the first place. By the middle of May the Russian armies had retreated more than 160km (100 miles) and by the end of the month they had lost an astonishing 410,000 men.

Success followed on success. In late June, the Austro-Hungarians got a bit of their pride back by retaking Lvov and changing its name once again to Lemberg. They then invited the Kaiser to come to

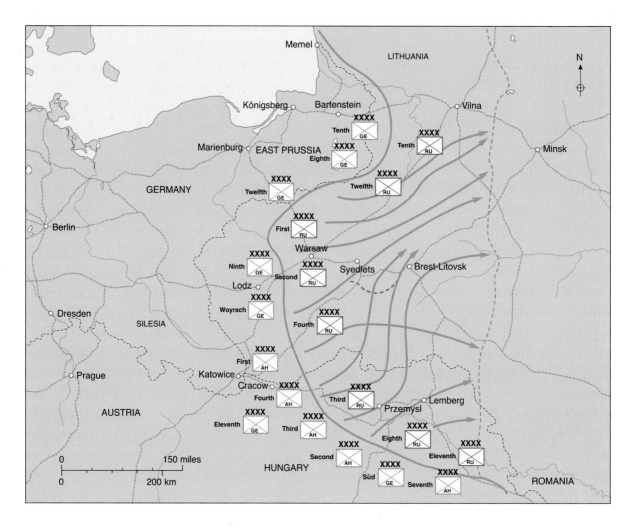

The massive Russian retreat that followed the breakthrough at Gorlice-Tarnow seemed to confirm in German minds their superiority to the Russians. The great victory, however, still failed to force Russia from the war, and the Eastern Front remained a persistent distraction for the Germans.

Lemberg for a celebratory dinner, which he ungraciously held in Berlin instead, and without the presence of any Austro-Hungarian officials. Promotions flowed, with both Mackensen and Conrad being named field marshals. Austro-Hungarian supply problems eased with the capture of mountains of Russian guns and ammunition.

The Gorlice-Tarnow Offensive went so well for the Germans that in July they launched a second major offensive that aimed at the long-awaited capture of

Warsaw. The original plan to encircle the city and its hinterland simultaneously from the north and south (and thereby trap hundreds of thousands of Russian soldiers) proved too ambitious, even for the Germans. They did, however, cut the main railway lines into the city and began a general attack all along the Eastern Front with what one reporter called 'the most formidable [force] yet launched against the Allies'. Alongside the operations against Warsaw the Germans sent six corps into the Baltic provinces, where significant Baltic German populations, and thus sympathy for Germany, existed.

Toward the end of July the Germans concentrated a remarkable 45 corps with the final mission of securing Warsaw. The Germans planned to use these massive forces in a series of flank attacks aimed at cutting off all the roads leading into the city rather than attempting an urban battle in the city's narrow streets. They hoped that the Russians would see that the threat was not just to Warsaw but also to the entire Russian Army if it committed itself to defend the city at the risk of encirclement. They knew that the Russians would have no choice but to sacrifice the city voluntarily in order to save what was left of their army.

The jaws of the Central Powers advance thus began to close on Warsaw. On 23 July the Germans crossed the Narew River and captured some key fortifications to Warsaw's south. On 28 July, they began to cross the Vistula north of the city, bringing with them heavy siege guns and threatening both flanks. The last major fortification protecting Warsaw fell in due course, leading Hindenburg to invite the Kaiser to come to the

The Russians were reduced to taking extreme measures to stop the retreat. These men are local militia soldiers enlisted into the Russian Third Army. They were no more able to halt the retreat than the Russian regulars.

> 'The forest for miles looks as if a hurricane had swept through it. Trees staggering from their shattered trunks, and limbs hanging everywhere showed where shrapnel shells had been bursting.'

An eyewitness account of a battlefield near Warsaw, 1915

front to witness the German capture of Warsaw, expected in a few days. More than 350,000 of the city's residents were already in flight, clogging the roads and making any orderly Russian withdrawal (which Grand Duke Nikolai finally ordered) all that much harder to conduct. Rather than defend the city, Russian soldiers turned to dismantling as much of it as possible, taking factory equipment and metals with them to prevent them from falling into German hands.

Russian Changes in Command

In the wake of the Gorlice–Tarnow disaster, the Tsar made the fateful decision to replace his uncle, the Grand Duke Nikolai, as commander of the Russian Army. Nikolai had led reasonably well to manage the disaster, reorganizing Russian forces and helping the retreat avoid becoming a rout. Nevertheless, the disaster was too great for the Tsar to keep the commander in his place. Having no one else of senior rank to turn to, the Tsar named himself as commander. He had virtually no understanding of the complexities of the army or of modern warfare, but hoped that his assumption of command would rally Russian morale. Most of the real work was done by the loyal but unpopular General Mikhail Alexeev, but when Russian military fortunes declined, the Tsar, not Alexeev, took most of the blame, with dramatic consequences for his regime's survival.

On the night of 3/4 August, the Russians gave the order for the withdrawal of the final units from the Warsaw region. At 3am on 5 August, Russian engineers blew up the last remaining bridges over the Vistula River. The first Germans pursued in pontoon boats, crossing the river just three hours later and walking into an eerily calm city. The Kaiser ordered public celebrations all across Germany. Perceptive German generals, however, noted that the seizure of Warsaw alone meant little to the overall German strategic picture. The Russians still showed no sign of quitting and were instead taking a page from Napoleon's book. The Germans continued the pursuit and the Russians continued the retreat, surrendering the strongpoints of Brest-Litovsk on 26 August, Grodno on 2 September and Vilna on 19 September before heavy rains gave them some breathing space.

German soldiers make a triumphant entry into Warsaw. Poles who had hoped that the expulsion of the Russians would lead to Polish independence were quickly disappointed when they faced an intense German occupation and exploitation instead.

The loss of territory was one problem for the Russians. The front line moved more than 480km (300 miles), forcing the Russians to give up Poland and significant parts of their Baltic provinces. The loss of men was even more serious. The Russian Army, in the words of one of its senior commanders was 'melting like snow'. More than 800,000 Russians became prisoners of war or deserted. Exact figures remain a matter of conjecture, but most sources agree that the Russians lost two million men between May and September, losses that even the massive Russian Army could not easily replace.

In a rare moment of clarity and lucidity, Falkenhayn suggested using the massive victory to cut a deal with the Russians. He proposed to give them back most of what they had lost in 1915 in exchange

For Austrian soldiers like these cavalrymen, the success at Gorlice-Tarnow was a mixed blessing. The Russians had been driven away from the Carpathian Mountain passes, but the Germans had assumed virtual control of the Austrian military, and would remain in charge for the rest of the war.

for a peace that would enable the Germans to transfer men to the Western Front for a massive 1916 campaign. Few Germans heeded his advice. They looked aghast at giving back what they had conquered and worried that opening talks with the Russians would send the wrong signs to the British and the French. German industrialists, salivating at the chance to get access to natural resources in Poland and Russia, pressured the government to fight for even more territory. The war in the east would thus continue into 1916 and beyond.

CHAPTER 3

Russia's Recovery

Russia's catastrophic defeat in the wake of the Gorlice–Tarnow Offensive signalled to most Germans and Russians alike that the Russian Army was on the verge of collapse. Nevertheless, the Russians conducted a successful offensive in 1916 that temporarily revived their fortunes and proved part of the old adage that Russia is never as weak as she looks.

A t the end of 1915 the Germans could be forgiven for presuming that the Russians were at the end of their rope. They had been chased from Poland, had suffered repeated massive defeats and had shown that their system of war was wholly unsuited to the modern, industrial battlefields of 1914 and 1915. Russian generalship had ranged from uninspiring to abysmal, and the Russian transport and economic systems were already showing serious signs of cracking. Despite their ability to retreat into their own massive territory and call upon seemingly endless manpower reserves, Russia appeared to most Germans

At the Chantilly Conference in December 1915, the Russians agreed to conduct an offensive in summer 1916, even though many people doubted that they had the capacity to do so. At approximately the same time, the British, French and Italians would also take the offensive.

as a fatally wounded nation whose last death throes could not possibly be far away.

The view in Paris and London was broadly similar. British and French military attachés reported on the mismanagement of the Russian armies and the manifest incompetence of the Russian state to handle the war. Russian offensives in the Caucasus theatre had gone little better than those in Poland, drawing Russian resources away from what the British and French saw as the main theatre of Russia's war, Galicia. The Russians countered by reminding the British of their failure to help Russia's cause by mismanaging their own campaign in the Gallipoli Peninsula, but the fact remained that after the Gallipoli debacle there were precious few places where the French and British might hope to provide some direct help to their faltering ally, even if they could spare the resources from their own fronts. Had the Gallipoli operation succeeded, the Russians could have closed down their Caucasus theatre and they would have had a reliable warm water link to their allies.

Nevertheless, almost as if to prove the second half of the adage that Russia is never as weak as she looks, the Russians decided they would attack in 1916. Russia still held an impressive overall numerical advantage over their Central Powers foes and still believed that they were militarily superior to at least one of the Central Powers, the Austro-Hungarians whom they had already beaten in Galicia. Russian generals with a sense of history looked back to a campaign a century earlier when long retreats had led to problems for an invading army, which eventually overextended itself and left itself exposed to a massive counterattack before withdrawing in disgrace, leaving Russia master of the field.

THE CHANTILLY CONFERENCE

The Russians, therefore, showed up to a high-level inter-Allied conference at the Château de Chantilly in December 1915 in an optimistic mood and ready to discuss resuming the offensive. The conference was held in French commander Joseph Joffre's palatial headquarters near Paris to discuss the coordination of Allied strategy for the coming year. The basic idea was

to get all of the Allied nations to agree to launch more or less simultaneous attacks on the enemy sometime in the early summer of 1916. Joffre's intention was to pressure the Germans so that they would be unable to transfer men and munitions from the Western Front to the Eastern Front as they had done that spring after the Second Battle of Ypres to help them prepare for the Gorlice-Tarnow Offensive.

The senior Russian representative at Chantilly was Yakov Zhilinski, the man who had so badly mismanaged the events that led to the Tannenberg and Masurian Lakes disasters. Zhilinski was, however, a familiar and welcome face to many French generals and for that reason had been sent to Paris to act as the Russian liaison officer to Joffre's General Headquarters (GQG). After the drubbing the Russians had taken in 1915, the question of how to keep Russia in the war occupied many French and British strategists at Chantilly. Most feared a repetition of the 1905 Revolution in Russia that had been brought on by Russian failures in the war against Japan, although no one envisioned how much more fundamental a future revolution would be. The men at Chantilly saw the coordinated offensive scheme as a way to provide some desperately needed, if indirect, help to the Russians.

Zhilinski surprised many of the conferees by proclaiming Russia's eagerness and ability to participate in the proposed joint offensive. He added Russia's official support to two critical concepts enshrined in the Chantilly agreements. First, Russia would be prepared to launch a major offensive in June 1916 to coincide with a major Franco-British offensive to be launched on both sides of the Somme River. They would be the largest offensives yet conducted on the Western Front, using new French heavy artillery pieces and volunteer British Pals' battalions then finishing their training in Britain and preparing to ship to France in large numbers. Second, the conferees agreed to launch local supporting offensives if one of

A Russian trench at Lake Naroch. It was part of the new defensive line the Russians constructed in the wake of the great retreat out of Poland. Russian soldiers were beaten, but not yet completely defeated.

Yakov Zhilinski bore a considerable amount of the blame for the twin disasters at Tannenberg and the Masurian Lakes in 1914. Nevertheless, he knew the French better than any other Russian officer and represented Russia at the Chantilly conference which decided Allied plans for 1916.

close it just a month before the Chantilly conference), keeping it open seemed a small price to pay to gain Russian agreement to resume the offensive in the near future. The agreement to launch supporting attacks was also a way to compensate for French and British inability to provide any more direct support to the Russians than a few Murmansk convoys carrying food, artillery pieces and ammunition. Little did the attendees know that the British and French would need the Russians to honour the agreements at Chantilly first.

The Russians did what they could to prove that they were far from vanquished. They used an unusually mild winter to conduct small, localized offensives designed to test the strength of the new German defensive line. Most of these attacks failed in the face of withering German machine-gun fire. In late January, the Russians turned their attention to the south, attacking along the Dniester River and capturing the Austro-Hungarian stronghold of Usciezko with a daring infantry attack. The success gave the Russians back a small bit of confidence and helped them to form a more or less defensible line across the Eastern Front.

the Allies were attacked before midsummer in order to prevent the Germans from redirecting their forces against one front exclusively. In exchange, Zhilinski demanded, and received, grudging French and British acceptance to keep the Salonika front open in Greece in order to draw some Central Powers troops (mostly Bulgarians) to the south.

At the time, most Allied generals saw the agreements as ways to help the Russians and keep them in the war. Although they saw Salonika as a sideshow (Joffre had agreed to a British request to

But events in the west soon took centre stage. The careful planning at Chantilly became obsolete and irrelevant in late February when the Germans launched their massive assault on the French fortress city of Verdun. Erich von Falkenhayn had seen the attack as a way to attrite the French and thereby 'knock England's best sword' out of her hand. Without France, England would have to leave the war and end the blockade. With the Western Front and overseas shipping lanes secured, the Germans could turn east and deal a deathblow to the Russians in 1917. Falkenhayn had not even bothered to inform his Austrian counterpart, Conrad, of the plan, revealing that inter-allied relations in the Central Powers were significantly worse than they were among the French, Russians, British and Italians.

The offensive at Verdun created a genuine crisis for the Allies. Joffre and the French GQG had been so obsessed with their plans for their midsummer offensive that they had left Verdun scandalously unprepared to meet the German attack. The unprecedented size and scale of the attack inflicted massive casualties and put the French in serious peril. Until they were able to recover and make some critical changes, it appeared that they might indeed lose Verdun, which would in turn have had serious, perhaps fatal, implications for their ability to continue the war.

Joffre urged his allies to meet their Chantilly agreements and launch offensives designed to distract the Germans and buy him and his new commander at Verdun, Henri Philippe Pétain, some badly needed time. The British demurred, arguing that their new soldiers were not yet ready to attack, a judgment Joffre reluctantly had to accept. The Italians launched a half-hearted and ineffective offensive in the Isonzo River valley that failed much as their others had. The

The Nagant firm in Belgium designed this pistol for the Russian Army, just as it had designed the standard-issue rifle. It held seven 7.62mm rounds, but was underpowered owing to a design defect that was never fully corrected.

Russians, who had originally seen the Chantilly agreement as a guarantee of French support if the Russians were threatened, now had, ironically enough, to launch an offensive of their own.

THE BATTLE OF LAKE NAROCH
They decided to attack in Belarus with the ultimate goal of turning north and eventually recovering some of the ground they had lost in the Baltic provinces. The Russians had spotted a weakness in the German defences, where just 75,000 men guarded the southern approaches to the Baltic region. Against these German forces, the Russians assembled more than 300,000 soldiers and their heaviest concentration of artillery pieces to date, more than 1000 guns. The artillery would, presumably, compensate for the hasty preparations of the offensive and the relatively green quality of Russian troops engaged in the operation.

On 18 March, the Russian guns opened fire. Although the weight of shells fired was the heaviest yet seen on the Eastern Front, the accuracy left a great deal to be desired. Russian spotting techniques were primitive and correction of fire proved to be very difficult to organize. Consequently, the German positions, especially the machine-gun nests hidden in the woods, remained undamaged. The shelling continued for more than two days, giving the Russians

Russia's War in Turkey

Russia and the Ottoman Empire fought one of the war's most brutal and unforgiving campaigns in the snowy, frigid heights of the Caucasus Mountains. Amid poor communications networks and primitive supply systems, men died of diseases like typhus, cholera and frostbite as often as they died from enemy bullets. In February 1916 the Russians accomplished the stunning feat of capturing the Ottoman stronghold of Erzerum, which temporarily lifted the spirits of the Russian Army. In the following year, however, the Russian position in the Caucasus deteriorated as new Ottoman leaders found ways to move supplies to the region by sea. Although often forgotten by historians, the Caucasus theatre occupied much of the energies and resources of the Russians well into 1917.

Russian field artillery crews pause for a break in the sunshine. The Russians faced shortages of almost everything from artillery tubes to ammunition to horses. The large losses of 1915 also meant a crucial shortage of trained crews and officers.

a great deal of unwarranted confidence that the Germans would offer little resistance.

The Russians followed the artillery with a daring night attack by their infantry. They hoped that the darkness would provide further protection and cover for their inexperienced troops. It did not. German machine guns opened fire on Russian formations, which were unusually dense and thick in order to prevent separation in the darkness. Spring thaws turned the ground to mud and muck, slowing down the attacking waves and making command and control virtually impossible.

The first two Russian waves were destroyed well before they reached the German line. A third wave of attacks managed to seize a small portion of the German line, but the Russians soon lost it during a daring pre-dawn German counterattack. As dawn broke, the German artillery opened a devastating fire

on the remaining exposed Russian positions over a 56km (35-mile) front.

Further to the north, the Russians had launched two supporting drives, one aimed at pressuring German forces west of Riga and the other at reaching Lake Naroch, the largest lake in Belarus. Russian troops managed to use a dense fog to infiltrate German positions and advance to the shores of the lake itself, but the Germans recovered and re-established defensive lines. The Riga Offensive went nowhere and the Russians soon called it off. The Germans responded with carefully planned attacks preceded by massive artillery fire and, by late April, had recovered almost all of the lost ground.

The so-called Battle of Lake Naroch was a failure in every sense of the word. The Russians lost 70,000 men in the fight around the lake and another 30,000 around Riga. German losses were less than 20,000 combined. The Russians had taken no territory worth the losses nor, more importantly, had they done anything to cause the Germans to divert men or resources from Verdun. They had therefore bled themselves to no real purpose and seemingly proved once again their general inferiority in combat against the Germans, who read Russian methods as crude and Russian infantry tactics as suicidal.

The Lake Naroch and Riga attacks did, however, have the benefit of lulling the Central Powers into a sense of confidence. With German efforts in 1916 directed in the west, the Central Powers forces in the east would have to hold on as best they could with the resources they had on hand. As the French recovery at Verdun continued, moreover, the Germans found themselves having to commit more and more

resources to a battle that was quickly devolving into a slaughterhouse for both sides. Most Germans in the east, however, were not worried. Riga and Lake Naroch had seemingly demonstrated to them that they could contain and reverse any offensives the Russians attempted. They remained concerned about the ability of their Austro-Hungarian allies to do likewise, but with all eyes fixed on Verdun, there seemed little cause for worry.

THE BRUSILOV OFFENSIVE

The failures at Lake Naroch and Riga did nothing to dim Russian enthusiasm for keeping their promise to launch a midsummer offensive. The crisis at Verdun remained, as did Russian desires to prove their mettle

This photograph shows a handful of the hundreds of thousands of Russians who died in World War I. Russian losses were appalling, leading to charges of both incompetence and corruption at the Tsar's court.

and recover their lost territories from the occupying Germans. Joffre continued to urge both the Russians and the British to offer any help they could by launching any offensives at all to distract even a small part of Germany's efforts away from Verdun. In May, the Italians added their calls for help when the Austro-Hungarians launched an offensive in the South Tyrol. Italy's King Victor Emmanuel III personally appealed to Nicholas II for help. Although then serving as nominal commander-in-chief of the Russian Army, the Tsar had a difficult time finding any enthusiastic generals for another offensive designed to help out a distant ally, especially at a time when Russia herself seemed to be teetering dangerously on the edge of collapse.

The only commander anxious to attack was the aggressive and talented Alexei Brusilov, recognized then and now as Russia's best general of the war. In April, he had been named to replace Nikolai Ivanov as commander of the Southwest Front, encompassing all of the armies south of the Pripet Marshes. He had led well in the war's first months and had worked hard to rebuild his shattered armies after the disastrous retreat that followed the Gorlice-Tarnow breakthrough. He believed that his men were ready to attack and that he had a plan that stood a more than a reasonable chance

> ## 'Russia has not yet reached the zenith of her power, which will only be approached next year, when she will have the largest and best army since the beginning of the war.'
>
> Brusilov's official report on his offensive

of success. Not coincidentally, his Southwest Front faced the Austro-Hungarians, whom the Russians believed were ripe for destruction.

Brusilov had examined the Russian failures at Lake Naroch and Riga and rejected fashionable (and exculpatory) views inside Stavka that blamed the poor quality of Russian munitions or the low state of

Alexei Brusilov (1853–1926)

Brusilov was an aristocrat by birth and a cavalryman by background. He had, however, come to understand the changes in modern warfare much better than most of his peers. He was meticulous about training his men and very careful about staff work. He was also one of the first aristocrats to realize that the Tsarist system was broken beyond repair and needed to be replaced. Accordingly, he supported the Tsar's abdication and later even offered his services to the Bolsheviks, helping to lead the Red Army to the gates of Warsaw in the Russo-Polish War. He published a memoir of his wartime experiences that provides one of the best looks inside the Russian Army at war.

Russian morale. Instead, he concluded that the offensive and its supporting artillery had been too narrowly concentrated. Concentrating fire had seemed sensible enough given the inaccuracy of Russian gunners and the paucity of Russian artillery reserves. But Brusilov thought that this method had channelled Russian soldiers through gaps in the enemy line that were far too narrow, exposing them to the full fury of devastating German machine-gun and artillery fire.

Convinced that Russian soldiers could still fight effectively if properly led and trained, Brusilov set to work. He aimed to launch his offensive over a broad front to give Russian forces the chance to break through at several points (as the Central Powers had done at Gorlice-Tarnow) and remove the flanks from which the enemy could pour his deadly enfilading fire into advancing Russian formations. This method required a massive artillery preparation, something the Russians were incapable of producing. Thus the offensive would need to safeguard itself by ensuring absolute secrecy. Only at the last minute would Russian gunners open up a brief, but devastating fire to clear the way for the infantry.

Secrecy would also help Brusilov solve another problem, that of the reserves. Typically, when the Russians had made sizeable gains in offensive operations, they had stalled when the Central Powers had rushed reserves forward. To overcome this problem, Brusilov wanted to mass Russian reserves just behind the front lines. These men could launch simultaneous attacks on multiple parts of the front to confuse and disorient the enemy, forcing him to stretch his reserves dangerously thin. They could also be used to exploit areas of success and conduct pursuit of enemy soldiers in the open field.

Aware of the limited number of shells that Russian gunners would be able to fire, Brusilov knew that accuracy would need to be improved. He forced gunners to spend time in the front lines in order to acquaint themselves with the problems infantry faced. He also had them work out better methods of communication so that field artillery units could provide fire support on the move. Although cavalrymen were not generally noted for their acceptance of new technologies, Brusilov embraced aviation and its capacity for high-level aerial reconnaissance. He ordered his aviators to photograph the Austro-Hungarian lines, helping his gunners

find the locations of the majority of the enemy's artillery pieces, which they could then target in the opening phases of an attack in order to silence the enemy's most powerful weapons.

Secrecy was vital. Brusilov would need to conduct training in new methods to thousands of soldiers and amass reserves close to the front line, normally a sure sign of an impending attack. Secrecy and subtlety had

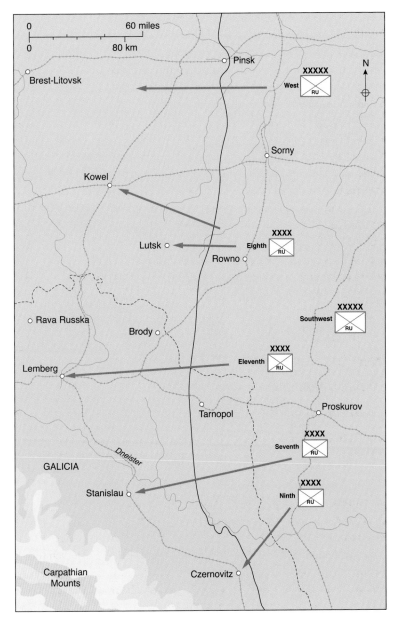

Russian lines after the great retreat from Poland were straight, thus eliminating salients, or exposed bumps in the line. Salients were hard to defend and required extra manpower to guard against attacks from several directions at once.

not normally been associated with the Russian Army, so Brusilov took many precautions. He was noticeably tight lipped around officers from the Stavka and people with connections to the Tsar's notoriously gossipy court. He also kept his own counsel, guarding his plans even from several of his key subordinates. Although he routinely visited the trenches to make sure that his preparations were being carried out as ordered, he did not often chat with junior officers or take them into his confidence. Like many Russian aristocrats, he was uneasy his social inferiors and this desire for remove helped to underscore his secrecy.

Brusilov also ordered minute preparations uncommon for most Russian operations and supervised them personally. He ordered the

construction of scale model Austro-Hungarian trenches behind the lines based on aerial reconnaissance, as well as new communications trenches to move men and supplies forward efficiently. Extra dugouts in the trenches safely concealed masses of Russian troops from enemy aviators and observation posts. Lastly, he replaced commanders he found wanting and struck the appropriate level of fear into many others. Brusilov's forces soon became a model for the Russian Army, although few other commanders were able to do what he had done.

For their part, the Austro-Hungarians were not expecting a Russian offensive at all. They had become obsessed by what they saw as the treasonous behaviour of Italy and had dedicated most of their staff energies to planning the South Tyrol Offensive. To give that offensive every chance of success, they had moved six infantry divisions away from Galicia, much

These Austrian infantrymen were the lucky ones. They were still alive in 1916. Thousands of the men they went to war with in 1914 were already dead. Casualties were especially high among junior officers, who often led from the front.

These men were not as lucky. They are Austrian POWs being marched off to Russian camps. There they faced a grim and uncertain future – many of the camps were in Siberia. Thousands of men died in captivity, although the exact numbers remain unknown.

to the consternation of the Germans, who doubted that the South Tyrol Offensive would achieve any goals worth the men and munitions dedicated to it. The weaknesses of Austro-Hungarian forces in Galicia meant that their units were pushed far forwards in what was derisively known as a 'shop-window' defence, with a lack of reserves to the rear. Brusilov had a reasonably accurate picture of the Austrian defences from aerial reconnaissance and had guessed that if he could smash the window, his men might be free to range almost at will against the Austro-Hungarians, taking them from behind and scoring a great victory.

Brusilov had four field armies under his command. He intended to use them to strike consecutive blows along a front line of more than 30km (19 miles). Among the targets of the first waves of attacks were the town of Lutsk, where several key roads converged, and the town of Kowel, which commanded the north to south railway that led to Lemberg. In the region of the two towns, Brusilov had deftly and carefully concentrated a numerical superiority of 125,000 men. By mid-May he had completed his preparations, but at the last minute had to convince an anxious Tsar and Stavka that he could attain his goals and achieve success where previous Russian offensives had failed. Two of Brusilov's own army commanders practically begged him to call off the attack; they were afraid that the secrecy needed for so large an offensive could not be maintained and that the Austro-Hungarians must surely have picked up some sign of the impending attack. One of the army commanders may have even suffered a nervous breakdown, which required Brusilov to make several trips to his headquarters in order to bolster his confidence. The risks were indeed

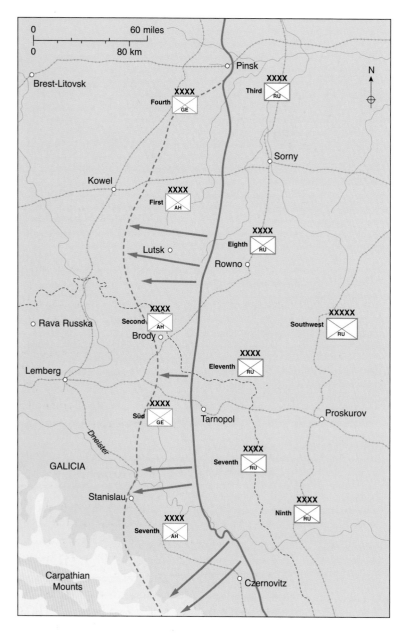

coincidentally also the birthday of the Austro-Hungarian Fourth Army commander, Archduke Josef Ferdinand. He was the godson of Kaiser Wilhelm II and, out of family courtesy, had been spared the kinds of direct German oversight that other officers had experienced. He was arrogant and unwilling to listen to the advice of the professional officers around him. His domineering and manipulative wife, the Archduchess Isabella, burned for the chance to become empress and played politics both in Vienna and at her husband's army headquarters. For his part, he spent much more of his time womanizing and hunting than he did preparing his army for war. For her husband's 44th birthday Isabella had planned a massive dinner at the castle of Teschen and had drafted several members of the Fourth Army staff to help her deal with the myriad of details involved. She had invited Conrad who, believing that no military operations were imminent, had accepted.

Thus when the Russian guns opened fire on 4 June they caught the Austro-Hungarians utterly unprepared. Reports of massive Russian attacks filtered in to Conrad's headquarters, which relayed them to Teschen. Conrad saw nothing in the reports serious enough to cause him to risk offending the Archduchess by leaving the party early. He told his staff officers that the Russians had made a temporary gain and that his men would correct it after the Russians had moved forward a few

great. Running low on both supplies and public faith, the Russians could not afford another disaster, and morale was still unsteady after Gorlice-Tarnow and the subsequent Great Retreat from Poland.   •

Brusilov fumed at the delays imposed upon him by men thousands of kilometres away, but the extra few days inadvertently helped him. The day Brusilov finally set to start his offensive was 4 June,

The Hansa-Brandenburg C.I biplane was a German-built reconnaissance plane flown mainly by Austro-Hungarian pilots. Although it was not designed as a fighter, 12 Austro-Hungarian airmen became aces while flying it.

hundred metres. He sent directives to his field commanders to hold the line, then, as one version of the events had it, returned to his card game with his apologies to the ladies for his absence.

He might well have made the right choice, because by then the situation was already out of his control. Brusilov had ordered his artillerists to fire a fast and furious hurricane bombardment that chased Austro-Hungarian defenders into their deep dugouts. Lighter field guns targeted the thin layers of barbed wire that protected the Austro-Hungarian trenches and the known placements of Austro-Hungarian artillery pieces and machine guns. The artillery did most of the work; Russian infantry then only had to follow up, surround the trenches and wait for their enemies to come out of their dugouts with their hands up. Thousands did so, especially ethnic Slavs who had little desire to fight and die for the Austro-Hungarian Empire.

The Fourth Army's shop window had shattered and elements of the Russian Eighth Army were moving behind it, taking Austro-Hungarian units in the flank and creating chaos. The demolition of the Austro-Hungarian Fourth Army necessitated the staged withdrawal of its neighbour, the Seventh Army. It had no choice but to retreat south, placing it hard against the Carpathian Mountains. The First Army also withdrew, thereby putting the entire Austro-Hungarian position in considerable danger. Whole units began to melt away. In some cases, regiments,

mostly Czech and Ruthene, walked to the Russian lines and surrendered as a unit. Some men even switched sides and joined the Russians, believing that the final collapse of the Austro-Hungarian Empire could not be far away.

By the third day of the offensive, the severity of the situation was plain for all to see. The Russians had torn open a sizeable hole 32km (20 miles) wide in the Austro-Hungarian front. Hundreds of thousands of Austro-Hungarian troops were prisoners of war or

Alexei Evert (1857–1918)

Evert was a strong monarchist and a close confidant of the Tsar. Upon naming himself commander-in-chief of the Russian Army, Nicholas II overlooked Evert's many shortcomings and promoted him to commander of the West Front. His poor performance at the Battle of Lake Naroch failed to convince the Tsar to remove him. Instead, he accepted Evert's arguments that he had failed owing to insufficient stocks of artillery shells. Evert's caution caused the Brusilov Offensive to lose steam far too early, but again he successfully deflected all criticism, at least in the Tsar's eyes. When the Tsar abdicated, Evert was removed from command. He went into hiding when the Bolsheviks took over and died under mysterious circumstances.

had simply fled from the battlefield. By 8 June, the Fourth Army, which had had a field strength of 110,000 men one week earlier, had just 18,000 men under arms. Reports suggested that as many as 60 per cent of the Austro-Hungarian casualties were deserters from their units.

Brusilov had designed a masterpiece. Austro-Hungarian units were in retreat along a massive 400km (250-mile) front from the Pripet Marshes to the Carpathian Mountains. Several Russians began to boast that their country would prove 'the saviour of

the Entente' and that the Brusilov Offensive would save the French from the killing at Verdun. Dreamers at Stavka headquarters began to envision a massive Russian crossing of the Carpathians into Hungary and the recapture of Lemberg.

A combination of German action and Russian inaction soon turned the tide, however. Conrad became awake to the terrible peril his army faced, but was aware that he could do little to stop the bleeding without more help from the Germans. He therefore headed to Berlin for a meeting with Falkenhayn on 8 June. He began in undiplomatic fashion by telling Falkenhayn that his offensive in the South Tyrol was working whereas the German attack at Verdun was not. He therefore asked Falkenhayn to wind down the

Alexei Evert (right) conferring with other senior officers at Russian headquarters. He did not share Brusilov's faith in the offensive and reacted too slowly and too cautiously. His inaction gave the Germans time to recover and reinforce.

Verdun offensive and transfer troops to the South Tyrol so that the Austro-Hungarians could move men from the South Tyrol to the Carpathians. He also suggested that all German forces moved to the South Tyrol be placed under Austro-Hungarian command.

Whatever Conrad was expecting to accomplish, he got quite a rude reception. Falkenhayn screamed at him, belittling Conrad's strategic vision and lecturing him for his senseless obsession with a meaningless operation in the South Tyrol. Falkenhayn all but ordered him to shut the offensive down and move four divisions to the Carpathians before it was too late. He then informed Conrad that German reinforcements were already on their way to railway stations for immediate dispatch to the Carpathians but that they would only arrive if all Central Powers forces came under direct German control on the model of Mackensen's Ninth Army. Falkenhayn then warned Conrad that if he failed to accept the terms, Germany would send no help at all and Russian forces would be free to cross the Carpathians whenever they wished.

Falkenhayn was most likely bluffing. He knew that the Germans still needed the Austro-Hungarians, even if he often derided them as 'childish' and 'military dreamers'. Conrad sheepishly accepted Falkenhayn's terms, but the two were never on good terms again. Falkenhayn dispatched German forces east under the command of General Hans von Seeckt, who soon assumed command of all Central Powers forces in the southern theatre, much as Mackensen had in the northern. The Austro-Hungarian general staff retained control of its operations in the Italian and Balkan theatres, but in Galicia it had become a virtual subordinate formation to the Germans.

The next day, 9 June, was supposed to witness the opening of Brusilov's second phase. The troops that

Archduke Josef Ferdinand (right) had family connections in Austria and in Germany that allowed him to stay in command despite his lack of military acumen. His poor generalship was painfully exposed by the Brusilov Offensive in 1916.

had fought in the first few days of the attack were to rest and await supplies. Brusilov did not want his men to outrun their supply lines and thereby leave themselves exposed to a Central Powers counterattack. To keep the momentum of the offensive going, the West Front, under the command of Alexei Evert, was to have begun its attack. But Evert demurred, arguing that he was not ready and that he needed to wait for more artillery shells before going on the offensive. Brusilov accused him of turning a hard-won victory into a humiliating defeat, but Evert could not be budged. With the men of Evert's front not moving forward and those of Brusilov's front in need of time, the offensive stalled.

The Germans used the time very wisely. By the end of the first week in July, the Germans had moved four divisions from France (although these had little

Russian soldiers pose with trench mortars. These weapons had a high enough angle of fire to place shells inside trenches and were light enough to move easily. They gave a measure of local firepower to infantry units.

impact on the fighting at Verdun or the fighting that began on the Somme) and five more divisions from reserves in the east, along with 98 artillery batteries, to the Carpathians. Hindenburg later added another division out of his general reserve. Falkenhayn also made certain that the Austro-Hungarians moved the four divisions out of the South Tyrol as promised. These reinforcements secured the Carpathians and helped to restore order.

As the situation stabilized and no second Russian attack materialized, Conrad's spirits soared. Incredibly, Conrad chalked up the disaster to bad luck and the poor decision making of a few subordinates. He began to prepare for a resumption of the offensive, asking Falkenhayn once again to move men from Verdun to the east in preparation for a double envelopment in the region east of Lemberg. Falkenhayn instead told German troops to set up solid defensive lines, restore discipline and assume command of Austro-Hungarian units as small as companies. Conrad was only deluding himself by dreaming of renewing the offensive. In Vienna, senior officials began to scheme to get rid of him. Although he held on to his job for a while longer, he was no longer the commanding authority he had once been. Instead, he was boxed in both by the domineering attitude of his German allies and the suspicions of many in the Austro-Hungarian government.

Many military historians point to the Brusilov Offensive as the effective end of the Austro-Hungarian Empire. Thereafter, it began a steep descent into irrelevance, becoming an effective state of the German Empire without much say in its own future. The Austro-Hungarians were also deeply in debt to German bankers, adding further to the reliance on Berlin. On 27 July,

Russian officers occupy trenches in the Austro-Hungarian front line following the early successes of the Brusilov Offensive. The initial advances were so successful that second- and third-stage objectives were taken with ease; however, the momentum did not last.

Hindenburg received control of all military operations in the east and a new title of supreme commander of the Eastern Front. On 6 September, this military move was followed by an essentially political one with the creation of a United Supreme Command, with Wilhelm II as the titular head.

Although these moves meant the end of their sovereignty, the Austro-Hungarians were aware that they had little choice. Without German help, they feared that the Russians would in all likelihood cross the Carpathians and begin to pillage or occupy Hungary. They needn't have worried quite so much. Russia was certainly ascendant, but Russia was not as strong as she looked. Russian casualties had been nowhere near as high as Austria-Hungary's, but the Russians could ill afford the losses. Even in victory the losses led many to

question the value of the war and the ultimate benefits to the average Russian even if they did win. Desertions increased, as did indiscipline.

Evert's failure to attack increased the demoralization of many soldiers. At Stavka, Alexeev generally accepted Evert's rationales, but railed at the opportunities Russia was missing. The Austro-Hungarians were reeling and Russia had a chance to attack them and finish the job before the Germans had the time to arrive in strength and reinforce the line. According to some estimates, the

Russian forces advancing during the Brusilov Offensive. Their initial success was dramatic, but also very costly and, in the end, it could not be sustained.

Russia's aviators did not earn themselves a great deal of distinction during the war, but their reconnaissance efforts paid off in 1916. They also used machine guns to strafe and terrorize retreating Austro-Hungarian soldiers, echoing developments in air combat on the Western Front.

Russians had a manpower advantage of 800,000 to 450,000 in Galicia, but if the Russians did not attack, the advantage would come to naught. Alexeev therefore ordered Brusilov to attack again. Brusilov, still furious that Evert was remaining in place, objected at first before finally relenting.

Brusilov attacked again on 27 July and routed the remnants of the Austro-Hungarian First Army. The next day the Russians moved against what was left of the Fourth Army and routed it, too. Still, Evert stayed in place, leaving Brusilov to try again alone. From 7 August to 20 September, the Russians kept pushing, but stiffer resistance from German units made the going much slower and much costlier. Alexeev and the Tsar demanded that Russian forces finish off their enemy, but even though Evert reluctantly began to

send units into combat, Brusilov understood that the offensive had reached the point of diminishing returns. Although they had inflicted one-and-a-half million casualties on the Austro-Hungarians (leaving the Austro-Hungarian Army with just 700,000 men in arms), the Russians had also taken one million casualties, most of them in the offensive's later stages. Along with the manpower losses came the losses of tonnes of equipment that could not easily be replaced. Russia had achieved its most spectacular victory of the war, but it had proved in the end to be Pyrrhic, further weakening and destabilizing the Tsar's already shaky hold on his empire.

The Brusilov Offensive also had ramifications for Poland. The Kaiser discarded a plan to transfer the crown of Poland to the Habsburg royal family, and instead announced the creation of a new Polish vassal state under the control of the German Empire and with its capital at Lublin. Ludendorff and others drew up plans to recruit hundreds of thousands of Polish soldiers, whom they presumed would want to defend their new homeland against Russian aggression and what the German foreign ministry termed 'Jewish masses'. In the end only 4700 Poles volunteered.

ENTER ROMANIA

Poland was not the only small nation whose fate hung in the balance. Romania sat in a geographic position that gave it many options. Although a small and poor country by great power standards, it bordered Russia, Bulgaria, Austria-Hungary and Serbia, and also sat close to the Ottoman Empire. Thus it presented at least the possibility of opening up new fronts for both sides. Sitting on valuable grain and oil fields, Romania in theory offered quite a lot to a prospective ally, but its army had performed terribly in the Balkan Wars and few Europeans thought Romania was ready for

modern warfare. Its general staff was regarded as worthless, even by foreign observers generally sympathetic to the Romanians. The country had had little money to modernize its armed forces after the Balkan Wars and by almost every material measure, the Romanians looked more like a nineteenth-century army than a twentieth-century one.

Like Italy, the Romanians had no vital national interests at stake, and therefore had little reason to worry about being dragged into the war. Such ties as had existed for the Romanians all pointed to the Central Powers. Fears of the Russians had led to a

Austro-Hungarian soldiers retreating in the wake of Brusilov's success. The attack soon turned into a rout, with thousands of Austrians surrendering or deserting, another indication of the cracking morale.

secret treaty with Austria-Hungary in the 1880s, although the terms did not require Romania to go to war in 1914. Most of Romania's key economic links were with Germany and the Romanian royal family was a branch of the Prussian Hohenzollerns. The Prime Minister and most senior government officials were also pro-German. Although Queen Marie was the granddaughter of an English and Russian monarch (Queen Victoria and Alexander II), both of the king's brothers had chosen service in the German Army.

Nevertheless, the Romanians, again like the Italians, had political aims that could only be satisfied through war against Austria-Hungary. As Italy sought territories with large Italian populations like Trieste and Fiume, so too did the Romanians seek Transylvania with its large number of ethnic Romanians. The Bukovina and the Banat also held Romanian populations that many nationalists coveted. Not coincidentally, these regions were also lucrative from an economic standpoint. War against Russia could only gain the Romanians a non-Romanian territory like Bessarabia and the undying enmity of a powerful neighbour. Perhaps most importantly, few Romanian generals liked the idea of joining the Central Powers and thereby fighting on the same side as their recent Ottoman enemies.

Ironically, what settled the Romanians on entering the war was the success of the very Russians they feared. The Romanians assumed that a Russian victory would mean Russian control of the Carpathians and, perhaps, Constantinople and its hinterland. In early

Hans von Seeckt (1866–1936)

With his monocle and his icy stare, Hans von Seeckt seems to be almost a caricature of a German general. Assigned to be August von Mackensen's chief of staff in early 1915, he received the lion's share of the credit for the planning that led to the Gorlice-Tarnow breakthrough. He then served in a variety of positions aimed at reforming the Austro-Hungarian Army and making it more like its German counterpart, earning a number of enemies in Vienna in the process. Known for his organizational and management skills, he rose through the ranks quickly. After the war he replaced Hindenburg as chief of staff and built the 100,000-man German Army that the Versailles Treaty permitted. He later turned to the Nazis and died in 1936.

1915 the Romanians concluded secret agreements with the British in which the British pledged that they would support Romanian acquisition of Transylvania if Romania entered the war. Shortly thereafter, the Russians collapsed during the Gorlice-Tarnow disaster and seemed more likely to be knocked out of the war

This Romanian 75mm field gun was manufactured by the German firm of Krupp. It symbolizes the tight links between Romania and Germany before the war. Nevertheless, Romania entered the war against Austria-Hungary in hopes of gaining Transylvania.

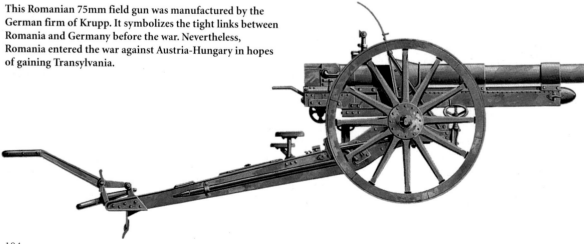

than win it. Germany had made no promises about any future Romanian control of Transylvania, so remaining on the sidelines seemed to make the most sense to Romanian officials.

All that thinking changed when Brusilov brought Russian troops to the foothills of the Carpathians in June 1916. It seemed obvious to everyone in Bucharest that the Austro-Hungarian Empire was ready to implode and that Transylvania, Bukovina and the Banat would be ripe for the taking. If Brusilov and his Russians succeeded in crossing the Carpathians, they would be the most likely to acquire the desired provinces, a situation too dangerous for the Romanians to contemplate.

In August, therefore, the Romanians went back to the Allies with a new proposal. If the Allies (including Russia) would guarantee post-war Romanian control

of not only Transylvania, but Bukovina and the Banat as well then the Romanians would enter the war. They also demanded that the Russians continue their offensives against the Austro-Hungarians and that the British and French continue the Salonika offensive to pin down the Bulgarian troops fighting there. Most Allied (especially Russian) diplomats thought the price too steep, but they agreed because they were anxious for some good diplomatic news and they hoped a Romanian declaration of war might have a positive effect on other neutral nations, who might be persuaded to enter the war on the Allied side.

At the end of August, Romania declared war on Austria-Hungary with the following justification:

'All the injustices our brothers thus were made to suffer maintained between our country and the monarchy a continual state of animosity. At the outbreak of the war Austria-Hungary made no effort to ameliorate these conditions. After two years of the war Austria-Hungary showed herself as prompt to sacrifice her peoples as powerless to defend them.

Romanian cavalry advance toward Transylvania in 1916. The Romanian Army was badly outclassed and still suffering shortages incurred during the Balkan Wars. Militarily, it was far from ready to fight a war in 1916.

'The war in which almost the whole of Europe is partaking raises the gravest problems affecting the national development and very existence of the States.

'Romania, from a desire to hasten the end of the conflict and to safeguard her racial interests, sees herself forced to enter into line by the side of those who are able to assure her realization of her national unity. For these reasons Romania considers herself, from this moment, in a state of war with Austria-Hungary.'

Almost immediately, Romanian forces crossed into a lightly defended Transylvania with the aim of seizing it before the Russians did so. The war had been extended to yet another country, once again with disastrous consequences.

EXIT ROMANIA

The Romanians had been careful not to declare war on Germany, a country with which they had no direct quarrel of any kind. The distinction failed to make an impression on Kaiser Wilhelm, who exploded in rage.

He saw the Romanian declaration of war as a family betrayal and a reneging on an alliance commitment. He immediately ordered Germany to declare war on Romania and made clear his desire that it be erased from the map as quickly as possible. The Ottoman Empire and Bulgaria, both of which nursed grievances against the Romanians from the Balkan Wars, eagerly followed Germany's lead.

Hindenburg decided on a swift and punitive expedition against the Romanians. He formed two large Central Powers armies, each featuring a combination of German, Austro-Hungarian, Bulgarian and Ottoman troops and placed them under German control. One of the armies was given to the ruthless and battle-hardened Erich von Falkenhayn, fresh from

German soldiers pose at the Romanian fortress of Turtukai. Sitting on the Danube River, it was a key strongpoint in Romanian defences. Its rapid fall, along with the loss of its 25,000-man garrison, exposed nearby Bucharest to assault by German forces.

his dismissal after his failure to take Verdun. Anxious to restore his reputation and prove his worth, he seethed with the chance to execute the Kaiser's orders. The other army went to August von Mackensen, one of the architects of the Gorlice-Tarnow breakthrough. Romania was about to face a double pincer movement led by two of the most efficient and merciless generals the Germans had.

Until these forces could assemble, the Romanians enjoyed considerable success. They ranged 80km (50 miles) deep into Transylvania with more than 350,000 men against the barely 30,000 men the Austro-Hungarians could muster to stop them. It soon became obvious, however, that the Central Powers response would be much stronger than the Romanians were prepared to handle. Like a schoolyard bully who had angered one too many classmates, the Romanians looked around for help. They naturally turned to the biggest kid on the block, the Russians. Alexeev refused

Without Turtukai to guard it, the Romanian capital of Bucharest fell. Residents of the city felt the full weight of German fury, with some senior Germans arguing that the Reich should annex the city directly in order to exploit it more fully.

to send any help at all, accusing the Romanians of acting like vultures only interested in carving up the Hungarian corpse after the Russians had fought and died for it.

By early September, Falkenhayn was ready to use what he learned at Verdun and elsewhere against the Romanians. His Ninth Army would clear Transylvania and enter Romania from the west, slicing southeast through the Ploesti oil fields and toward Bucharest. At the same time, Mackensen's Army of the Danube would invade from the south, using Bulgaria as its base, and overrun Romania's border fortifications. It would then advance northeast into the Dobrwa region, seizing the Black Sea ports as it went. The only

Erich von Falkenhayn (1861–1922)

A cool professional in the Prussian tradition, Falkenhayn had come to the Kaiser's attention as a result of his ruthless actions in China to protect German interests during the Boxer Rebellion. He had become a court favourite, and had done well in all the tasks assigned to him in the years before the war. He replaced Helmuth von Moltke in charge of German forces at the end of 1914 and, as a committed westerner, had launched the bloody Battle of Verdun early in 1916. Ironically, the westerner was sent east to dispatch the Romanians, a job he took on with great energy. He was a ruthless general who advocated the bombardment of civilians from the air, unrestricted submarine warfare, and the use of poison gas.

help the Romanians could expect was from the Allied units in Salonika, but they would have to cut through the Germans and Bulgarians opposite them to have any effect at all. As it turned out, the demoralized Salonika garrison was barely able to fight off the mosquitoes, let alone the Germans.

On 5 September, Mackensen began his concentrations against Romania's most powerful fortress complex, Turtukai. It boasted 15 separate fortifications and, in a fit of hubris, its commander promised that it would become the east's Verdun and hold up any and all German attempts to take it. Made up mostly of earthworks instead of the steel and concrete of Verdun's Forts Douaumont, Souville and

Vaux, Turtukai was no match at all for the powerful German siege guns. Within 24 hours of the first German shell hitting it, the commander surrendered along with the majority of his garrison of 39,000 men. The fortress of Silistria followed in due course, leaving Mackensen free to begin his movements on schedule.

At the end of the month, Falkenhayn began his movements as well. It took him just a few days to clear the only important strongpoint opposite him, the fortress of Hermannstadt (built with German money and German technical help) and capture its garrison. He then began to push the Romanians back out of Transylvania and against the city of Kronstadt. Only rainy weather and their own extended supply lines slowed the German pursuit. Seeing the desperation, a Russian detachment finally came to the aid of the Romanians, but when they arrived on the battlefield, the Romanians mistook them for Bulgarians and surrendered. The Russians responded by pillaging and looting whatever they could find before withdrawing back into Russia.

In November, Mackensen's men crossed the Danube in pontoon boats. At roughly the same time, Falkenhayn's men crossed the 1830m (6000ft) peaks of the Transylvanian Alps just before the first snows began to close the passes. There were now no natural barriers between the Central Powers forces and Bucharest. Supplies began

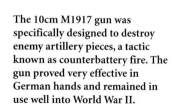

The 10cm M1917 gun was specifically designed to destroy enemy artillery pieces, a tactic known as counterbattery fire. The gun proved very effective in German hands and remained in use well into World War II.

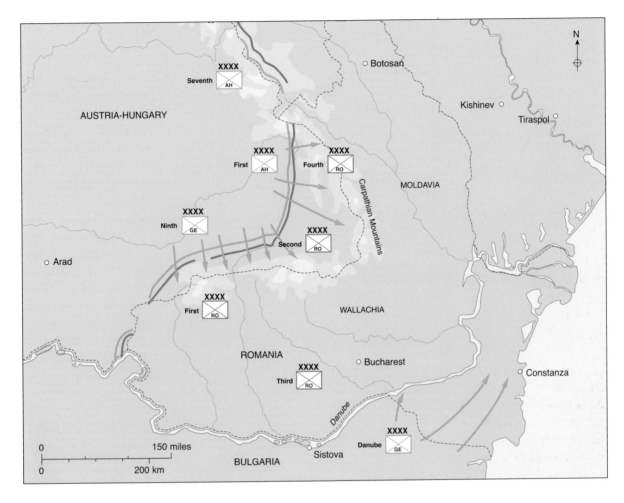

The Allies did what they could to help Romania, but to no avail. The ensuing Treaty of Bucharest made Romania a vassal state to Germany, Austria-Hungary and Bulgaria, which took most of Romania's precious mineral resources and grain supplies.

to run low, but all concerned could see that the campaign was fast coming to an end. The British looked on in horror but could do little to help, though they did send a commando team into the Ploesti oil fields, which destroyed 800,000 tonnes of oil and petrol to prevent them falling into German hands.

The French sent Henri Berthelot, a veteran of the Marne, to try to direct a Romanian counterattack. It was hopeless. Six entire divisions of the Romanian Army had disintegrated so badly that for all intents and purposes they no longer existed. Only 90,000

soldiers remained of the 700,000-man Romanian Army. The army had also lost almost 300,000 rifles, 350 machine guns and an equal number of artillery pieces. On 25 November, the Romanian Government left Bucharest and headed north to Jassy. Four days later Mackensen entered the city, effectively ending the Romanian campaign and forcing the Russians to move divisions to cover their previously undefended border with Romania.

The Kaiser's generals had delivered on their promises. The Central Powers added Bucharest to the list of key cities they occupied along with Belgrade, Brussels and Warsaw. Like those other cities, Bucharest and the rest of Romania soon faced the full fury of German occupation. Hindenburg and Ludendorff argued for annexing Romania to Germany in order to

execute the fullest possible exploitation of its mineral and agricultural resources. The Kaiser at first agreed, but his vengeance was soon counterbalanced by diplomats in the Foreign Ministry who argued that annexation would send the wrong message to other neutral nations.

The diplomats, however, could not keep the generals from enforcing a crushing armistice on the defeated Romanians. The Germans took more than one million tonnes of oil, two million tonnes of grain, 300,000 animals and 200,000 tonnes of wood out of

> 'The remembrance I keep of those days is of a suffering so great that it almost blinded me; I was as one wandering in fearful darkness wondering how much anguish one single heart can hear.'
>
> Romanian Queen Marie remembers the German Invasion

Romania, reducing the country to starvation conditions. The Treaty of Bucharest codified these harsh measures, giving the Germans a 90-year lease on all Romanian oil wells and mineral mines. Romania also lost all of its mountain passes and most of its Black Sea coastline, although the Germans were politic enough to grant the former to Austria-Hungary and the latter to Bulgaria. The Danube River delta fell under the authority of a joint Central Powers commission and Bulgaria took back the Dobruja region it had lost to Romania in the Second Balkan War in 1913. Romania had paid dearly for its ill advised decision to enter the war and served as a reminder to the French, British and Russians of the need to keep fighting in 1917 or risk the same fate.

The outmatched Romanian Army suffered enormous casualties at the hands of the much more experienced Germans. The Romanians nevertheless did well at the 1919 Paris Peace Conference, gaining the territories of Bessarabia, Bukovina and Transylvania.

CHAPTER 4

The First Russian Revolution

The failures of the Russian system in 1914 and 1915 underscored the fundamental weaknesses of the Tsarist state. The 1916 Brusilov Offensive's success fell far short of reversing Russia's battlefield fortunes. Russia's sufferings led to increasingly strident demands for change. By 1917 those calls had become irresistible and Russia underwent two revolutions.

In hindsight, it is easy to see that the Brusilov Offensive was Russia's last real chance to emerge from the war victorious. The Russians had more than redeemed themselves from the disasters of Gorlice-Tarnow, Lemberg and Warsaw in 1915 and had made one of the war's most impressive territorial gains. They could at last point with pride to a military accomplishment that had changed the very character of the war. Russian liaison officers in London and Paris could make favourable comparisons between the Brusilov Offensive and the bloody frustrations that the British and French forces had faced at almost the same time on the Somme.

Russian soldiers in Petrograd. Their relaxed demeanour evokes the decline in discipline among Russian soldiers by 1917. The presence of thousands of armed men near major cities added to the tension inside Russia.

But even so massive and crushing a campaign had failed to put the Russians in any kind of place to dictate favourable peace terms to their enemies. Instead, despite the ground and momentum gained, the offensive had inflicted heavy losses and had laid bare the essential flaws in the Russian command system. The Russians had proved themselves to be slow and inefficient at the very moment when a much larger victory might have been at hand. A few prescient observers (Brusilov among them) understood that the ground gained could not be held indefinitely and that Russia was in all likelihood incapable of conducting another such offensive in the near future. Even if it could, the result would probably be the same: a few kilometres of strategically insignificant steppe recovered for high losses.

The Russian Parliament or Duma photographed in session. The Duma was much weaker than its British and French parliamentary counterparts, its lack of independence symbolized by the giant portrait of Nicholas II that hangs over the Speaker's rostrum.

THE STRATEGIC SITUATION

The Brusilov Offensive notwithstanding, from the perspective of the winter 1916/17, the outcome of the war was still very much in doubt. For the Germans, crushing the Romanians had been easy enough and had provided a kind of cathartic release following the frustrations they had experienced at Verdun and on the Somme. Still, the Romanian campaign had absorbed resources that might have been better employed elsewhere. More fundamentally, Germany still faced its dreaded two-front dilemma and both of its principal allies were showing serious signs of cracking. The Brusilov Offensive had all but ended the Austro-Hungarian Army's ability to do anything more complex than static defence, and in the Middle East, the Arab Revolt and a renewed British interest in Palestine had marked the Ottoman Empire as a primary target for 1917. Germany would need to conduct offensives in the coming year to help both allies or risk their being vanquished.

Inside German circles, the mood was therefore hardly optimistic, despite the continued bombast that came from the Kaiser. He presented unrealistic schemes for fomenting a German-backed Muslim revolt in India and for arming the Japanese in return for their attacking the American possessions in the Philippines. Knowledgeable officers in the Germany Army simply shook their heads and took steps to cut

the Kaiser further and further out of the decision-making loop. Germany was becoming more and more a military dictatorship every day, with the generals setting not just military policy, but economic and diplomatic policy as well. Their war aims grew more and more ambitious, both cutting off any possibility of a negotiated settlement and committing Germany to fighting harder and longer.

The most fundamental problem the Germans faced was on the high seas where the British blockade continued to cut into the food supplies for both the army and the home front. Expecting a short war in

A workers' demonstration featuring caricatures of Rasputin, the influential monk, and Alexander Protopopov, a court favourite and syphilitic who had become Minister of the Interior. Both men were accused of using their influence against the Russian people.

1914, the Germans had not made anything like adequate preparations for feeding civilians during a prolonged war. The German Navy had tried to take over control of the North Sea in the summer of 1916, but the fleet had been chased back to its ports after the inconclusive Battle of Jutland. The Germans had inflicted more damage than they had taken, but they had also learned that the British fleet was too large and powerful for the Germans to ever hope to attain mastery of the high seas. The German surface fleet never engaged the British again.

After Jutland, the only way to deal with the blockade was to resume unrestricted submarine warfare, a course that risked bringing the United States and its immense economic assets into the war on the Allied side. Falkenhayn and most senior admirals dismissed the power and potential of the Americans and urged the Kaiser to unleash the U-boats. Advocates of unrestricted submarine warfare argued that the U-boats could starve the British into submission well before the Americans could mobilize their assets for the war in Europe. Submarines, they believed, would sink American transport ships in any case, thereby destroying the nascent American Army before it even fired a shot.

By April 1917, the Kaiser had come to the conclusion that submarines were the only way out of Germany's dilemma. The Germans had already taken almost everything they could out of Belgium and the

Eduard Böhm-Ermolli (1856–1941)

Böhm-Ermolli's life and career shows the diversity and complexity of the Austro-Hungarian Empire. Born in what is now Italy, he served the empire for more than 40 years. When the war ended, he settled into the estate he had purchased while on active service, which sat in the part of the empire that became Czechoslovakia. The Czechoslovak Government granted him a reserve army commission and a pension. Later they promoted him to general in the active forces and he remained on service with them until his retirement in 1928. In 1938 his estate, which was in the Sudetenland, was annexed by Hitler's Germany and he became a German citizen as well as an honorary general in the Wehrmacht reserves. Three years later he died and was afforded a state funeral in Vienna, once the heart of the empire he had served for so long.

parts of France and Poland they occupied, reducing the local populations to near starvation conditions. They would do the same to Romania and later to the Ukraine as well. But seizing food created tremendous animosities and absorbed needed resources. As a long-term policy it was doomed to fail, as peasants responded by hoarding more of their grain or refusing

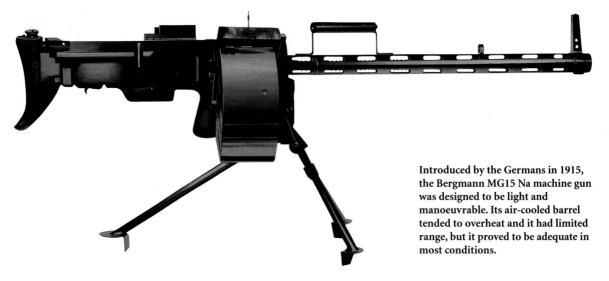

Introduced by the Germans in 1915, the Bergmann MG15 Na machine gun was designed to be light and manoeuvrable. Its air-cooled barrel tended to overheat and it had limited range, but it proved to be adequate in most conditions.

Rasputin (centre) gained influence at the Russian court by claiming that he could cure the haemophilia that afflicted the royal family. The 'Mad Monk' was a negative presence at court and in December 1916 he was assassinated.

to plant crops they believed would just be taken from them anyway. Like most of his advisers, the Kaiser assumed, with a breathtaking insouciance, that the Germans would win the war long before the Americans could do anything to stop them. Therefore, there was no reason to let the possible American response force the Germans to keep a powerful option off the table.

Given all of these risks, a negotiated compromise settlement would have been in the interests of both sides in the east, but neither Germany (which was calling the shots for Austria-Hungary as well) nor Russia expressed any interest in such a solution. The Germans presumed that once they had taken firm control of Austro-Hungarian assets, further setbacks like the Brusilov Offensive would be avoided and a massive offensive could deal the final deathblow to the Russians. For his part, the Tsar had staked the survival of his regime on winning the war when he had assumed supreme command in 1915. At the end of 1916 he dismissed his Prime Minister, a Baltic German who had expressed interest in opening up negotiations with the Germans through a neutral third party. In his place came a Slavophile from the Russian Parliament (the Duma) who had repeatedly depicted the war as a struggle for the very survival of the Russian people. The move was widely seen as a rededication of the Tsarist regime to winning the war at all costs.

The Russians also felt that they needed to resume the offensive to help out their allies. The British and the French had had a miserable 1916. Verdun and the Somme had bled their armies for little gain and, as a result, the French had experienced a major command shake-up. The new French commander, Robert Nivelle, had pledged to resume the offensive in the west, but even the massive Somme offensive had done little to help Russia the year before; therefore few Russians expected much direct help from whatever offensive Nivelle designed for 1917. Instead, Russian generals argued for a new offensive in order to take some heat from the western Allies, who were also their primary sources of credit and hardware.

The western Allies saw the war in just the opposite terms, believing that the Russians would be the first to crack. In a symbolic gesture, the western Allies greeted the arrival of the new Russian Prime Minister with a renewal of their support for Russian control of Constantinople at the war's end. The move was designed to infuse the Russians with more motivation to keep fighting and to show that the British and French were willing to offer their support, at least in the diplomatic arena. The Russian Government responded with a statement promising to continue the war in order to realize the 'age-long dream, cherished in the hearts of the Russian people', of annexing Constantinople.

But the willingness of the Russian Government to continue the fight was not matched in spirit by its people. Inflation was rampant: goods that would have cost 100 roubles at the start of the war cost more than

1100 roubles by the start of 1917. Wages did not rise to keep pace with this inflation; thus whatever food did reach the cities was usually beyond the reach of the average Russian. Transportation difficulties greatly reduced the amount of food available for purchase in the cities in any case. Most opponents of the government lambasted the Tsar, not for his failure to advocate a common-sense compromise peace, but for his inability to prosecute the war more efficiently. Even

some generals, including Brusilov, had concluded that the system would need massive, fundamental changes if Russia were to win the war. Russian industry had in fact made some impressive gains and had begun to fill the orders for shells that the War Ministry sent to the factories, but morale was low and the enthusiasm of new recruits for the war was even lower. The mythic notion of pan-Slavism no longer seemed a reasonable justification for continuing the war and all of its suffering, both on the front lines and at home.

An unseasonably cold winter had shown how deeply the war was cutting into Russian life. Food and fuel became increasingly scarce and the rigours of war had so denuded the Russian transportation system that although the 1916 harvest had been generally good, food could not get from the countryside to the cities where it was most needed. The death of the

> ## 'At one o'clock in the morning [16th] I left Pskov, with a heavy heart because of the things gone through. All around me there is treachery, cowardice and deceit.'
>
> The Tsar's diary entry on the day of his abdication

notorious adviser to the Tsarina, the mysterious and (some said) pro-German monk Rasputin, had added a great deal of uncertainty about what exactly was going on at the Russian court. The Tsar's regular absences from court to be seen closer to the front lines had not helped matters much. His absence from court led to more intrigues and his presence with the armies did little to bolster morale.

Desertion and indiscipline in the Russian Army was matched by revolutionary sentiment on the home front. It became harder and harder for the Russian

Russian soldiers gather for a meeting of revolutionaries. Revolutionary ideology, with its promises of peace, had great appeal to many men in uniform. Even many officers saw the lure of revolutionary thinking.

Government to track and catch the thousands of draft evaders who were wandering the streets and the countryside. Many of them became anti-war agitators urging men to avoid military service or to mutiny. Draft evasion had been a long tradition in Russia and peasants had found many ways over the years to hide their sons from the army.

In the cities, strikes and protests became more and more common, shutting down production of military hardware and contributing to the general sense of unease. Public discussion of a future without the Tsar became more common. Strikes were the largest problem, because they both threatened the industrial

order and were a manifestation of public mistrust in the system. The Duma reconvened in February amid some of the largest and most widespread strikes of the war to date. The Tsar left for a routine trip to his military headquarters at Mogilev on 7 March. The next day another massive wave of strikes began and lasted for three days. Russian troops had been ordered to put the strikes down with force if necessary, but they had refused. A detachment of Cossacks, normally

Revolutionary ideology, influenced heavily by the ideas of Karl Marx and Friedrich Engels, also held great appeal among Russian industrial workers. The men shown here are on strike at a metals factory in Lysva, Perm Province.

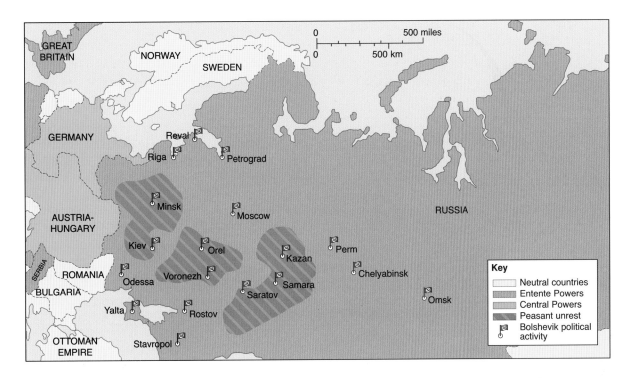

among the most loyal units to the Tsar, had refused to bring their rifles with them into working-class districts of St Petersburg (renamed Petrograd to give it a more Russian-sounding name) and a machine-gun unit disobeyed orders and replaced their live ammunition with blanks. The men of one regiment went even further, shooting their officers and joining the strikers, taking their weapons with them.

The Duma, whose leaders had concluded that the Tsarist system was incapable of dealing with the crisis, formed the Provisional Government and deposed several of the Tsar's ministers. Nicholas responded by leaving his military headquarters to return to Petrograd and announcing that he would dissolve the Duma once he arrived. He never got the chance to carry out his threat. Strikers had paralyzed the Russian railway system, preventing loyal Russian units from getting into the cities and generally bringing the entire Russian system to a standstill. Strikers had also pulled up the railway line Nicholas was to use to get back to Petrograd, forcing him to go to the town of Pskov on 14 March, where railway workers stopped his train and forced him to get out.

At Pskov, Nicholas re-established contact with his Army chief of staff, Mikhail Alexeev and the Northwest Front commander, Nikolai Ivanov. They presented him with reports of massive indiscipline in the army and widespread unrest on the home front. They then told him that the situation demanded drastic action and urged him to abdicate. They advised him that the Duma would no longer recognize his authority and that his stepping down was the only way to avoid civil war. The Tsar reluctantly agreed and then signed a manifesto to that effect that Duma leaders had already drawn up. He then issued his own statement, abdicating in his name and the name of his son as well. He transferred power to his brother, the Grand Duke Michael, whose marriage to a twice-divorced commoner had put him on bad terms with the court. A group of Duma representatives had foreseen this eventuality and sought out Michael to

Nicholas II's Abdication Statement

In the days of the great struggle against the external enemy, who has striven for nearly three years to enslave our homeland, the Lord God has willed to subject Russia to yet another heavy trial. The popular disturbances which have broken out threaten to have a calamitous effect on the further conduct of the hard-fought war. The fate of Russia, the honour of our heroic army, the welfare of the people and the whole future of our beloved Fatherland demand that the war be brought to a victorious conclusion. The cruel foe exerts his last efforts, and the time is near when our valiant army, together with our glorious allies will decisively overcome him. In these decisive days in Russia's life, we have deemed it our duty in conscience to our nation to draw closer together and to unite all national forces for the speediest attainment of victory. In agreement with the State Duma we have acknowledged it as beneficial to renounce the throne of the Russian state and lay down

Supreme authority. Not wishing to separate ourselves from our beloved son, we hand over our succession to our brother, the Grand Duke Michael Alexandrovich, and give him our blessing to ascend the throne of the Russian State. We command our brother to conduct the affairs of state in complete and inviolable union with the representatives of the nation in the legislative institutions on such principles as they will establish, and to swear to this an inviolate oath. In the name of our deeply beloved homeland, we call on all true sons of the Fatherland to fulfil their sacred duty to it by obeying the Tsar in the difficult moment of national trials, and to help him, together with the representatives of the people, lead the Russian State to victory, prosperity and glory. May the Lord God help Russia!

Pskov, 2 March 1917
15 hours 5 minutes
Nicholas

urge him not to accept the throne. They told him that no solution other than a full transfer of power from the royal family to the Provisional Government would be acceptable. Michael, who had little desire to rule in any case, agreed. The Romanov dynasty was over with surprising speed and equally surprising loss of life.

THE PROVISIONAL GOVERNMENT GOES TO WAR

The abdication of the Tsar did not necessarily mean the end of Russia's war. A few anxious days followed, but some measure of calm did return to the cities and the army. Most of the senior officers of the army and navy pledged their allegiance to the Provisional Government; many of those who did not were court favourites of no particular competence in any case. Even Alexeev, the Tsar's former senior military adviser, obeyed orders from the Duma to place his former master under arrest and transfer him to Tsarskoe Selo before his dispatch to Siberia. In Britain and France, there had been few admirers of the Tsarist system and

many hoped that the new government would prove to be more representative and more inspiring to the Russian people. In Paris and London (and on the Western Front as well), people cheered the Provisional Government's statement that it would continue to fight the war in the name of the Russian people.

The March Revolution solved a major ideological problem for the Allies. Claiming to be fighting a war for the defence of liberty and freedom had always been a shaky rhetorical trick when the largest of the Allied armies was commanded by the most regressive and repressive regime in Europe. With the Tsar gone and a new, plausibly representative, government in place in Russia, however, Allied politicians could more reasonably state that they were fighting a war of democracy against autocracy as the Central Powers comprised three distinctly unrepresentative regimes. Thus could politicians more convincingly sell the continuation of the war in the Allied nations as an essentially defensive war of free people against the aggressive regimes of their autocratic enemies.

Such rhetoric was especially important for the American President, Woodrow Wilson, who led the United States into the war shortly after the Tsar's abdication. Wilson's high-minded idealism bewildered many Europeans, but it led him to see great possibilities in the future of a representative Russia. The United States was the first country to

German Chancellor Theobald von Bethmann-Hollweg was one of a very few German voices arguing for a compromise peace with Russia, although he expected such a peace to be favourable to Germany. He was forced to resign in July 1917.

recognize the new government on the principle that it had been determined by the will of the Russian people. Wilson's hopes for what this new Russia could achieve help to explain his anger and disappointment at the later Bolshevik success, and thus his decision to intervene in the Russian Civil War.

For their part, the Germans hardly knew what to make of the new situation in the east. Some saw an opportunity to take advantage of the chaos by conducting a quick offensive, although others were cautious about attacking and thereby giving the new Russian nation a cause that might rally them. They advocated playing a waiting game and letting the Russian system collapse in against itself. Most German leaders despised the inefficiency and corruption of the Tsar's court, but the forced abdication of a monarch by a war-weary and hungry populace boded ill for the future of Germany as well. As food became increasingly scarce in Germany, opposition to the Kaiser had grown, although it had not reached anywhere near the level of Russia. Still, the similarities did not go unnoticed. The German Chancellor, Theobald von Bethmann-Hollweg, gave a speech shortly after the Tsar's abdication in which he said, 'Woe to the statesman who does not recognize the signs of the times and who, after this catastrophe, the like of which the world has never seen, believes that he can take up his work at the same point at which it was interrupted.' The speech was widely interpreted as a call for democratic reforms in Germany after the war to forestall the possibility of a similar revolution in Berlin.

CHANGES IN RUSSIA

Removing the Tsar was one thing. Finding a government that could replace the Tsar's and compel the loyalty of the Russian people was quite another. The new

Tsar Nicholas II (seen standing, centre right, with spade) was one of the world's most powerful men in 1914. Three years of war later he was a prisoner under house arrest and forced to tend a garden, a symbol of the powerful and rapid changes the war had brought to Russia.

Provisional Government was headed by a Russian prince, Georgi Lvov, a political moderate who had been among the first aristocrats to advocate the Tsar's abdication. His participation in the government helped convince many members of the middle class to support it in the hope of Russia gaining liberal reforms and a basic statement of rights. The most important member of the new government, however, was Alexander Kerensky, a lawyer and a moderate socialist. A powerful public speaker with support from urban industrial workers, he had used his seat in the Duma to oppose Russian entry into the war in 1914 and then became a vocal critic of the Tsar. Illness had forced him to go to Finland for treatment during parts of 1915 and 1916. From there he observed the changes inside Russia and had reversed his stance on the war, concluding that Russia's participation was necessary and just in order to combat German militarism. But he had also concluded that the Tsar's mismanagement of the war risked disaster, not just for Russia but for all of Europe. Russia therefore had an obligation to continue the war, but the nation had to find ways to fight it more effectively.

Upon joining the Provisional Government, Kerensky began to give patriotic speeches in which he urged Russians to continue the war, but as a way of safeguarding their own newly won liberty, not for the maintenance of the repressive regime of the Tsar. In his capacity as Minister of War, he gave Brusilov command of the Russian armies and began a massive reorganization of Russian industry. He also oversaw the extension of some basic civil rights to Russians and built links to the voice of many members of the working class, who agreed to work with him even though many of them did not support a continuation of the war. Before long the young and energetic Kerensky had eclipsed Prince Lvov as the key figure of the provisional government.

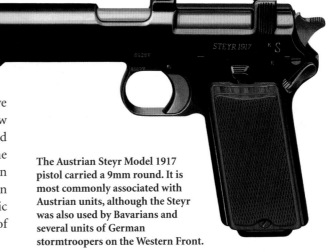

The Austrian Steyr Model 1917 pistol carried a 9mm round. It is most commonly associated with Austrian units, although the Steyr was also used by Bavarians and several units of German stormtroopers on the Western Front.

As one contemporary had observed, the changes in Russia had been so revolutionary (and, in most people's eyes, so positive) that 'men looked for other miracles to follow'. Among those anticipated miracles was a change in Russia's military fortunes. Kerensky reiterated Russia's commitment not to make a separate peace with the Germans, and Britain and France soon followed suit with a declaration that they would not sign a separate peace either. High-level representatives like France's well respected socialist Minister of Munitions, Albert Thomas, and America's Elihu Root (a former Secretary of War, senator and a Nobel Laureate) came to Russia with diplomatic delegations to offer their support and express their joy at having a democratic Russia on their side. Root told Kerensky

that the Revolution had brought 'universal satisfaction and joy' to the American people and that Russia had to win the war because 'the triumph of German arms would mean the end of Russian liberty'. The internationally respected Root became Wilson's senior representative in Russia, a symbol of how important the new relationship was in American eyes.

The idea of harnessing all of this positive energy into another military offensive seems to have come first from Alexeev, who, despite his close links to the Tsar, had remained an important adviser to the Provisional Government. Kerensky was careful to follow proper channels and insisted that the Duma, the people's representative, be made a full part of the

Austro-Hungarian Emperor Karl (1887–1922)

Franz Joseph, who had sat on the Austro-Hungarian throne since 1848, died in November 1916. He was succeeded by his grandnephew, who became Emperor Karl. A cavalry officer by training, Karl had served in a variety of military assignments. Influenced by his pro-Allied wife, he came to the throne anxious to end Austria-Hungary's participation in a war that he knew would eventually disintegrate his empire. He sent out secret peace feelers to the French, but his refusal to

cede Austro-Hungarian territory ended this initiative. The Germans, however, found out about his overtures and never trusted him again. Throughout 1918 he continued to plan for the transformation of Austria-Hungary into a federation with himself still at the head, but few of his former subjects were interested in hearing what he had to say. When the war ended, he fled first to Switzerland then to Spain, where he died virtually penniless of pneumonia in 1922 aged 34.

military process. The government formally presented the idea of an offensive to a secret session of the Duma in mid-June. Among the goals the government laid out for the offensive were forestalling revolution at home by showing the competence of the Provisional Government to handle military matters, bolstering Russia's place in the post-war peace conference, and proving Russia's value to its alliance partners. The Duma passed a resolution approving the idea and declaring peace 'or prolonged inactivity on the battlefront' to be an act 'of ignoble treason … for which future generations never would pardon the Russia of the present day'. Shortly thereafter the Congress of Workmen's and Soldiers' Delegates voted their support for the idea and their confidence in the Provisional Government. The news served to boost morale in the trenches and put a temporary brake on the waves of strikes. Brusilov and others were welcomed at the front with ecstatic receptions. Russia seemed to have come back from the brink.

In the enthusiasm that accompanied the heady days of spring, the Russians had decided to take the field. That enthusiasm, however, made for hasty planning and unclear purposes. Within two short weeks of the Duma approving the offensive, Russian troops were to launch a major attack on the Germans and Austro-Hungarians. There was little time to see to all of the myriad details that necessarily have to accompany a major offensive. Moreover, the ultimate operational goals were unclear. In short, no one knew quite what the offensive was supposed to accomplish other than showing the will of the Russian people to continue the war. In lieu of planning and preparation, the Russians hoped that the new revolutionary ardour of their people would carry the day much as the French revolutionary armies had done at the watershed Battle of Valmy in 1792.

Brusilov set out to plan the offensive, but even he recognized that the government had made inadequate

Emperor Karl I took over the Austro-Hungarian throne upon the death of his grand-uncle in November, 1916. Finding himself and his empire in a hopeless situation, he sought a separate peace, but got little but German anger in exchange for his efforts.

Elihu Root won the Nobel Peace Prize in 1912 and served as American Secretary of War before serving in the US Senate. He accepted Woodrow Wilson's offer to become head of a special diplomatic mission to Russia in 1917.

the Bolsheviks, which had begun to influence the views of many enlisted men and even many officers. The Bolsheviks argued for an end to the war, which they claimed was a capitalist imperial struggle that had nothing to do with the interests of the average Russian. Their influence was so pervasive that many commanders were afraid that their men would not obey orders, or, worse yet, might turn their rifles on their own officers and mutiny.

The offensive was therefore certainly not without its serious risks. In his fiery oratory, Kerensky had linked the future of the Provisional Government to the success of the Russian military. As war minister, he had also linked his own personal future to the performance of the upcoming offensive. Although most of the political factions inside Russia had offered their support to the attack, the signs were not all positive. The Russians had launched a 'Liberty Loan' with great fanfare to help fund the war in 1917. The Russian finance minister hoped that the loan would show the public's faith in the war and the government, as well as leave Russia far less dependent on foreign creditors. The loan, however, was a failure. Russian workers had too little money to contribute, and most members of the middle class had no faith that they would get their money back or that inflation would not far exceed the promised returns.

preparations and really had no clear idea of what it wanted. He nevertheless assembled 31 divisions and prepared them for a major campaign as best he could in the limited amount of time available to him. Brusilov concentrated his forces in the south against the Austro-Hungarians. He aimed for the sector held by the Second and Third armies. They guarded the approaches to strategically important oil fields in the Drohobycz area and, beyond them, the symbolic fortress of Lemberg, whose recapture might provide the Provisional Government with the important morale boost it sought.

Brusilov and others were worried about the influence of radical propaganda from groups such as

Finding money overseas proved to be a problem as well. The Americans were willing to extend credits, but the Provisional Government decided to turn to the

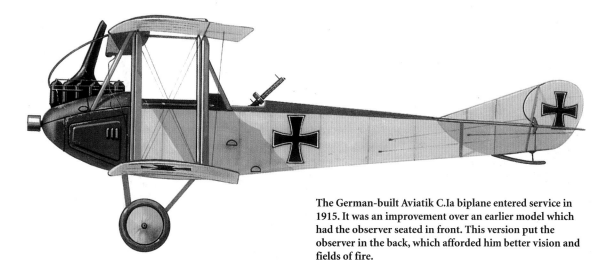

The German-built Aviatik C.Ia biplane entered service in 1915. It was an improvement over an earlier model which had the observer seated in front. This version put the observer in the back, which afforded him better vision and fields of fire.

British and French they already had business dealings rather than open discussions with Americans with whom they did not. Bankers and diplomats in London and Paris made grand promises but the money did not show up, leaving the Russians with little credit and even less hard currency.

Without money, the Russians could not solve their munitions shortfalls. The ripple effects of the strikes were still being felt across Russian industry, creating dangerous shortages of all kinds of military hardware. Without overseas credit, the Russians could not buy munitions from the British and the French, the only countries that could possibly have met their orders. Facing uncertain futures of their own, the British and French were understandably reluctant about committing too much to the Russians. The Americans and the Japanese might have filled at least some orders, but neither had fully converted their industrial plants from civilian to military production, and both wanted to see most of their money up front something the Russians struggled to provide.

Morale had improved, but many commanders still reported rampant acts of indiscipline and fraternization with the enemy. Members of ethnic minorities like the Ukrainians often refused orders

The first Russian Revolution was a great boon to American President Woodrow Wilson. With the Tsar gone, Wilson could, at least for a time, claim that the war was one of democracy versus autocracy and despotism.

until their homelands were given more local autonomy by the Provisional Government. Kerensky responded to the morale problem by announcing the reimposition of the death penalty, a move designed to bolster morale by cracking down on dissenters. Instead, soldiers read it as a return to the

indiscriminate punishment and brutality of the Tsar's regime. Rather than raise the fighting spirit of the Russian Army as expected, the decision caused a sharp drop in morale.

Across the front lines, the Austro-Hungarians were hardly in better shape. Most units were well below their allotted strength, short on weapons, and in a fragile state of morale. Those units opposite Brusilov were commanded by Eduard Böhm-Ermolli, whose military career had thus far seen a great deal of ups

> ## 'Natural love of law and order and capacity for local self-government have been demonstrated every day since the revolution.'
>
> Elihu Root's report on his visit to Russia, June 1917

and downs. The son of a legendary soldier who had risen from the enlisted ranks to general's rank and a noble title, in 1914 Böhm-Ermolli had been the commander of the Austro-Hungarian Second Army that had spent the early part of the war shuffling back

and forth to no effective purpose. His units later moved to Galicia where he had the honour of leading the recapture of Lemberg from the Russians. The retaking of Lemberg had been the high point of his career and had led to his promotion to command of an army group. Brusilov had routed this army group in June 1916, temporarily eclipsing Böhm-Ermolli's star. By 1917, however, he had not only recovered his command, but had managed to convince the German officers in his army group to follow his general operational guidance. He therefore had much more freedom of action from the Germans than did most of his peers.

Böhm-Ermolli's army group was to be the target for Brusilov once again. On 1 July 1917, the Russians attacked using most of the same methods that had worked so well for the Brusilov Offensive the previous year. Brusilov had packed his artillery and the bulk of his most reliable infantry into a 48km (30-mile) wide zone that would encompass the main axis of the attack. Subsidiary and diversionary attacks extended the range of the battle to the same length as the front, almost 160km (100 miles) long. Kerensky himself came to the front line to oversee the start of the offensive. For four days he toured Russian front-line positions, talking to the men and urging them to fight for Russia and for their own freedom. He personally

gave the order to start the offensive from the Russian front trench line.

Kerensky moved along the line, urging the men on and putting heart into some of the army's least willing units. When one regiment refused to advance, Kerensky stood on the trench line in plain view of the Austro-Hungarians and told the men that if they would not attack, he would fight the enemy alone. The speech inspired the men (one observer said the men were 'reborn') and they went over the top, with many soldiers pausing to embrace Kerensky before they did

Kerensky (left) travelled the length of the front line after taking control of the Provisional Government. He hoped to use his oratorical skills to rally Russian soldiers and urge them to continue the war.

so. Kerensky was swept away by the emotion and tried to join the attack, but was dissuaded from doing so by the very men he had just inspired to risk their lives. A journalist who saw the scene said it 'promised to go on record as one of the historic feats in war operations'. Word of Kerensky's behaviour at the front reached Petrograd where a jubilant crowd gathered outside his home and, not knowing what else to do, began singing 'La Marseillaise'.

Although there were some exceptions, most soldiers of the Russian Army showed a willingness to fight in the offensive's early stages. Among the most

The last major Russian offensive of the war is known as either the Kerensky Offensive or the Second Brusilov Offensive. By either name it was a complete failure and laid bare Kerensky's outlook for the future of Russia.

highly motivated units was a group called the Czech Legion. Its members were ethnic Czechs and Slovaks who had been prisoners of war captured in Russia's successful campaigns earlier in the war. They were offered the chance of leaving squalid Russian prisoner of war camps in exchange for their service in the Russian Army, and later received a promise from the Provisional Government that Russia would support the formation of an independent Czechoslovakia at the end of the war. The Czech Legion formed two brigades of the Russian Eleventh Army, which became one of Russia's most dependable large units in the forthcoming offensive.

The Eleventh Army and the Seventh Army formed the vanguard of Brusilov's attack. Brusilov's old unit, the Eighth Army sat in reserve. Known as the Kerensky

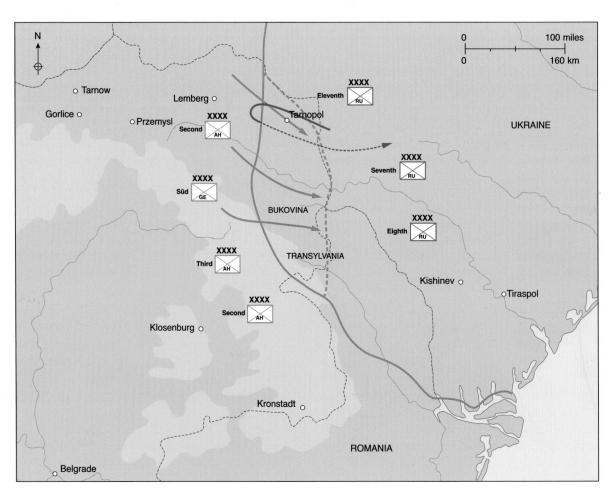

Kerensky Calls for the Soldiers of the Russian Army to Rally to their Country

I came to you because my strength is at an end. I no longer feel my former courage, nor have my former conviction that we are conscientious citizens, not slaves in revolt. I am sorry I did not die two months ago, when the dream of a new life was growing in the hearts of the Russian people, when I was sure the country could govern itself without the whip.

As affairs are going now, it will be impossible to save the country. Perhaps the time is near when we will have to tell you that we can no longer give you the amount of bread you expect or other supplies on which you have a right to count. The process of the change from slavery to freedom is not going on properly. We have tasted freedom and are slightly intoxicated. What we need is sobriety and discipline.

You could suffer and be silent for ten years, and obey the orders of a hated government. You could even fire upon your own people when commanded to do so. Can you now suffer no longer? We hear it said that we no longer need the front because they are fraternizing there. But are they fraternizing on all the fronts? Are they fraternizing on the French front? No, comrades, if you are going to fraternize, then fraternize everywhere. Are

not enemy forces being thrown over on to the Anglo-French front, and is not the Anglo-French advance already stopped? There is no such thing as a 'Russian front', there is only one general allied front.

We are marching toward peace and I should not be in the ranks of the Provisional Government if the ending of the war were not the aim of the whole Provisional Government; but if we are going to propose new war aims we must see we are respected by friend as well as by foe.

If the tragedy and desperateness of the situation are not realized by all in our State, if our organization does not work like a machine, then all our dreams of liberty, all our ideals, will be thrown back for decades and maybe will be drowned in blood.

Beware! The time has now come when everyone in the depth of his conscience must reflect where he is going and where he is leading others who were held in ignorance by the old regime and still regard every printed word as law. The fate of the country is in your hands, and it is in most extreme danger. History must be able to say of us, 'They died, but they were never slaves'.

Offensive or the Second Brusilov Offensive, it began with great success. Brusilov had placed the Czech Legion opposite the Austro-Hungarian 19th Division, which contained two regiments of ethnic Czechs. These two regiments refused to obey orders to fight against fellow Czechs, and a mutiny soon ensued, sending shock waves back to Vienna. More than 3000 Czechs had simply left the army; some had even joined the Russian attack. The incident was an ominous sign. If ethnic identity had finally superseded imperial loyalty to this extent inside the army, then the empire itself could not have much longer to exist.

The greatest first day success of the offensive came in the capture of a strong point near Brzezany, where Russian forces took more than 10,000 prisoners. The Russians noted with some glee that many of the

prisoners were German, not Austro-Hungarian. Böhm-Ermolli's Second Army collapsed, as did the Eighth Army on its flank. Austro-Hungarian units began to flee in panic. A gap opened in Austro-Hungarian lines that was 72km (45 miles) long and more than 32km (20 miles) deep. The American major-general Hugh Scott personally witnessed the offensive and saw the Russians break three separate Austro-Hungarian trench lines. He reported that what he saw of the Russian Army led him to believe that it was 'excellent' in its use of artillery and in the quality of its officers.

Scott could be forgiven for having such an inflated opinion of the Russian Army. For the first few days of July the Russians did indeed look like they had designed a masterpiece once again. The Russians had

Ethnic Czechs and Slovaks in the Czech Legion, formed from former prisoners of war. In 1918, they tried to get to France via Murmansk and then Vladivostok, but instead became embroiled in the developing war between the Red and White factions inside Russia.

advanced to Halicz on the Dniester River, thus giving them command of the southern approaches to Lemberg, about 80km (50 miles) away. Southwest of Halicz, the Russians made their furthest advances of the campaign, establishing bridgeheads across the Lommica River, and in the course of doing so, driving a wedge between the German Army Group South and Böhm-Ermolli's units. Farther to the south, Russian forces had cleared most of the Bukovina region of enemy forces and advanced once again to the passes of the Carpathian Mountains.

This advance provided badly needed (if largely unintended) help to the Romanians, who responded by cancelling their signing of the armistice with

Germany. It was to be a rash and unwise move that only brought further German vengeance later in the year and harsher terms at the Treaty of Bucharest.

The Romanians, however, believed that the Russian advance had changed the situation in the east. And indeed it had. In the first two weeks of July, the Russians reported that they had captured 36,634 enemy soldiers, 93 artillery pieces and 406 machine guns. The Central Powers had been forced to cede two important river lines and the Russians had cut all but one road leading to Lemberg.

Russia also received a new hero in Lavr Kornilov, a man already well known in the army, whose units advanced furthest and with the most success in July 1917. Having served the Tsar in a variety of positions around Asia, he received command of a division in 1914. He was among the Russian officers captured at Przemysl, but he had made a daring escape from his captors and the story had gained much in the telling over the months. He was returned to service as a corps commander and later was placed in charge of the military district of Petrograd. In charge of that city's defences, he had repeatedly urged the provisional government to use lethal force to put down demonstrations. Although his urgings and his advocacy of the return of the monarchy made him extremely unpopular among the industrial classes of Russia, he was sent to the front to serve under Brusilov, where he had performed well during the earlier offensive.

On 19 July, however, German Army Group South counterattacked and, using nine German and two

The disintegration of Imperial Russia unleashed nationalist feelings in ethnically non-Russian areas. These Estonians are marching for a federated Estonia after the war. The national issue proved to be one of the most daunting facing the Bolsheviks, whose ideology was ideally non-national.

Brusilov from command and replace him with the only soldier in the Russian Army who had proved his ability to fight, the volatile monarchist Kornilov. He soon made rampant use of the death penalty for soldiers who had deserted or fled in battle, but the policy failed to stem the precipitous drop in morale.

The collapse of the offensive destroyed whatever momentum and confidence the Provisional Government had built. The moderate, centrist position it had occupied soon withered away. On the left the Bolsheviks, with their call for 'peace, bread and land', began to attract more and more followers. On the right, calls for the return of the Tsar or another member of the royal family also began to grow shriller. Kornilov himself repeatedly made statements critical

Eduard Freiherr von Böhm-Ermolli was born in Italy to a recently ennobled ethnic German military family and rose quickly through the ranks of the Austro-Hungarian Army. His Second Army was the target of the Kerensky Offensive.

Lavr Kornilov (left) came from a long line of Central Asian Cossacks. His intrigues in favour of the return of the Tsarist system helped put in motion the events that led to the October Revolution, which in turn resulted in eventual victory for the Bolsheviks.

Austro-Hungarian divisions, crashed into the northern flank of the Russian advance. Low on supplies and fully unable to withstand the assault, the Russians began to flee, often in panic. A tired and physically ill Brusilov ordered a retreat that in many places turned into a rout. Kornilov and Brusilov had furious arguments about the future conduct of the campaign that did not help matters. Within a few weeks the Russians had lost all that they had gained and more. In the final weeks of July, the Russians lost more than 40,000 men to the Central Powers' losses of just 12,500 men. Central Powers' forces only stopped their pursuit when they ran out of supplies. On 1 August, Kerensky saw no choice but to remove

Two of Lenin's Ten Theses, Announced in April 1917

I have outlined a few theses which I shall supply with some commentaries. I could not, because of the lack of time, present a thorough, systematic report. The basic question is our attitude towards the war.

The basic things confronting you as you read about Russia or observe conditions here are the triumph of the traitors to Socialism, the deception of the masses by the bourgeoisie. ... The new government, like the preceding one, is imperialistic, despite the promise of a republic – it is imperialistic through and through.

One

In our attitude toward the war not the slightest concession must be made to 'revolutionary defence', for under the new government of [Prince Georgi] Lvov and company, owing to the capitalist nature of this government, the war on Russia's part remains a predatory imperialist war.

In view of the undoubted honesty of the mass of rank and file representatives of revolutionary defence who accept the war only as a necessity and not as a means of conquest, in view of their being deceived by the bourgeoisie, it is necessary most thoroughly, persistently, patiently to explain to them their error, to explain the inseparable connection between capital and the imperialist war, to prove that without the overthrow of capital it is impossible to conclude the war with a really democratic, non-oppressive peace.*

This view is to be widely propagated among the army units in the field.

Two

The peculiarity of the present situation in Russia is that it represents a transition from the first stage of the revolution – which, because of the inadequate organization and insufficient class-consciousness of the proletariat, led to the assumption of power by the bourgeoisie – to its second stage which is to place power in the hands of the proletariat and the poorest strata of the peasantry.

This peculiar situation demands of us an ability to adapt ourselves to the specific conditions of party work amidst vast masses of the proletariat just wakened to political life.

of the Provisional Government. The army he now led was in tatters and grew less and less able to defend Russia every day. The high revolutionary spirits of 1 July were gone, their hopes dashed. Men deserted the army in droves, either to escape further bloodshed or to defend their homes from the civil war that many now feared.

Amid this tense environment, Kornilov's political intrigues grew. He had determined that the Provisional Government had no right to govern because it had lost the faith of the Russian people, thereby defeating its own democratic logic. In late August, he ordered a Russian army to march to Petrograd and called upon the Provisional Government to hand power over to the army and

resign. Kerensky understood that Kornilov's demands amounted to a virtual coup that would place all power in the hands of a dangerous monarchist. Acceding to Kornilov meant rolling back all of Russia's gains since March. More seriously, there were signs that the Germans were preparing to launch an offensive in the Baltic provinces and Kerensky needed to know that he had an army commander upon whom he could rely. Accordingly, Kerensky removed Kornilov from command and ordered him to come back to Petrograd. Kornilov refused, setting in motion the events that would lead to the second Russian Revolution. This time, the results would be far more fundamental and have far more dramatic outcomes for the course of the war.

CHAPTER 5

Russia Capitulates

By 1917 the external and internal pressures on the Tsarist state led to its collapse and the introduction of the Provisional Government headed by Alexander Kerensky. That state, too, proved unable to deal with the myriad problems Russia faced. By the end of the year, the Bolsheviks had taken power, with grave consequences for the other great powers.

The Germans moved quickly to take advantage of the chaos and confusion inside Russia after the failure of the Kerensky Offensive. They sensed that the Russians were at a crucial material and morale breaking point, and they wanted to place as much pressure on that breaking point as they possibly could. They chose to attack at the port city of Riga, the centre of a multi-ethnic region known to have large numbers of people who were openly hostile to the Russians. They included a sizeable population of Baltic Germans and Finns who had given up any lasting associations they felt towards either the Tsarist system or the provisional government that replaced it.

German stormtroopers advance on the Eastern Front. Although many armies had worked on the idea, the Germans were the first to put all of the tactical elements of the system into one operational plan.

Oskar von Hutier (1857–1934)

Marked early on in his career as an intelligent and hard-working young officer, Hutier's connections inside the army included such key figures as Erich Ludendorff (a cousin) and Paul von Hindenburg (a former instructor). Hutier made his name on the Eastern Front, where he was one of the principal innovators of infiltration tactics. Although many of the central ideas he used were in fact British or French, Hutier was the first to make large-scale practical use of infiltration tactics. Later becoming known as 'stormtroop' tactics, they temporarily restored mobility to the static conditions of the war. Used at Riga on the Eastern Front and at Caporetto on the Italian Front, Hutier's tactics seemed to have unlocked the secret of winning of the war. Hutier was sent to the Western Front, where he oversaw the implementation of his system in time for the great Spring Offensives of 1918. Like his cousin, he became a key proponent of the stab-in-the-back myth and a supporter of the Nazis before his death in 1934.

Riga also had great strategic value, sitting just 320km (200 miles) from Petrograd, at once the centre of Russian decision making and anti-governmental revolutionary activity.

The responsibility for the attack on Riga fell to Oskar von Hutier, the new commander of the German Eighth Army. Once a large conventional army that had won the great victories at Tannenberg and the Masurian Lakes, the Eighth Army had recently begun to adopt new tactics, sometimes called 'Hutier' tactics, although Hutier himself played little to no role in their origins. Also called stormtroop tactics, the basic ideas were mostly French and British. By late 1917, however, the British and the French had come to the quite reasonable conclusion that with the entry of the United States into the war on their side, they did not need tactical innovation. Rather, their best chance to win the war was to await the incorporation of American men and resources, then conduct a series of large set-piece campaigns in 1918 and 1919 with fresh men and large numbers of heavy weapons.

Not so the Germans, who were still haunted by the two-front dilemma and also knew that they could not hope to match the men and material of the Allies. They also knew that they could not afford to fight

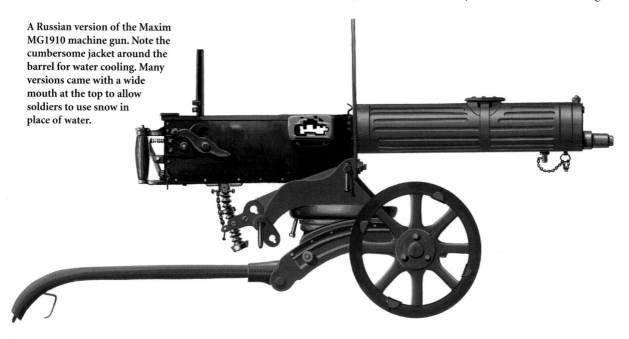

A Russian version of the Maxim MG1910 machine gun. Note the cumbersome jacket around the barrel for water cooling. Many versions came with a wide mouth at the top to allow soldiers to use snow in place of water.

General Oskar von Hutier (left) did not originate the tactics that sometimes carry his name. He was, however, the commander of the first army to use such tactics on a wide scale. His success created a new operational model for the German Army.

Foremost among them was the introduction of the new 'Hutier' tactical system. It involved the use of specialized stormtroops backed by a very careful synchronization of artillery and infantry. The infantrymen were volunteers who agreed to join these special assault detachments in return for extra rations, more leave time and excusal from fatigue duties. They were trained in the use of new and more portable weapons like the light machine guns, portable flamethrower and field mortar. They were also trained to use initiative and think as they moved instead of waiting for orders from their officers.

Hutier tactics were quite complicated and varied considerably from battle to battle, but they shared several features. A stormtroop attack was normally preceded by a carefully designed artillery bombardment that relied heavily on gas instead of high explosive. The gas was targeted at enemy command and control posts with the intention of slowing the enemy commander's ability to discern the nature of the offensive and his ability to issue rapid orders to meet it. Gas also left the ground relatively undisturbed in order to permit specialized infantry to advance quickly through it.

Those specialized infantry were trained to bypass the enemy's strongpoints and advance through the holes created by the artillery bombardment. They would then range behind the enemy's lines looking for enemy command posts, communications infrastructure and any other targets of value. Once the enemy's 'head' had thus been decapitated, the regular German infantry could come forwards to fight its body. Ultimately, the goal of a Hutier operation was to encircle and capture enemy units rather than try to

many more set-piece battles like Verdun or the Somme and, more importantly, that until they could eliminate one of their two fronts time was not on their side. The arrival of the Americans would make these problems all the more acute. A way therefore had to be found to win on one of the two fronts before the Americans could make their presence felt on the battlefield. Despite the disastrous Allied offensives along the Chemin des Dames and near Passchendaele in 1917, the French and the British were not yet ready to break. That meant attacking the seemingly faltering Russians. Nevertheless, although the Russians certainly appeared weak, no one in the German high command knew how many Russian soldiers remained loyal to the regime or if someone like Kornilov might rally the men and resume the offensive. Russia therefore had to be defeated soon and the Eastern Front eliminated as a German operational and strategic concern.

As part of the effort to capture Riga quickly, the Germans decided to take a number of calculated risks.

trade casualties man for man, a system that the Germans knew their numbers did not favour.

THE FALL OF RIGA

An attack on Riga in September was to be the first test of the new system. On 1 September 1917, German artillery fired more than 20,000 shells, most of them gas shells, without warning. The attack struck Russian defenders like a bolt of lightning, catching them completely unprepared. German stormtroops soon began to cross the rivers and streams around Riga in specially designed boats, establishing bridgeheads and directing the fire of more conventional artillery to prevent Russian counterattacks. With both banks of a river secured, the Germans could build pontoon bridges for the safe crossing of regular infantry in large numbers. Some of these bridges were even strong enough to allow field artillery to come forward and support the attack.

Using these methods, the Germans were able to land nine divisions of troops across the Dvina River in just 48 hours. Once they did so, the Russian defenders knew the battle was lost and made quick plans to evacuate a now indefensible Riga. Setting some buildings on fire to, the Russians evacuated as many men and supplies as they could amid scenes of chaos and sheer panic. German artillery pounded the city and many of the bridges leading east in the hopes of capturing as many Russian soldiers as possible. By the third day of the operation, German forces had entered parts of Riga, and by day four they had complete control of the city and its port.

The effect of this battle on both sides was electric. The Germans estimated their casualties at 4200 and

The campaigns of 1917 destroyed most of what remained in the Russian arsenal. The Russian Army soon found itself short of almost everything, especially heavy artillery pieces and the shells they fired.

Russian casualties at more than 25,000. The Russians also lost 250 of their precious artillery pieces, leaving five Russian divisions without significant artillery support. Many smaller Russian units simply melted away in the face of the attack, underscoring the essential morale problems of the army. The Russian officer corps tried everything it could think of to stem the tide of desertion. Commanders ordered deserters shot on sight, tried to create their own stormtroop detachments and even formed a special all-female battalion. The Russian soldier, however, had begun to give up the cause.

The Germans rightly saw Riga as a great success and a validation of their investment in the new methods. In stark contrast to the frustrations and indecisiveness of the Western Front, the victory at Riga was dramatic and relatively cheap. The Kaiser decorated Hutier with the Pour le Mérite, Germany's highest military award, and ordered a day of national celebration, the first since the fall of Bucharest. Hutier then ordered an even more daring amphibious assault to capture the Baltic islands of Ösel, Moon and Dagö. The Germans used aircraft to spot and target enemy positions, torpedo boats and cruisers to clear away the

A unit of German cavalry enters Riga, a city with a large Baltic German population. The fall of the city symbolized a major turning point in the war for the Germans and the Russians alike, and set in motion the final end of the Provisional Government.

Russian surface fleet from the islands, and marines to secure landing areas. Although there were many problems and much more work clearly needed to be done before the Germans could repeat an attack of this kind, the assault on the Baltic islands represented one of the very few successful amphibious and joint operations of the war and was a crushing morale blow to the Russian Army, which now seemed powerless to stop the German onslaught.

The Germans used methods broadly similar to those used at Riga in Italy later in the year. At Caporetto in late October, they caved in the Italian line and sent two Italian armies retreating in conditions resembling a rout. Only the difficulty of supplying their fast-moving men and the limited goals the Germans had set for the operation kept the disaster from becoming even worse. The new system had now been tested twice, albeit against armies suffering from low morale and poor commanders. Hutier was

German troops climb aboard ship on their way to the
Russian Baltic island of Ösel as part of an operation code-
named 'Albion'. The Russians saw the attack coming, but
could do little to prevent it. German control of the Baltic
proved to be decisive.

transferred west with much of his staff to put the new
methods in place along the Western Front in
preparation for a major last gamble offensive against
the British and the French in the spring of 1918 before
the Americans could arrive in force.

The tactical lessons of Riga were clear. For the
Germans, Riga showed the value of new methods of
war that, when well executed, were parsimonious with

German lives, but created panic in enemy lines. Thus
large victories by a smaller German army against a
larger Russian army were still conceivable. This
conclusion was welcome to the Germans because they
knew that they would soon need to begin large-scale
troop transfers from the east to the west to meet the
arrival of the Americans. Whether the new methods
would work against the French and British as well as
they had against the Russians and the Italians,
however, remained to be seen.

Nevertheless, alongside the tactical successes stood
the strategic shortcomings that Riga also revealed. The
capture of Riga did not materially change the situation

in the east as much as the Germans had hoped. The Germans might be able to use Riga's port to ease some supply problems, but the port would soon ice over, thus limiting its utility. The Germans also expected to receive a warm welcome from the Finns and Baltic Germans living around Riga, but it remained far from clear how much their support would translate into usable military assistance. Like the Poles, the Germans expected the Finns to be grateful for liberating them from the Russians, but they anticipated that few Finns would seek military service in the German Army. Even many Baltic Germans had their doubts about trading a Russian regime that had generally treated them well for a German regime that looked upon them as alien and suspicious, notwithstanding the ethnic links that bound them together.

Most importantly, Moscow and Petrograd were still far away. The Russians had set up a reasonably strong defensive line between Riga and Petrograd and most Germans expected Russian soldiers to fight harder for the latter than they had for the former. Even the capture of Petrograd or Moscow, moreover, provided no sure guarantee that the Russians would

leave the war. Nightmarish visions of 1812 still burned deeply into German strategic and operational thinking. Germany had won an important battle (and one the Kaiser thought worth celebrating), but it was far from clear how the Germans might still win the war. No one in Germany welcomed the thought of chasing the Russians to and beyond Moscow as Napoleon had done.

For their part, the generals of the Russian high command intuitively understood the German dilemma. They concluded that the loss of Riga itself was no great calamity for Russia. Many Russians in and out of uniform had seen Riga as a hotbed of Baltic German treason and radical revolutionary sentiment. They therefore responded to its loss with mixed emotions. On the one hand the loss of a key city of the Russian Empire with so little effort expended in its defence was an embarrassment; on the other hand, the city had not done much to help the Russian cause and not a few Russians greeted the news of its fall with a sense of good riddance.

The real importance of the fall of Riga lay in what it meant for the Russian political system. The loss of

A German Agent Describes an Officer of the Russian Women's Battalion

In May 1917 a Russian peasant woman named Maria Bochkareva convinced Kerensky to allow her to form a 2000-person-strong women's battalion. Desertions and casualties soon reduced the number to a few hundred, but they made news across the world and helped to shame more Russian men into staying with the army, which many suspected was Kerensky's goal all along:

'Among the passengers once standing in a car, I saw an officer of the Women's Battalion of Death. With a white fur cap saucily perched on her head, her hair combed high under it, and spurs on her boots, she was a sturdy and pleasing figure. Standing in front of her was a slovenly looking sailor, the band of his cap so loosely fastened that it hung almost over one eye. On it I read the name of his ship, the Pamjat Asowa, *In Memory of Asow – Asow, the revolutionist.'*

The creation of an all-women's battalion in the Russian Army was one of the few such examples in history to that time. It would be an example to a future generation of Russian women.

the city, on top of the failure of the summer offensive, proved to most Russians beyond a doubt that the Kerensky government was little better at fighting wars than the Tsarist system it had replaced. The wild optimism and hope that had accompanied the change of government was quickly replaced by pessimism and fear. Perhaps most importantly, the failure of the Kerensky government meant that the already weak Russian centre could not hold. The fate of Russia would soon turn into a struggle between factions on opposite sides of the Russian political spectrum, with important consequences for the last year of the war.

REVOLUTION AND RETREAT

After the failure of the Kerensky Offensive, Lavr Kornilov, the most powerful Russian general still holding a field command, had determined that the only way to save Russia was to remove the Provisional Government by force and restore the Romanov dynasty to its proper place in Russian governance. Conservative newspapers in Russia had turned Kornilov into something of a folk hero and saw him as the best way to prevent a radical revolution from breaking out in Russia. He seemed the last best hope for stopping the rise of the urban-based soviets, which had grown tremendously in influence and power since the summer. Many Russian conservatives had begun to talk openly about Kornilov seizing power for himself rather than trying to resuscitate the Tsar and his incompetent regime. Kornilov proved more than receptive to their ideas and his relationship with Kerensky subsequently deteriorated.

The situation grew much more tense after the fall of Riga. Kerensky and Kornilov each blamed the other for the military failure and, while both recognized the need for change, they shared too much mutual mistrust to work together, even in the face of a common threat to both of them from the revolutionary parties. In an exchange of notes sent through intermediaries (the two were no longer communicating directly with one another), Kerensky and Kornilov discussed Russia's future (as well as their own projected places within it), but it soon became clear that they had diametrically opposed visions of

Leon Trotsky (1879–1940)

Born Leon Davidovich Bronstein in the Ukraine in 1879, he was an early opponent of Nicholas II and an advocate of Marxism. Escaping from a Siberian prison in 1902 he took on the name Trotsky and soon became an important adviser to Lenin, especially on military matters. As the Red Army's Commissar for War he played key roles in ending Russia's participation in World War I as well as directing Soviet military policy during the Russian Civil War and the Russo-Polish War. In 1924, after Lenin's death, he lost the succession struggle for control of the Soviet Union to Joseph Stalin, who then exiled him to Turkey. In 1937 he moved to Mexico on the invitation of his friend, artist Diego Rivera. There on 21 August 1940 a Soviet agent assassinated him. George Orwell based Snowball the pig in the book *Animal Farm* on Trotsky.

what a future Russian government might look like. Leftists and moderates began to worry that Kornilov was plotting a coup that would roll back all of the many gains Russia had made since the abdication of Nicholas II.

On 9 September, Kerensky concluded that the danger of coup had become too great to ignore. He ordered Kornilov removed from command despite veiled promises in the exchange of notes that he would not do so. An enraged Kornilov felt that he had been betrayed and defied the order. Claiming that the revolutionary threat to Petrograd put the nation in grave danger, he sent a detachment of soldiers toward the city on the ostensible grounds of providing the law and order that the provisional government could not. Petrograd workers, most of whom loathed Kornilov for his advocacy of the Tsar and his repeated insistence on being allowed to restore the death penalty for desertion, reacted to the news with alarm and panic. So, of course, did Kerensky, who presumed that the coup he had so feared was about to begin.

The tensions inside Russia were reflected as well in an increasingly tense environment in the cities. The number of strikes was on a dramatic increase, as industrial workers voted with their feet much as deserting Russian soldiers had been doing. Amid food shortages, fears of a German occupation and general uncertainty about the future, the numbers of Russian workers on strike increased from 41,000 in March to 385,000 in July. These numbers, generally corresponding to the period of the Provisional Government, were frightening enough. But the failure

Leon Trotsky used his ideological fervour and his passionate speeches to inspire Russian workers to take up arms. He famously declared, 'You may not be interested in war, but war is interested in you.'

of the Kerensky Offensive and the loss of Riga were met with newer and larger waves of strikes. In August, 380,000 Russian workers went on strike, with an amazing rise in September to 965,000 workers on strike. More and more radical leaders began to assume leadership of these strikes, with many calling for industrial sabotage, class warfare and revolution.

Among the rising stars of the radical revolutionaries was a member of a long-standing revolutionary family in Russia. Vladimir Ilyich Ulyanov was born into a family of schoolteachers and civil servants. In 1887, when he was just 17, his brother was executed for his part in an unsuccessful plot to kill Tsar Alexander III. The young man, who changed his name to Lenin, was expelled from school for his revolutionary talk and later exiled to Siberia. In 1900 he left Russia to study and think about Marxism and how it might be useful to Russia's future. In 1905 he returned to Russia amid the revolutionary events of

the end of the Russo-Japanese War as a dedicated member of the Bolshevik Party, which was committed to a violent overthrow of the Tsarist regime by a dedicated revolutionary vanguard. When the Tsar kept his hold on power, Lenin went back into exile, initially in Finland and then in Western Europe.

> 'Russian soldiers who had fought brilliantly under Brusilov and won victories under Kornilov were on the run.'
>
> A journalist describes the Russian Army in August 1917

He spent most of World War I in neutral Switzerland where he had concluded that the war was an imperial struggle of no possible gain or benefit to the working class. Lenin believed that imperialism was the last stage of capitalism and that therefore the time was right for moving to the next stage of the Marxist struggle, the destruction of the capitalist classes. He urged workers in the belligerent nations to stop fighting one another and take up arms in an international class struggle to rid the world of the capitalists who had created the conditions that made the war possible. In February 1917, the German Government saw the value of

Russian revolutionaries storm the Winter Palace in Petrograd after it became clear that the palace's guards would not fire upon them. The incident marked the end of the Provisional Government and the culmination of the October Revolution.

inserting Lenin and several other revolutionaries into the Russian maelstrom in the hopes that they might further destabilize the Russian political system. The Germans transported the Russians in a sealed train through Germany, Sweden and Finland, and arranged for them to enter Russia.

Lenin's appearance at first made little real difference to the political situation in Russia. Seen even by many of his supporters as an intellectual who had had little practical experience of the war or the social changes inside Russia, he had trouble assuming the leadership mantle of the Bolsheviks he had so craved. In July, the Bolsheviks had made a clumsy attempt to gain power, but it had failed, and this had temporarily reduced the profile and the power of the party. It had also sent Lenin running to Finland for fear that Kerensky might order his arrest. By the time of the Kornilov crisis, however, he and the Bolsheviks spoke for a large and growing number of Russian workers. They advocated an end to the war, a

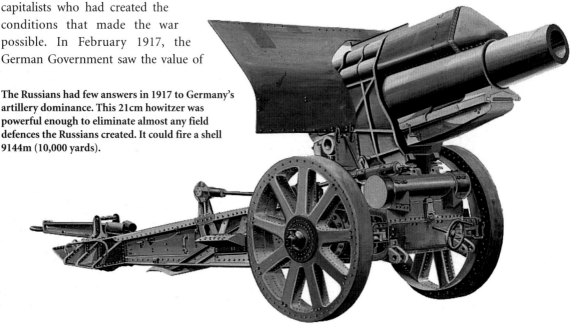

The Russians had few answers in 1917 to Germany's artillery dominance. This 21cm howitzer was powerful enough to eliminate almost any field defences the Russians created. It could fire a shell 9144m (10,000 yards).

redistribution of land, and the immediate delivery of food to the starving Russian cities. 'Bread, peace and land' was a simple and alluring slogan to Russian workers amid the chaos and anxiety of 1917.

To meet the threat that Kornilov seemed to pose, Petrograd's highly motivated and disciplined revolutionary workers made a temporary alliance with Kerensky's Provisional Government. Lenin and the Bolsheviks supported the alliance. At this stage, each of them feared Kornilov's anticipated coup (and with it, the return of the monarchy and all of the retribution it could be expected to mete out to its enemies) more than they feared one another. With the army in complete disarray and some of it probably still

Sailors check papers in Petrograd during the tense days of 1917. The imminent collapse of the Tsar's government created a whirlwind of tensions and mutual suspicions across Russia, but nowhere as intensely as in Petrograd.

following Kornilov's orders, the workers provided the only large source of power upon which the government could call. Speaking on behalf of the Bolsheviks, Lenin made it clear that the alliance was temporary and that he was only cooperating because he saw Kerensky as the lesser of two evils.

Inside the city, workers were quick to form militias and units for self-defence against any forces Kornilov sent against them. These forces were organized under the authority of the Congress of Soviets, a body dominated by many key Bolshevik leaders. Throughout the crisis, the Bolsheviks proved to be the best organized and most enthusiastic members of the militia, which both heightened their overall prestige and gave them important advantages in the days to come. In large part thanks to their boldness and initiative, the workers of the city were now armed and organized to resist.

Revolutionaries take to the streets in a show of force. Many of them were former soldiers, as is indicated in the photograph by the weapons and uniforms of the Imperial Army. The Revolution soon dissolved into the Civil War, which lasted until 1921.

Kornilov's coup, which probably never stood a chance of succeeding, quickly fell apart. Railway workers refused to help transport either Kornilov's men or their arms toward the city, forcing them to approach the city on foot. The delay gave the soviets more time to organize and the Bolsheviks more time to assume the most important leadership positions. Workers from the Petrograd Soviet marched out to meet the force Kornilov had ordered into the city. They convinced the soldiers that Kornilov's plot was an attempt at counterrevolution and the soldiers ended their march with virtually no bloodshed on 12 September. Thousands more soldiers deserted, many of them to the Bolsheviks. Kornilov and several other generals were arrested, although Kornilov himself eventually escaped from jail and later died in the Russian Civil War as a general for the 'White', or Tsarist side. The threat to Petrograd was over, although to many the crisis had also shown the unwillingness of Russian soldiers to keep fighting.

With Kornilov in jail, the Bolsheviks no longer needed Kerensky. The leader of the Provisional Government tried to make some adjustments to their liking by forming a new cabinet with more socialists, but Kerensky no longer had the power to hold Russia

together. In late October the Bolshevik Central Committee decided on an armed revolution to eliminate the provisional government and seize power for themselves. By 25 October, Leon Trotsky had done much of the work to set up a leadership organization for the Revolution based around 20,000 members of the Red Guards, all of them members of the party and almost all of them armed. Trotsky also worked to build links to the leaders of 150,000 soldiers and 80,000 sailors willing to support the Revolution.

On 24 October, Trotsky and the Bolshevik leadership put their carefully crafted plan into action.

A famous photograph showing the street violence outside the Duma that underscored the tense and unstable environment in Russia after the October Revolution. The Bolsheviks emerged from the chaos as the best organized and best disciplined of the groups.

It was timed to take place as the second Congress of Soviets was set to begin its session. Pro-Bolshevik members of the soviets stormed the Winter Palace, the seat of the provisional government, and arrested several government ministers. Kerensky himself fled from the city, never to return. Soldiers, sailors and workers took control of most of the key centres of

After his abdication, Nicholas II was sent with his family to the Siberian city of Ekaterinburg. On 18 July 1918 revolutionaries from the Ural Soviet executed him, his wife and all of their children.

power inside Petrograd as tens of thousands of loyal Bolsheviks fanned out through the city. Partly because of its audacity and partly because of the careful planning, the seizure of power took place with almost no violence. The second Russian revolution of the year (called the October Revolution) was underway.

The next day the Congress of Soviets met. Over 60 per cent of the members were Bolshevik. Many of the non-Bolshevik members withdrew in disgust at what they saw as an illegal and provocative seizure of power. Still, no group had the power or the boldness to try to remove the Bolsheviks, and most of the senior officers of the army showed little sign of wanting to involve themselves in the crisis. The Bolsheviks proposed a wide and far-reaching programme of reform throughout Russia,

The Death of Nicholas II

After his abdication, the fate of Nicholas hung precariously in the balance. British Prime Minister David Lloyd George offered to give Nicholas refuge in Great Britain, but King George V (Nicholas's cousin) blocked the offer, most likely because he did not want to be associated with Nicholas's brand of royal absolutism. After the Bolshevik seizure of power, Nicholas was moved to Siberia where we was executed on 17 July 1918 and placed in an anonymous grave. In 1979, his remains were found, but they were not unearthed until the end of communism in 1991. In 1998 he was given a proper funeral and entombed in St Petersburg. The Russian Orthodox Church canonized him two years later.

but what interested most foreign observers to these incredible events was the position the party planned to take on the war. Although the leaders of the Bolsheviks had denounced the war in their speeches what would they do now that they actually held power? Would they pull Russia out of the war or would they do as Kerensky had done and harness the war to the new Russian revolutionary spirit? Would they try to export their revolution across Europe, especially to Germany or Austria-Hungary where food shortages and accusations of government incompetence had become increasingly common?

Lenin gave the world part of the answer in his first speech to the Congress of Soviets on 8 November. He called for 'all warring peoples and their governments to open immediate negotiations for a just, democratic peace'. He also proposed an immediate armistice for a minimum of three months. The manifesto was approved unanimously and ending the war became a key Bolshevik policy, although Lenin, Trotsky and other leaders were careful to keep their exact conditions for ending Russia's part in the war secret. They seem to have held out the belief that they could appeal to German reason to assure a reasonably just end to the war. They were to be sorely disappointed.

Alexander Kerensky (1881–1970)

Kerensky's fall from power was swift. After the Bolshevik takeover a warrant was issued for his arrest. He was saved by an American diplomat who smuggled him out of Petrograd in a car flying an American flag.

Although he initially wanted to build an army to march back on the city, he was persuaded that the Provisional Government had ended. Still just 36 years old, he accepted an American offer of passage to the United States. He lectured at several universities and for a time became a sought-after public speaker on matters of the war and how to defeat communism. He moved to New York where he died in 1970.

Members of the 'Red Guard of the Proletariat', as the Worker's Army was renamed, stand guard at the gates of the Winter Palace. The Red Guard gave the Bolsheviks an armed presence that could be used on the streets or as a veiled threat of violence against their enemies.

Unlike Kerensky, the Bolshevik leaders had little interest in working with the capitalist western Allies. They soon published the texts of secret treaties and diplomatic understandings that they found in the Winter Palace and the government archives. These agreements showed French and British support for Russian territorial gain, especially at Turkey's expense with regards to Constantinople. This seemingly revealed what the Bolsheviks had been arguing all along, namely that the war had been fought for imperial interests, not out of self-defence. The publication of these terms embarrassed Allied diplomats who had claimed in public that no such agreements existed. This also angered the American who had advocated a peace without annexations.

True to their promises, the members of the new Russian Government made overtures to the Germans about an armistice. No longer bound to the western Allies, they had no reason to honour the Provisional Government's promise not to sign a separate peace treaty with Germany. Facing the real possibility of civil war with several different anti-Bolshevik factions inside Russia, the Bolsheviks hoped to end the war with Germany and move on to the primary task of completing the success of the revolution and ending all possibilities of counter-revolution. Trotsky took charge of the negotiations, hoping to acquire peace without having to surrender much of the territory that Russia had held in 1914. His was an impossible task given German attitudes on the subject of peace in the east, but he managed to obtain an armistice with the Germans that temporarily ended active

A German armoured car patrolling the streets of Kiev. The Germans found that defeating the Russian Army was only half the battle. They still had to impose their will on the Ukraine and other parts of Russia they occupied.

combat on 5 December 1917. Trotsky then headed to the formerly Russian fortress of Brest-Litovsk (in modern-day Belarus) for negotiations with the Germans on the treaty that would end Russia's participation in the war.

THE TREATY OF BREST-LITOVSK

If Trotsky thought that the ongoing war in the west would make the Germans more likely to negotiate a compromise peace, he was soon disappointed. The Germans had already concluded that they would exact a winner's peace on the Russians. They believed that they had acquired the right of conquest over anything and everything their armies had taken. Moreover, they looked aghast at any proposal to give back voluntarily what German soldiers had fought and died to win. They also had decided that they would need to take as many natural resources out of Russia as possible to give their forces the best possible chance of winning

Key

Front line,
3 December 1917

Line set by Treaty of
Brest-Litovsk,
3 March 1918

N

Petrograd

Reval

Pskov

Riga

Moscow

Danzig

Minsk

Kursk

Warsaw

Lodz

Brest-Litovsk

Kiev

Kharkov

Rostov

Odessa

SEA OF
AZOV

Stavropol

Sevastopol

Belgrade

Bucharest

Constanza

BLACK SEA

Varna

Sofia

Trebizond

Constantinople

Salonika

0   300 miles

0   400 km

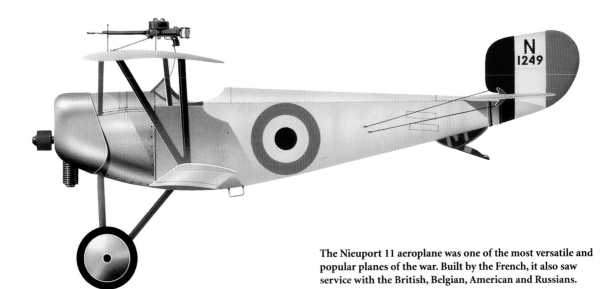

The Nieuport 11 aeroplane was one of the most versatile and popular planes of the war. Built by the French, it also saw service with the British, Belgian, American and Russians.

the war in the west. Seized grain and fuel from Russia would compensate for losses to the British blockade, even if the seizures reduced whole sections of occupied Russia to starvation conditions, as happened in the Ukraine and Belarus.

There had been voices for moderation inside the German Government, especially that of Foreign Minister Richard von Kühlmann. He had hoped that a quick peace treaty with only small border adjustments would allow the Germans the chance to focus their energies on the war in the west and perhaps find a way to insert some provisions that might help Austria-Hungary avoid disillusion and dismemberment. Although few Germans paid any attention to the desires of Austria-Hungary, the empire's representative, Ottokar von Czernin, also favoured a lenient peace. The two foreign ministers had issued a joint declaration stating that the Central Powers sought a 'general peace without forcible annexations and indemnities'.

Hindenburg and Ludendorff, however, showed who really ran Germany by rejecting the diplomats

The Treaty of Brest-Litovsk was one of the most lopsided agreements in history. It gave the Germans more than 1,600,000 square kilometres (620,000 square miles) of Russian territory, but it also inspired the British and French to fight even harder.

and their talk of a compromise peace out of hand. They demanded that Russia be dismembered, and that the Germans annex all the territory they could. The two soldiers demanded border adjustments that would make a future round of war with Russia easier to conduct and envisioned removing all Russians from the Baltic states and turning them into 'settlement areas' for Germans. Their plan would have deprived the Russians of virtually all access to the sea, turning the Baltic into a 'German lake'.

Ludendorff also spoke of creating permanent barriers between Germans and Slavs in the east. The powerful duo threatened the German Government with a joint resignation if the diplomats altered these demands or failed to attain all that the generals demanded. Much to Kühlmann's disappointment, several key leaders of Germany's business community sided with the soldiers and demanded heavy reparations and annexations of key Russian mines and oil wells.

Thus the German plan was clearly staked out. Although Kühlmann sat as the titular head of the German delegation to Brest-Litovsk, the real head of the mission was General Max Hoffmann, the same man who, as a lieutenant-colonel in 1914, had designed the operational plan for Tannenberg. Frustrated at what he saw as German military arrogance and domination, Czernin threatened to sign a separate Austro-Hungarian peace with the Russians. The Kaiser responded by comparing Austro-Hungarian 'perfidy' to that of Italy in 1915, and Hoffmann threatened that he would reassign the 25 German divisions protecting the Austro-Hungarians from a renewed Russian offensive to the Western Front if the Austro-Hungarian delegation made any separate overtures to the Russians. The German Army had won the internal struggle to set the terms of the peace treaty. Now it had to deal with the Russians.

For their part, the Bolshevik leaders favoured signing a peace with the Germans, even on disadvantageous terms. Lenin and Trotsky knew that

they needed to prepare to fight a civil war and that their regime could not possibly survive a civil and foreign war at the same time. Lenin preferred an immediate peace in order to allow the Bolsheviks to move forward. Trotsky favoured stalling for as long as possible because he believed that a Bolshevik revolution in Germany was imminent. The rising of Europe's working classes that he expected would give him all of the bargaining power he would need. Still, he must have known how little he had to offer at the peace negotiations, having already publicly stated his support for ending the war on almost any terms.

Discussions at Brest-Litovsk began on 17 December. The Germans had already concluded that the Russians had no cards to play at the bargaining table and had proceeded accordingly. They had ignored the clause in the armistice that had forbidden the two sides from moving forces across the front and

German soldiers head to Finland, which was formerly a province of Imperial Russia but became an independent state after 6 December 1917. The Germans fought on the 'White' side in the Finnish Civil War that followed.

The Bolshevik delegation arrives by train at the city of Brest-Litovsk for negotiations with the waiting Germans. Leon Trotsky (centre, in the fur hat) headed the Russian negotiating party. Max Hoffmann, one of the victors of Tannenberg, represented Germany.

had instead redeployed their units to make any resumption of hostilities easier to begin. They had also begun separate negotiations with a provisional, generally pro-German, Ukrainian Government, even though the Bolshevik Government still claimed control over the Ukraine.

Early negotiations were tense and acrimonious from the start. Even though their insertion of Lenin into Russia had helped to make the October Revolution a possibility, the Germans looked down their noses at the Russians. They despised having to negotiate at all with Slavs and equally despised the

political ideology of Bolshevism. More importantly, Hoffmann saw no need to give in at all to a people he believed had been fully conquered and beaten. Despite the ongoing discussions about peace, German soldiers talked openly of 'the eventuality of energetic military measures against the Russians' being resumed in the near future. Hoffmann made it clear to Trotsky that the Russians were at Brest-Litovsk to sign documents prepared by the Germans, not to haggle over terms.

Despite the pressures on him to sign a treaty, Trotsky could not accept German terms and walked out of the negotiations in February 1918. Kaiser Wilhelm responded by announcing a plan for the unilateral division of European Russia. Poland was to be given to the House of Württenberg, Lithuania to the House of Saxony, the rest of the Baltic states to his own House of Hohenzollern and Finland to his son,

---

Trotsky Describes Armistice Negotiations, December 1917

The conference opened in the presence of representatives of Germany, Austria-Hungary, Turkey and Bulgaria. Field Marshal [Paul] von Hindenburg and Field Marshal [Conrad] von Hötzendorf charged Prince Leopold of Bavaria with the negotiations, and he in his turn nominated his chief of staff, General [Max] Hoffmann. Other delegates received similar authority from their highest commander-in-chief. The enemy delegation was exclusively military.

Our delegates opened the conference with a declaration of our peace aims, in view of which an armistice was proposed. The enemy delegates replied that that was a question to be solved by politicians. They said they were soldiers, having powers only to negotiate conditions of an armistice, and could add nothing to the declaration of Foreign Ministers [Ottokar] von Czernin and [Max] von Kühlmann.

Our delegates, taking due note of this evasive declaration, proposed that they should immediately address all the countries involved in the war, including Germany and her allies, and all States not represented at the conference, with a proposal to take part in drawing up an armistice on all fronts.

The enemy delegates again replied evasively that they did not possess such powers. Our delegation then proposed that they ask their government for such authority. This proposal was accepted, but no reply had been communicated to the Russian delegation up to 2 o'clock, December 5th.

Our representatives submitted a project for an armistice on all fronts, elaborated by our military experts. The principal points of this project were: First, an interdiction against sending forces on our fronts to the fronts of our allies, and, second, the retirement of German detachments from the islands around Moon Sound [near Riga].

The enemy delegation submitted a project for an armistice on the front from the Baltic to the Black Sea. This proposal is now being examined by our military experts. Negotiations will be continued tomorrow morning.

The enemy delegation declared that our conditions for an armistice were unacceptable and expressed the opinion that such demands could be addressed only to a conquered country.

Oskar. The Austrians got nothing. At a conference at Bad Homburg, Hindenburg promised to resume the war within one week and demanded the outright annexation of the Baltic states to Germany 'for the manoeuvring of my left wing in the next war'. Ludendorff went even further, proposing a new round of war in the east to eliminate the Bolsheviks and prepare for the addition to the German Empire of Armenia, Georgia and the western coast of the Caspian Sea. The French, British and Americans, presumably, could be dealt with in 1919 or even later.

The conference at Bad Homburg showed how badly divorced from reality the German high command really was. The diplomats thought about a mass resignation in protest, but there was no real point in an empty gesture. Instead, they completed the treaty

with the Ukraine, promising not to annex it in return for more than six months' worth of grain and minerals. The Germans and Austro-Hungarians also released all Ukrainian prisoners of war. As a result, the Russians invaded the Ukraine, plunging that country into a bloody civil war and forcing the Germans to leave more than 650,000 men in place to maintain order after the assassination of the German commander Field Marshal Hermann von Eichhorn by a Ukrainian nationalist. As a result of all the chaos, the Germans never realized even a fraction of the grain that they had hoped to get from the Ukraine.

In mid-February the Germans resumed the offensive against Russia with more than 50 divisions. Turkish units also renewed their attacks in the Caucasus Mountains. German troops advanced with ease against only light opposition from Russian troops who had been told to expect peace. The Germans gained hundreds of kilometres, taking key cities like Dvinsk and Kiev and preparing to move into Bessarabia and the Crimea. Helsinki, still under nominal Russian control, fell as well, along with 25,000 Russian defenders who surrendered en masse.

The German offensive, and the lack of an effective Russian response to it, finally proved to Trotsky and Lenin that they had little choice but to sign whatever the Germans offered. The Treaty of Brest-Litovsk was signed on 3 March 1918, and gave the Germans terms that led the Kaiser to dub it one of the great successes in world history. The territorial concessions forced Russia to cede control over more than two-and-a-half million square kilometres of territory. Russia recognized the independence of the Ukraine (in effect a German satellite) and Finland as well the transfer of

The famous Luger P08 Parabellum pistol. Although more commonly associated with World War II it had been issued to German officers since 1904. It could be converted into a machine pistol that fired 9mm ammunition.

Russian and German delegates sign the final Treaty of Brest-Litovsk. Both Trotsky and Lenin saw the lopsided treaty as a necessary evil needed to buy the revolution time to strengthen itself against internal enemies.

the Baltic states to German crown princes. Poland was also removed from Russia, with its final status to be determined after a conference between the Germans and the Austro-Hungarians. German gains ranged as far east as the Crimean Peninsula and the west bank of the Don River. The land Russia gave up held 62 million people.

The economic concessions of Brest-Litovsk were just as staggering. In the lands Russia ceded sat almost 90 per cent of its coal and half of its heavy industry. Russia also gave up tonnes of grain and oil, which the Central Powers divided among themselves. Austria-

Hungary took the lion's share, not out of German kindness, but because the lines of transportation were easiest to manage. The Germans also took mountains of rifles, artillery pieces, and ammunition for use in their grand offensive in the west, expected to begin soon. By October 1918. the Germans had taken away 47,174 tonnes (52,000 tons) of grain, 30,844 tonnes (34,000) tons of beet sugar, 45 million eggs, 53,000 horses and 48,000 hogs. Still, to enforce the treaty and ensure themselves of the ability to take such vast amounts from starving peasants, the Germans had to dedicate almost one million men to the Eastern Front for the duration of the war.

Despite the need to keep so many men in the east, for the Germans, Brest-Litovsk finally meant that they could focus on one front exclusively. The Germans

The Treaty of Brest-Litovsk ended the war for these Russian prisoners of war. Unfortunately for them, most would not see peace for four more years as Russia descended into a civil war that killed millions.

Trotsky's View of Bolshevik Foreign Policy, November 1917

By order of the All-Russian Workmen's and Soldiers' Congress, the Council of The People's Commissaries assumed power, with obligation to offer all the peoples and their respective governments an immediate armistice on all fronts, with the purpose of opening discussions immediately for the conclusion of a democratic peace.

When the power of the council is firmly established throughout the country, the council will, without delay, make a formal offer of an armistice to all the belligerents, enemy and ally. A draft message to this effect has been sent to all the Peoples' Commissaries for foreign affairs and to all the plenipotentiaries and representatives of allied nations in Petrograd.

The council also has sent orders to the citizen commander-in-chief that, after receiving the present message, he shall approach the commanding authorities of the enemy armies with an offer of a cessation of all hostile activities for the purpose of opening peace discussions, and that he shall, first, keep the council constantly informed by direct wire of discussions with the enemy armies, and, second, that he shall sign the preliminary act only after approval by the Commissaries Council.

hoped to move 45 divisions from the east to the west to reinforce the Spring Offensives and crush the French and British before the Americans began to arrive. A more lenient and reasonable treaty might have permitted them to transfer even more men to the west, but such was not the thinking at German high headquarters. The Germans hoped that Brest-Litovsk would provide enough resources to feed the home front and thereby bolster its morale for the final push in the west. They also hoped that the treaty might provide some badly needed succour to faltering allies as well. All in all, they thought that they had done quite well for themselves.

For the Russians, the treaty was a great humiliation. Lenin nevertheless urged that it be signed out of fear that the Germans might resume the offensive if the Russians refused. He had also seen how much more vindictive the Germans had grown as a result of Trotsky's first refusal to sign in February. He remained confident that the treaty's harsh terms would be temporary and that a working-class revolution would soon break out in Germany and reverse all of the concessions. He was also aware of how weak his domestic powerbase was and knew he had to reorganize his party's strength for the Civil War.

For France, Britain and the United States, the Treaty of Brest-Litovsk provided additional motivation to win the war in the west. Alongside the equally harsh treaty the Germans had signed with Romania, the western Allies had seen what the Germans did to vanquished nations. Defeat was therefore out of the question, no matter what the price of victory turned out to be. Germany's realization of some of its greatest desires, namely the humiliation of Russia and the chance to fight on only one front, ironically helped to sow the seeds of its final demise. The Germans, who failed to understand their countryman Carl von Clausewitz's famous dictum that war is the extension of policy by other means, had fought war for war's sake. It was to be their final undoing.

> 'Their knees are on our chest, and our position is hopeless. This peace must be accepted as a respite enabling us to prepare a decisive resistance to the bourgeoisie and imperialists.'
>
> Lenin urges acceptance of the Treaty of Brest-Litovsk, 23 February 1918

CHAPTER 6

The Allied Intervention in Russia

Following the Treaty of Brest-Litovsk the Allied powers looked on in alarm as the war on the Eastern Front ground to a halt. In order to rescue something from the collapse of Tsarist Russia the Allied powers decided to intervene militarily. At first this intervention was limited to North Russia, but it gradually spread in both its aims and locations, reaching South Russia and Siberia and involving tens of thousands of men.

The decision by the Bolsheviks to pursue a peace settlement with the Germans was a matter of great concern to the Allies, since the punitive nature of Brest-Litovsk offered the prospect of the Germans gaining pre-eminence in Eastern Europe. Some observers felt that the Bolsheviks' renunciation of the Pact of London in seeking a separate peace justified intervention against the new Russian Government, but this was not a view shared by Allied governments. Although the Bolsheviks' fundamental political position was diametrically opposed to that of

British troops were initially deployed to Murmansk to protect supplies that had been shipped there for the use of the Russian Army on the Easton Front. From left to right, General Edmund Ironside, General Evgenii Miller, Colonel Thornhill, General Savitch and Count Hamilton.

all the Allied governments, there were sound practical reasons for seeking to engage the new Russian regime rather than oppose it. The first rationale behind attempting to formulate some measure of cooperation with the Bolsheviks was simple – they might, perhaps, be persuaded to challenge the terms of Brest-Litovsk and reactivate the Eastern Front, a course that would have been a grave threat to the Germans. Second, the Allied nations had established many commercial links with Tsarist Russia, and there were good economic grounds for not taking action that might prompt retaliation against those interests. In addition, there were large numbers of Allied citizens in Russia who might be at risk if the Allies openly opposed the Bolsheviks.

The Allies were aware that opposition to the new regime had begun to coalesce almost immediately after the October Revolution, creating the movement that would ultimately become known as the 'Whites'. The sheer size of Russia, coupled with the turbulent political situation, meant that the Bolsheviks were far from

With armies committed to the war in Europe and a bitter power struggle between the factions at home, Russia's need for manpower was voracious. Some of those who 'voted for peace with their feet' and deserted the war in Europe ended up fighting their own countrymen instead.

being in complete control of the country. The prospect of the Bolsheviks losing their hold on power was a possibility, and it seemed sensible to some politicians in Allied nations that it would be best to adopt a position of attempting not to alienate the Bolsheviks, in the hope of maintaining their support in the war with Germany, while simultaneously giving aid to the opposition movement as part of an 'anti-Bolshevik crusade'. Other considerations were to influence the Japanese decision to intervene in Siberia, further complicating understanding of the way in which the intervention proceeded. A further complicating factor was that of the Czech Legion. This was a large force of troops drawn from Czech and Slovak nationals that found itself trapped in Russia after the Revolution and desperate to depart to continue the war effort. One aspect of the intervention by the French and British was to enable the Czech Legion to leave so that it could be redeployed to the Western Front.

Finally, the Allies were sympathetic to the claims of nationalists in the Baltic states of Estonia, Latvia and Lithuania, and particularly towards the Poles, who were to be granted their own state in the post-war settlement, but who would have to overcome the fact that much of the territory that they thought should be included in their new homeland was under Russian control. In many ways, then, securing the self-determination of new states was the firmest justification for Allied intervention in Russia.

The deployment of Allied troops in post-revolutionary Russia thus occurred in an atmosphere of confusion and chaos as the battle for control of the

Such was the confused and uncertain political situation in Russia that the Bolsheviks asked the Western Allies for help while negotiating peace with Germany. A token British presence in Murmansk gradually grew into a major force formed of British, French and local troops.

country took place between the Bolsheviks and their enemies, and as the Germans sought to exploit the Bolshevik commitment to withdraw from a war that had exhausted the Russian people.

THE DECISION FOR INTERVENTION IN NORTH RUSSIA

Earlier in the war a British naval presence had been established in northern Russia to provide an anti-submarine capability in northern waters. The task force operated out of Archangel in the summer months, and from the ice-free port at Murmansk from November to May. Large amounts of supplies were sent to Murmansk, both to sustain the Royal Naval units based there and for onward transmission to the poorly equipped Russian forces, who needed all the war *matériel* that they were sent. A single-track railway was built from Murmansk to Petrograd to take the supplies onward. After the October Revolution, the British became increasingly concerned about the safety of their supplies, a fear that was realized in late

January 1918 when a Bolshevik 'Extraordinary Commission' arrived in the port and began to commandeer the supplies stockpiled in Murmansk for use by their own forces. This was not the only problem confronting the British, since a number of Russian ships were harboured in the port and their crews were particularly enthusiastic supporters of the Bolshevik Government. This meant that the Russian ships presented a potential threat to the safety of the Royal Navy vessels. To complete the list of issues that were of profound concern to the British, the Germans had sent troops to Finland to support the White Finns, fighting a civil war against the communists (the Red Finns) who had seized power there. The degree of German support was over estimated, but it was a cause of considerable worry to the Murmansk Soviet, who were deeply fearful of the possibility of a German attempt to occupy the port. As a result, and indicative of the confused and sometimes almost farcical situation in post-revolutionary Russia, the Soviet hit

The aircraft carrier HMS *Vindictive*, converted from a *Hawkins*-class heavy cruiser, was dispatched to the Baltic in June 1919 to provide support for Admiral Cowan's assault on the Bolshevik naval base at Kronstadt.

upon the idea of making use of the British presence to sustain their own position. They sent a telegram to Leon Trotsky, asking whether they could seek help from the British. At this point, Trotsky was fearful that the peace negotiations with the Germans would end in failure, and that the war would resume. He had few illusions about the ability of the Bolsheviks to survive a sustained assault by the Germans, and therefore accepted the notion of a British intervention in Murmansk with equanimity. He told the Soviet that they should accept help from any of the Allied missions, and not just the British. However, the British were the first to be asked, and they dispatched a small force of Royal Marines, who landed in Murmansk on 6 March 1918.

While the company of marines was little more than a gesture to the Murmansk Soviet, it represented a foothold that could be exploited to deny the north Russian coast to the Germans; it also proved to be a precursor to a much larger commitment of British troops to the region. In May 1918, at the Abbeville Conference, the Allies reached the conclusion that intervention in Russia was a good idea, since it would permit the extraction of the Czech Legion and Serbian

Attack on the *Oleg*

The prospect of a Bolshevik naval attack on the Royal Navy's small force in the Baltic caused considerable concern to Admiral Cowan, and he signalled the Admiralty to point out that the units at Biorko were at considerable risk. The Admiralty was reluctant to allow Cowan to attack the Bolshevik base at Kronstadt to remove the threat, and he was forced to consider other options.

The answer lay in the detachment of coastal motor boats (CMBs) that had been sent to Terrioki, near the Finnish border, and which were being used for intelligence operations, particularly agent running. Cowan sent the detachment commander, Lieutenant Augustus Agar, a consignment of torpedoes, with the intention that these should be used should an opportunity to attack Bolshevik shipping present itself.

On 13 June 1919, an opportunity presented itself when the garrison of Krasnaya Gorka mutinied. Admiral A.P. Zelenoy, the commander of the Bolshevik Baltic Fleet, gave order for two battleships to bombard the fort; once this was known, Agar set out to attack the two vessels, using two CMBs. Unfortunately for Agar, one of the CMBs struck an underwater obstacle and the operation had to be aborted. Agar was dismayed to learn that the two battleships had departed overnight, but spirits amongst the CMB detachment rose when it became clear that they had been replaced on station by the cruiser *Oleg*. Although Agar only had a single CMB at his disposal, he decided that he would attack that night. At 11pm on 16 June, *CMB4*, commanded by Agar and with Lieutenant J. Hampshier and Chief Motor Mechanic M. Beeley as his crew, left Terrioki and headed towards the *Oleg*'s last known position. They negotiated their way through a minefield with little difficulty. Once this was accomplished, Agar began to manoeuvre *CMB4* into a firing position for its torpedo.

The CMBs carried a single torpedo, and this was launched in a rather unorthodox manner. The weapon was ejected rearwards from the stern by a cartridge-fired ram. One of the crew was required to place a cordite cartridge into the ram and then remove two stays that held the torpedo in place. The cartridge was then fired and the torpedo propelled into the water, where its motor would start running, taking it towards the target.

This complicated matters for the CMB, which had to take instantaneous evasive action to avoid being struck by its own weapon. As Agar moved into position, Hampshier prepared the cartridge to launch the torpedo. As he did so, something went wrong and the cartridge fired. As the stays holding the torpedo had not been removed, it remained in place on the boat. Hampshier, already suffering from seasickness, was in mild shock, and Beeley – renowned amongst his colleagues for his imperturbable nature – took over, priming a new cartridge and making the torpedo ready. This took some time, leaving *CMB4* and its crew vulnerable to detection as Beeley quietly went about his business, the small craft remaining unseen by the enemy.

There were no mishaps with the second cartridge, and Agar resumed tracking the *Oleg*, then picked up speed as he took the motorboat through the Russian destroyer screen. Aiming at the hull beneath the middle funnel of the *Oleg*, Agar released the torpedo and swerved out of the way to give it a clear run to the target. The torpedo struck home, and the *Oleg* shook under the explosion.

A massive hole had been torn in her side and within ten minutes the ship had gone under. Agar was unaware of this, since he was taking violent evasive action in the face of heavy fire from the destroyers and guns ashore. *CMB4* left the scene at high speed and reached the safety of Finnish waters early on the morning of 17 June 1919.

For his actions, Agar was awarded the Victoria Cross, while Beeley received the Conspicuous Gallantry Medal and Hampshier the Distinguished Service Cross.

Conditions in northern Russia were rather different from those the personnel assigned there were used to. As well as a political climate that changed almost from day to day, the rather primitive transport system made movement of troops, supplies and senior officers a considerable challenge.

troops then stationed west of Omsk from Russia. The story of the Czech Legion will be outlined below, and as will be seen, they did not leave via Murmansk as the Allied plan intended. By this point, however, the British intervention had expanded to a point that was rather more ambitious than perhaps originally conceived.

The British commander in Murmansk, Admiral Kemp, signalled London expressing the view that if Murmansk and Archangel were to be denied to the Germans, a force of least 6000 strong would be required, since the company of marines was quite insufficient for the task. No troops were immediately available to meet this request, not least since there was a distinct risk of a major German offensive on the Western Front. Instead, the British and French sent a cruiser each, later to be joined by an American ship, the USS *Olympia*. Matters were further complicated when Trotsky issued instructions to the Murmansk Soviet that they were no longer to cooperate with the British; having negotiated a settlement with the

Germans, Trotsky realized that any signs of cooperation with the Allies would be taken by the Germans as a breach of the Treaty of Brest-Litovsk, with the probable consequence that the Germans would resume fighting. The Murmansk Soviet was horrified at the thought of having to face what they perceived as an ongoing threat from the Germans alone, and disobeyed their instructions.

As the German Spring Offensives began to lose momentum, the British therefore decided to send more troops, influenced by a report from General Poole, the head of a British military mission to Russia in 1917 that aimed to extract British forces and citizens with the minimum of fuss in the confused situation. Poole had reached the conclusion that the only way of securing an orderly withdrawal from Russia was to ensure that there were sufficient troops in place to make sure that any hostile forces could not interfere with the evacuation. Poole was also well aware of the prospect that abandoning Murmansk and Archangel risked ceding the northern waters to the Germans, and this may have influenced his perspective. In the aftermath of Abbeville, the British sent Poole back to Murmansk as the head of an expeditionary force. The purpose of Poole's mission was fourfold. First, all British war *matériel* and personnel were to be withdrawn from Murmansk; second, any effort by the Germans to exploit Russian resources for their own war effort were to be resisted, while, third, Poole was to ensure that the Czech Legion was safely removed from Russia. Finally, Poole was to make sure that the Germans did not advance upon the northern ports. This was a fairly wide-ranging brief, but Poole did not allow himself to be constrained by it. He appears to have decided that the intervention should have a supplementary aim of assisting resistance against the Bolsheviks. Poole went so far as to tell some of his officers that he intended to link up

The British and French sent thousands more troops to Murmansk and it became possible to act against Bolshevik leaders who had been appropriating Allied supplies. This was a different situation than that envisaged when the intervention was first requested by the Bolshevik leadership.

with the Czech Legion and thus reopen the Eastern Front against the Germans. On 23 June 1918, 1100 more British troops under the command of Major-General Maynard arrived, with the intention that part of the force would move to Archangel and train anti-Bolshevik forces and any Czech units that managed to reach the British positions.

It was not obvious to Poole and Maynard how the Bolsheviks would respond to the increased number of British troops in the region, and they therefore took steps to take control of the railway to the south of Murmansk, a task they accomplished by mid-July when British troops reached the point at which the railway branched off towards Archangel.

By August, Poole felt it necessary to deal with the Soviet authorities in Archangel, since they were sending a large number of supplies on to Bolshevik forces elsewhere in Russia. The arrival of a battalion of

French colonial troops on 26 July gave Poole the confidence that he had sufficient numbers to attack Archangel. He therefore began the assault on 1 August 1918. Naval gunfire support and bombing by aircraft from the seaplane carrier *Nairene* destroyed the Bolshevik artillery positions at Modyugski, and this silenced the opposition. Poole's forces moved into Archangel to discover that the majority of the Bolsheviks had fled. Poole interned the remaining Bolshevik leaders – despite loud protests from the British ambassador – and it was quite clear that the intervention had changed from the parameters

initially set for the British forces. The British forces around Murmansk and Archangel would ultimately reach something in the region of 50,000 men, many of them local troops who wished to fight the Bolsheviks. Furthermore, local anti-Bolshevik elements had coordinated with the British to launch a coup in conjunction with the attack. A local government under the veteran socialist leader Nicholas Tchaikovsky was established, but while Tchaikovsky was more than amenable to working with the British – not least because he spoke English fluently thanks to spending over a decade living in Britain – his administration was less than effective. Nevertheless, the Allied forces pushed further south out of Murmansk and at the end of August held positions up to 190km (120 miles) south of Archangel.

ANGLO-AMERICAN OPERATIONS

The British had been joined at this point by an American force that President Woodrow Wilson had finally agreed to send, despite his having severe reservations about the wisdom of any form of intervention in Russia. He imposed strict conditions on the way in which the American troops were to be employed, instructing that they were to be used only for the purpose of guarding stores. He did, however, accept the idea that the troops should be placed under British command, a decision that he was to regret. By the time the Americans arrived in Archangel, the influenza pandemic that had broken out across the world had struck their transport ships; over 300 of the American troops – just under 10 per cent of the force – had succumbed to illness, and 70 of them had died. They arrived to discover that General Poole had decided that they should not be used simply for guarding stores as Wilson had insisted, but would be employed to hold positions on the Murmansk railway and in a projected attack on the Bolshevik positions at Bereznik.

General Edmund Ironside was an active officer with a good grasp of politics, who did much to improve relations between the various nationalities involved in northern Russia. He later served as Chief of the Imperial General Staff at the beginning of World War II.

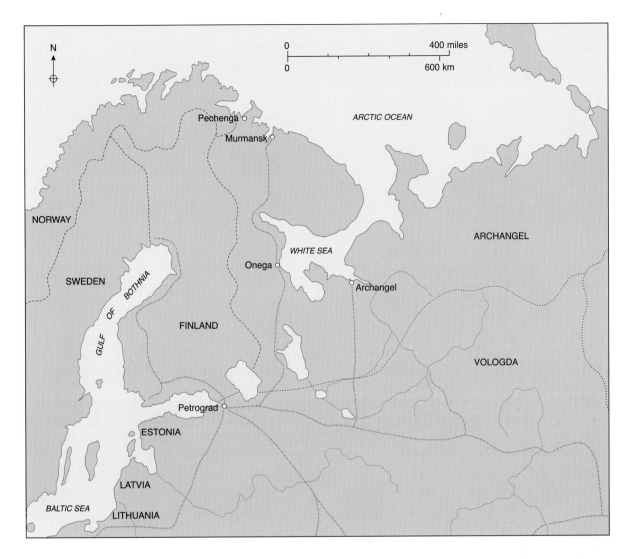

While the forces in place may have looked impressive on paper in comparison with the then rather disorganized Bolsheviks facing them, the reality was rather different. The British troops were made up of large numbers of men who had been categorized as unfit for front-line operations, but who were now being expected to fight in far more arduous conditions than those on the Western Front. The French colonial troops were utterly perplexed at their lot, being thousands of kilometres away from home and enduring conditions for which they were utterly unprepared – as a result, their morale and fighting effectiveness were low. The American troops were

The rail network was of critical importance as it provided the only means of moving large amounts of *matériel* or troops across very inhospitable countryside. Control of the railways was thus an important objective once the intervention moved beyond merely protecting stores in port.

recovering from the depredations of an influenza outbreak, which meant that it would be some time before they were effective. The only saving grace was that the Bolshevik forces confronting this less than healthy coalition of Allied troops were not of the highest standard.

To make matters worse, the American officers were less than impressed with the fact that President Wilson had agreed to place them under British command, and even less pleased to discover that Poole had no intention of taking them into his confidence or regarding them as being equal partners in the coalition in any way. The British, on the other hand, were intensely annoyed with the assertion by the Americans that they had in some way arrived to rescue

Once supplies were unloaded from rail transport, sledges such as these were the only viable way to get them to their final destination. This severely limited the mobility of forces, such as these French colonial troops from Africa, away from the towns and railheads.

the Allied mission from its inadequacies. British officers were concerned at the low quality of the American troops who had been sent, and many British other ranks were decidedly unflattering in their assessment of their newly arrived allies. This may have been influenced by the fact that a remarkably high number of the American soldiers were relatively recent immigrants to the United States who had volunteered to serve their new country long before they had mastered the English language. These frictions meant that it was extremely difficult to fashion the 8500 or so troops at Archangel into an effective fighting force. To

complete this unhappy picture, Poole's constant dabbling in matters of civil government – while understandable given the nature of the local administration in Archangel – meant that he was not paying full attention to building his forces and did nothing to win the support of the Russians.

CHANGE OF COMMAND

Although Poole now had over 20,000 men under his command, he wanted more. He requested that the British Government dispatch further reinforcements so that he could attack along the railway and the Dvina, with the aim of encouraging local men to join in the war against the Bolsheviks and continuing the push so as to join up with the Czech Legion, which was still at that point meant to be travelling to Archangel to join the Allied troops. Poole was invited to London to discuss the matter of reinforcements, little realizing that he would not return to Archangel. Doubts within the War Office about Poole's command style had been confirmed when President Wilson had complained strongly to Prime Minister Lloyd George about a variety of issues, not least the high-handed manner with which he had dealt with the American contingent. Poole was replaced by Major-General Edmund Ironside, who arrived at Archangel in the expectation that he would become Poole's chief of staff. Ironside was a physically imposing man and possessed of considerable intelligence. He spoke several languages very well – including Russian and French, something of considerable utility in the circumstances in which he found himself – and could manage to make himself understood clearly in several others. In addition, Ironside was a man of great tact and political skill, in direct contrast to his predecessor.

Ironside swiftly improved relations between the British contingent and the Americans, and the local

'The evacuation undoubtedly raised the enemy's morale, and for a time his continued attacks against our Vaga front were the cause of great anxiety.'

General Sir Edmund Ironside's official dispatch, the *London Gazette*, 6 April 1920

Russian leaders were most impressed with him, some said because of his ability (and willingness) to swear at them in their own language. He also took the trouble to visit his geographically separated commands on a regular basis, travelling between Murmansk, Archangel and all points between via sleigh.

Assessing the situation before him, Ironside reached the conclusion that the forthcoming winter would represent a formidable challenge to operations. This demanded a programme of instruction to all troops to explain to them the hazards of the fierce conditions that they were about to face, and serious consideration as to how to sustain the Allied positions dotted around the countryside at Murmansk and Archangel. Over 900 sleighs were procured to transport food, equipment and ammunition amongst the Allied lines. It was as well that Ironside ensured that a robust supply chain was established, since on 11 November 1918, the first major contact between Bolshevik and Allied troops occurred.

The Bolsheviks launched their attack along the Dvina, encouraged to do so by the fact that British gunboats that had patrolled the river until November had withdrawn so as to avoid being frozen in position when the winter came. The withdrawal proved to be premature, since the Bolsheviks were able to continue operating their own gunboats, a fact they exploited by using them to bring down heavy fire on British positions. Despite the various inadequacies of the British and American troops noted earlier, the Bolshevik attack bogged down in the face of stiff, if occasionally desperate, resistance.

CHANGING CIRCUMSTANCES

While the fact that the Bolshevik attack of 11 November 1918 was defeated was highly encouraging for the Allies, it in fact marked the point at which the nature of the Allied mission to Russia changed

Attack on Kronstadt

From the end of June 1919, Admiral Cowan's force in the Baltic was sent reinforcements, initially in the form of four cruisers. These were later joined by minesweepers and the aircraft carrier HMS *Vindictive*, along with more coastal motor boats (CMBs).

Augustus Agar's successful attack on the *Oleg* and the threat presented to his forces led Cowan to the conclusion that not only was an attack to cripple the Red Baltic Sea Fleet necessary, but that it could be conducted using the increased CMB force in conjunction with the newly arrived aircraft. While Cowan planned a combined air and sea attack, the RAF aircraft carried out a number of bombing raids on Kronstadt, although the most successful outcome of the attacks was unintentional: a bomb that had been aimed at a ship instead fell amongst a recently convened meeting of a soviet of sailors and killed over 100 of them.

By 17 August, Cowan had created a plan of attack against Kronstadt, and this began with a bombing raid as a diversion. While the defences were concentrating upon the air attack, they failed to notice the approach of seven CMBs led by Commander Claude Dobson. Dobson's small flotilla was guided into place by Agar, who knew the waters around Kronstadt well from his agent-running trips, and once in position, launched the attack. The CMBs moved in at low speed to avoid detection, but once in the harbour, they opened their throttles and attacked. The cruiser *Pamyat Azova* was sunk by Lieutenant W.H. Bremner, while Dobson, who was leading the operation from Lieutenant R. Macbean's boat, had the satisfaction of participating in a torpedo run that sank the battleship *Petropavlovsk*. Finally, *CMB88*, commanded by Lieutenant Dayrell-Reed, attacked another battleship, the *Andrei Pervozvanni*. As the CMB ran into the target, Dayrell-Reed was mortally wounded, and his number two, Lieutenant Gordon Steele, had to take over; he managed to do so just in time to launch his torpedo into the *Pervozvanni*, which promptly sank, and then skilfully manoeuvred his vessel, under heavy fire, to launch its second torpedo to deliver the *coup de grâce* to the *Petropavlovsk*. Three CMBs were destroyed: Bremner's boat sank after colliding with *CMB62*; *CMB62*, with Bremner's crew aboard, was lost after being hit by return fire; while *CMB24* was blown to pieces by the destroyer *Gavrill*. The remaining CMBs escaped. The remnants of the Bolshevik fleet now posed only a minor threat to the British forces operating in the Baltic. The success of the raid was such that all the participants were decorated: Dobson and Steele received the Victoria Cross, while Agar, along with three others, received a Distinguished Service Order to add to the Victoria Cross he had won two months before.

fundamentally. The attack occurred on the same day that World War I ended. There was now no need for the Allied mission to remain in Russia for the purposes of reopening a second front against Germany, nor to guard against a German seizure of war *matériel*. If the Allies were to stay, it would be to oppose the Bolshevik regime – giving the mission an entirely different purpose to that originally outlined. In addition, the fact that the war was over was likely to provoke questions amongst the soldiers, who would naturally wish to return home to their families now that the war was over. Whether volunteers or conscripts, they held firm expectations about their military service coming to an end shortly after the war, and it was questionable as to whether they would be content with being forced to continue to serve after the cessation of the war with Germany. This uncertain picture was further complicated in January 1919, with a second major attack by the Bolsheviks. An attack on Shenkursk began in the morning of 19 January, when American positions in the town came under heavy artillery fire. An assault by around 1000 Bolshevik troops followed the bombardment, and came close to dislodging the Americans, who fought a bitter rearguard action to remain in the town. The Bolsheviks responded to their failure to seize the town by putting in another intensive bombardment over the course of the next 48 hours. They accompanied this by sending small units to work their way around the Allied positions, both at Shenkursk and further along the line at Ust Padenga. It became clear that the position was untenable, and the Allied troops in the area conducted a skilful withdrawal at night back towards more defensible positions.

The loss of Shenkursk was a serious blow to the Allies, since the success of the Bolsheviks in taking the town and the surrounding area meant that it was now even more difficult to persuade local Russians that the anti-Bolshevik forces being built up by the Allies at Archangel and Murmansk had any chance of success. This had a deleterious effect on recruitment to the anti-Bolshevik army that was in the process of being established, and made locals wary of providing

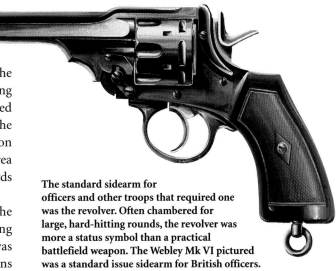

The standard sidearm for officers and other troops that required one was the revolver. Often chambered for large, hard-hitting rounds, the revolver was more a status symbol than a practical battlefield weapon. The Webley Mk VI pictured was a standard issue sidearm for British officers.

any support to the Allies for fear of retribution by the Bolsheviks.

This setback prompted Ironside to request reinforcements, which he received in the form of two battalions of British troops. Ironside had also been concerned about the quality of leadership displayed by the White Russian officers, and his observations led to the Whites deciding that General Durov should be replaced by General Marousheffski. Although

Some Bolshevik units were formed around a core of combat veterans and could be highly effective, while others were little more than a politically-motivated rabble. Many units had a rag-tag appearance but there was no shortage of weapons considering the numbers produced during the war.

Marousheffski was a much better general than his predecessor, the fundamental problem that had afflicted the Tsarist army remained – the officers had nothing in common with their men, and did nothing to engage with them; thus the motivation of their troops was low and building them into an effective and determined fighting force was a near impossibility. To make matters worse from Ironside's point of view, one of the battalions of British reinforcements he had asked for, from the Yorkshire Regiment, mutinied upon its arrival at Onega. The mutiny was swiftly suppressed, and the remaining troops subsequently performed well in combat. The combination of mutiny and poor leadership on the part of the White Russians meant that Ironside faced a major challenge in attempting to gain any sort of

The Czech Legion started out as a company-sized force formed of ethnic Czechs and Slovaks living in Russia, and grew into a large and professional force that played a major part in events during the Revolution.

success with the intervention. The Allies faced similar problems with all their interventions in Russia, be it in the south or in Siberia.

THE SIBERIAN INTERVENTION

Historians often forget the Japanese participation in World War I. Japanese forces did not make a major contribution in the main theatre of the war, namely the Western Front (they suffered a grand total of three casualties, all liaison officers, in France) and it is thus easy to overlook the fact that they were part of the Allied coalition. The Japanese rationale for involvement was simple, in that they sought to increase their influence in the Far East, not least in China. Japan declared war upon Germany in 1914, ostensibly because of the perceived threat presented in the Pacific by the ambitious Germans as they sought more colonies, but the possibility of being placed at a disadvantage if Russia were to be on the winning side while Japan remained on the sidelines, and the

prospect of territorial gains as part of the spoils of victory probably played a far greater part in the Japanese decision to intervene. The Japanese Government almost certainly feared the prospect of the Russians gaining some form of revenge for their defeat in the Russo-Japanese War of 1904–05 via the inevitable post-war settlement unless there was a Japanese presence on the side of the victors at the conference table.

The power vacuum that emerged in Siberia in the aftermath of the Treaty of Brest-Litovsk gave Tokyo considerable temptation to intervene, not least since there was a fear that the Bolsheviks would be as hostile towards Japan as the Russians had been in the past. Taking control of Vladivostok would remove a major naval base from Russian control and thus reduce the threat. The Japanese therefore concluded that it was desirable to send troops, but faced considerable opposition from the Americans, who suspected that Japan's motives were not in support of the wider Allied cause, but purely nationalistic. This was a source of annoyance to the British and French, who saw merit in bringing the Japanese into the complicated and uncertain Russian situation. The British, in particular, were concerned that the large stocks of war *matériel* located at Vladivostok and

Armoured trains allowed heavy and well-protected firepower to be brought to bear. Against an enemy free to manoeuvre as he pleased they were of limited use, but since they moved on the very rail lines that were the target of many attacks, they were at times highly effective.

along the Trans-Siberian railway line would somehow fall into the hands of the Germans and they therefore argued that it was necessary to ensure that these supplies were protected.

Japan's clear regional ambitions were a source of considerable concern to Washington, which enjoyed substantial amounts of lucrative trade with China. The possibility that the Japanese might exploit their involvement in Vladivostok to enhance their position at the expense of the United States was something that President Wilson was quite unwilling to contemplate.

The Japanese, though, were unconcerned by the view from Washington and on 5 April 1918 a Japanese expeditionary force landed at Vladivostok, nominally to ensure that the port continued operating. President Wilson expressed his displeasure at this move, but more seriously, the intervention at Vladivostok prompted Trotsky to give instructions that the trains carrying the Czech Legion to the port were to be stopped in retaliation for the violation of Russian territory. Under intense pressure from their Allies, the

Japanese withdrew. Ironically, while the fate of the Czech Legion aborted the initial Japanese involvement in Russia, it was soon to prove the justification for a much larger Japanese presence in the country.

THE SAGA OF THE CZECH LEGION

The Czech Legion, more properly the Czech and Slovak Legion, had its origins in the early days of World War I. Czech and Slovak nationalist leaders, anxious to seize any opportunity that might permit the establishment of a Czech and Slovak state independent of Austria-Hungary, petitioned Tsar Nicholas II for permission to establish a corps of Czech and Slovak troops under Russian command. Nicholas was only too happy to oblige, and the corps was established from volunteers living in Russian territory, as well as men who made their way over to Russian lines. The strength of the Czech Corps was boosted as the war went on, as all Czechs and Slovaks fighting as part of the Austro-Hungarian forces and taken prisoner of war were given the option of going to a prison camp or changing sides and continuing to fight. Many of the Czech and Slovak prisoners had been reluctant conscripts to the Austro-Hungarian cause, and willingly joined the Corps. The Corps fought alongside the Russians, and by the time of the October Revolution, they were in the Ukraine. The Supreme Allied War Council, the body coordinating the war for the Allies, exploited the fact that the Czechs were now (at least nominally) under French command, and could thus be given direction without the need for consultation with Petrograd. The Council sought to exploit the Czechs' presence in Ukraine to reopen the Eastern Front, albeit on a limited scale. On 20 January 1918, the Council gave directions to the Czechs that they were to move to the Vinnitsa–Mogilyov line and reopen fighting against the Germans. The Czechs, however, refused to move, not least since they were aware that the Ukrainian

Japanese cavalry at the charge. Although swept from the close confines of the Western European battlefield by machine guns and fast-firing rifles, cavalry were at times able to come to handstrokes with their long sabres, proving that when conditions were right they still had a part to play.

Government, already operating autonomously from Petrograd, was preparing to declare independence, which duly occurred two days later. The Ukrainian Government promptly headed to Brest-Litovsk to join in the peace negotiations, hoping to secure the creation of a separate Ukrainian state. This left the Allies facing the possibility that a force of some 50,000 men, eager to fight for the Allied cause, would be trapped in Russia. The decision was therefore taken to find some means of withdrawing them, and Trostsky's willingness to permit the Czechs to leave and join the fighting in France meant that it appeared that the

situation might be swiftly rectified. This was an illusory hope.

On 21 March 1918, the Germans moved into the Ukraine, prompting the Czechs to fall back. The Allies then issued instructions to the Czechs, transferring them from the Ukraine to Vladivostok and re-naming them as the Czech Legion. Plans for at least half, and possibly all, of the Legion to leave Russia via Archangel and Murmansk were mooted, since it appeared that the failure to reach consensus over the need for intervention in the far east of Russia would make it difficult to conduct the evacuation from Vladivostok

as had been planned. As it transpired, circumstances meant that a withdrawal from Archangel and Murmansk became impractical, not least because of the actions of the Czechs as they sought to escape from Russia.

THE CZECH 'REVOLT'

The Czech withdrawal to Vladivostok depended upon the goodwill of the Bolsheviks, since Russian trains were required to facilitate the movement of the Legion and all its supplies. An initial draft of 70 trains proved inadequate, and more had to be provided. The

opening moves of the Legion went reasonably smoothly, albeit slowly thanks to the lack of rolling stock available. The French consul in Vladivostok reported that the first elements of the Legion had arrived there on 28 April 1918. The Czechs discovered that there was no shipping to take them any further, and were left kicking their heels while they awaited transport. The Allied failure to reach agreement on involvement in Vladivostok and the surrounding area now presented a problem, since without consensus on how this was to be achieved, it was unlikely that any ships would be forthcoming. The British refused to send any of their ships for transport purposes, claiming that fighting in the Middle East and maintaining supply routes to India meant that they had none to spare. The French Government was irritated by this, protesting that the British were, in effect, going against the Abbeville agreement by denying the French the use of the Czech troops. This began a process that would finally see a pan-Allied intervention; by the time this happened, though, circumstances had changed dramatically.

Machine-gunners aboard an armoured train. The firepower that could be put down by such a force was awesome, though limited in its reach. An enemy that retreated away from the rail lines was essentially untouchable unless troops capable of fighting dismounted were carried by the train.

At the same time that the Czechs started their journey, the implications of the Treaty of Brest-Litovsk wrecked the smooth running of the Czech evacuation eastwards. The peace treaty provided for the return of all German and Austro-Hungarian prisoners of war held by the Russians. Some 800,000 men had to be returned to their homelands, and the Russians sought to achieve this by moving the men by rail. The majority of the prisoners were held in Siberia (with the aim of making escape to friendly territory all but impossible), and this meant that the trains carrying the prisoners had to pass along the same line as those conveying the Czechs. On 14 May, a train carrying members of the Legion stopped at Chelyabinsk alongside a train heading in the opposite direction that was taking Austro-Hungarian prisoners back home. Although the circumstances of what happened next are confused, it appears that the Hungarians shouted abuse at the Czechs, and one of them unwisely threw a missile of some description at the Czech train. The Czechs, who had little regard for the Hungarians at the best of times, responded by dragging the man responsible for throwing the missile away from his comrades and killing him. The local soviet arrested the Czechs responsible for the lynching and took them to the town jail. This was the final straw for the Czechs, who formed up and marched into the town. They then forced their way into the jail, removed their comrades and marched onto the local armoury, removing all the weapons and ammunition they could find. When news reached Moscow, the Bolsheviks arrested the Czech representative there and ordered him to send a telegram to Chelyabinsk appealing to the Legion to lay down their arms immediately. This met with no response. On 23 May, orders were given to all local soviets to disarm the Czechs; unfortunately for the Bolsheviks, they seem to have forgotten that Chelyabinsk was now under the control of the Legion,

which meant that the Czechs were running the local telegraph office and saw the instruction. Two days later, Trotsky issued orders that all Czechs seen carrying weapons were to be shot if they refused to surrender. Again, the Czechs read the orders, and this was the final straw, prompting a decision that they should no longer rely upon the Russians, but instead make their own way east, using whatever force was necessary.

The Legion therefore decided that it would fight its way to Vladivostok. Although it was deep within Russia, the Legion was an organized and proficient fighting force, something that could not be said of most of the military forces in central and eastern Russia at that point, most of which lacked the clear aim that the Czechs had set themselves. The Czechs promptly set about taking control of the Trans-

US troops were committed to the Far East to protect the line of supply and assist the Czech Legion in escaping from Russia. The policy was to try not to escalate the situation, though President Wilson made it clear that other nations were free to do as they thought best.

'It was left for the Czecho-Slovaks to set the hesitating Allied Powers a shining example, and to lead the way in the task of rescuing Russia. There is nothing more amazing in history than the meteoric insurgence of the Czecho-Slovak troops beyond the Volga and beyond the Urals.'

Lovat Fraser 'Russia and the Czecho-Slovaks' from *The War Illustrated*, 8 October 1918

Siberian railway, occupying a considerable band of territory either side of the railway line, with the aim of ensuring that the Bolsheviks could not deny them use of this essential transport link. One of the major consequences of this came on 16 July 1918, as the Legion moved towards the town of Ekaterinburg, where Tsar Nicholas and his family were being held prisoner. The Bolsheviks in the town became increasingly concerned that the Czechs intended to launch a rescue attempt, and decided that the royal family had to be neutralized. The family was awoken in the middle of the night and taken to the basement of the house in which they were imprisoned, supposedly to ensure their safety from an imminent attack by the Czechs. When the Tsar and his family were in the basement, the local commissar read out a death sentence and, before the royals could

react, a firing squad killed every member of the royal family and a number of their aides.

As the Czech Legion headed eastwards, linking with White Russian forces to aid its passage, a series of bitter battles occurred, notably at Penza on 28/29 May 1918 and in the Volga region, as the Red Army responded to the challenge to the Revolution that the Czechs appeared to present. It now became obvious to the Allies that they needed to intervene in the east to ensure that the Czech Legion could be extricated; the Archangel option was now a non-starter, and only Vladivostok was viable. This meant that the inter-Allied expedition that the British and French favoured was much more likely, since the Americans would, it seemed, have to withdraw their opposition to Japanese involvement as only the Japanese could provide the shipping needed to achieve the removal of the Czechs, and the consequences of giving the Japanese a foothold in Manchuria now seemed less important.

VLADIVOSTOK

The deteriorating situation in Russia finally led to American approval for an Allied intervention at Vladivostok and along the Trans-Siberian railway. President Wilson accepted that a small-scale operation was needed, but made it clear that the United States was opposed to intervention beyond that necessary to

Soldiers of the Czech Legion in Siberia. Although the Czechs had been warned to stay out of Russian affairs they really had no choice but to get involved if they wanted to survive. Control of the Trans-Siberian railway increased their influence upon regional affairs.

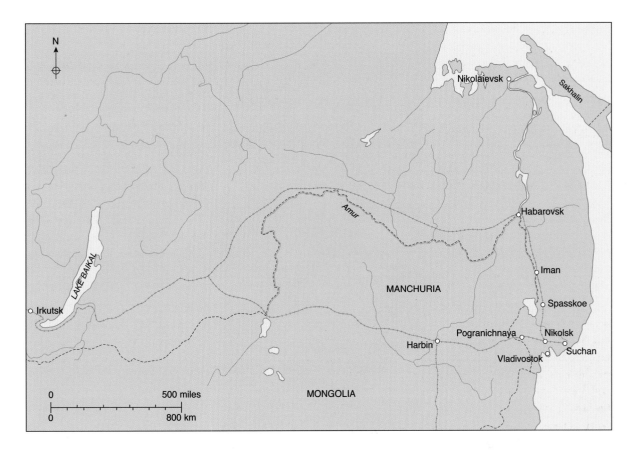

help the Czechs and to ensure that former German and Austrian prisoners of war did not interfere with the withdrawal of the Legion from Russia, or take control of military supplies at the port. The Americans would therefore contribute 7000 men for the purpose of aiding the Czechs and guarding military stores. However, while Wilson was clear that a military intervention was undesirable, he made clear in the memorandum that his views applied only to the Americans. The memorandum included an explicit line in which it was made clear that the Americans had no desire to constrain any decisions regarding intervention that were reached by Allied governments.

This gave the Allies a free hand to send troops to Russia, since the utter chaos prevailing in Siberia meant that it would be relatively easy to justify sending a large number of troops to meet the desired aim of the intervention. The Japanese were delighted with the decision, and set about creating an expeditionary force

The vast area of Siberia that formed the battlefield for the Czech Legion, White Russians, Bolsheviks and the various Allied intervention forces. Control of the Trans-Siberian railway allowed the Czechs to fight their way towards the port of Vladivostok.

to contribute to the operation, while the British, French and Americans formed rather smaller contingents.

On 3 August 1918, British and Japanese troops arrived at Vladivostok, and the Americans followed on 16 August. The British force, based upon the 25th Battalion of the Middlesex Regiment, was the first to move into position, having been asked by the Czech representative at Vladivostok for assistance in a battle that was taking place on the river Ussurie. Czech and Cossack troops were facing a strong force of Bolshevik troops, which was rumoured to be led by German and Austrian officers. The commanding officer of the Middlesex, Lieutenant-Colonel John Ward, sought permission to send half of his battalion to help, and the War Office gave permission. Ward took 400 of his men and a mixed force of Czech infantry and Cossack horsemen to the front line. After a fortnight of waiting, Ward received news that a contingent of French troops would be arriving in due course, and that the Middlesex would come under the command of the French officer. However, just as the French arrived, the Bolsheviks launched an attack and sought to outflank the Allied positions. The action began with combat between two armoured trains, one Bolshevik the other British manned, and the Bolsheviks were able to manoeuvre into a position that threatened the Allied lines. A battalion of Japanese troops was sent from Vladivostok, along with an artillery battery, and they helped to stabilize the situation. Ward's next set of instructions revealed the depth of the Japanese commitment in Siberia, since he was told that an entire Japanese division would be arriving in due course, and that the Middlesex battalion would come under the command of the Japanese commander, General Oie. The Japanese division arrived on 22 August, and Oie decided that the main attack would be conducted by his troops and the Middlesex, supported by the French and the Czechs. The British soldiers were highly impressed with the quality of the Japanese troops, and the Bolsheviks were routed. Following this success, the Allies moved along the railway to positions at Omsk. The British left Vladivostok on 24 September and took up their new positions a month later.

It soon became clear that the Japanese regarded their allies with nothing more than polite tolerance (and occasional obstruction), seeing them as an

Lieutenant-Colonel Ward of the Middlesex Regiment was forced to operate in a complex political environment. He led part of his force to the assistance of Czech and Cossack forces fighting in Siberia, and later fought under the command of a Japanese general.

obstacle to Japanese occupation of eastern Siberia. To complicate matters for Ward and his men, the local government at Omsk was promptly deposed in a coup, with Admiral Kolchak being appointed as Supreme Governor of the area. Kolchak managed to bring some degree of organization to the White Russian forces, and they enjoyed a number of successes, finally managing to reach a position only 480km (300 miles) from Petrograd. However, the Czechs despised Kolchak, and he was unable to make any use of the Legion as it headed towards Vladivostok.

By March 1919, the Allies had over 100,000 men in Siberia, dominated by the Czech Legion with 55,000 men, and an ever-expanding Japanese contingent that would eventually reach a strength of 70,000. However, by this point, only the Japanese Government remained enthusiastic about the commitment to Siberia. The British, American and French governments faced increasing pressure to withdraw from a commitment that was little understood and even less appreciated by their electorates. The Czechs and Slovaks had been granted their homeland in the peace treaties that ended the war, and their only motivation was to leave Russia for their newly created state. Suspicions about Bolshevik cooperation with the Germans were now irrelevant to them, and the Allied powers had little to concern them with regard to the progress of the war, even though they hoped that the Bolsheviks might be overthrown. By early 1919, then, the lack of a clear end-state for the

Allied mission, coupled with the fact that a quick end to the Civil War appeared unlikely, led to a situation where the Allied powers were more than willing to extricate themselves from Russia.

SOUTH RUSSIA

With the main objective behind Allied intervention in Russia being to attempt to renew an Eastern Front against Germany, it was perhaps inevitable that there would be an intervention in South Russia. There were a number of generals in the Russian Army who thought that it was in the nation's interests to continue to fight, recognizing that hopes of creating a greater Russia would disappear once a peace treaty was signed with Germany. Whether the Allies or the Central Powers won the war, the conclusion of a separate peace would leave Russia without a meaningful voice at the conference table, and the dissident generals felt that it would be a failure of duty if they did not attempt to continue the war – a step that would inevitably require the defeat of the Bolsheviks. A

further factor in South Russia came in the form of the Cossacks, who could not accept the notion of a Bolshevik-run country, and who were eager to see the removal of the new regime.

A number of prominent Tsarist generals managed to flee from Petrograd and Moscow in the aftermath of the revolution, notably General Alexeev, who had been the Tsar's chief of staff, and General Kornilov, leader of the failed coup against Kerensky. Both reached south Russia in December 1917 and established a 'Volunteer Army'. The Cossacks were unimpressed with the new arrivals, feeling that they would interfere with their ability to run their own affairs, not least because the Bolsheviks would attempt to suppress any counter-revolution. Furthermore, Kornilov and Alexeev were not of the same views about how to overcome the

The British sent assistance to White Russian forces fighting in the south of the country, arriving in November 1918. It was hoped that British, French and other Allied forces could shelter those opposed to Bolshevism while they formed an effective army to retake the country.

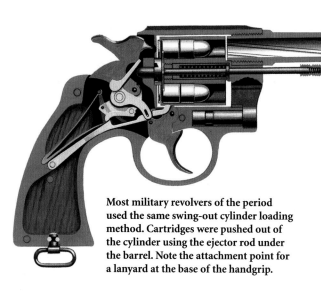

Most military revolvers of the period used the same swing-out cylinder loading method. Cartridges were pushed out of the cylinder using the ejector rod under the barrel. Note the attachment point for a lanyard at the base of the handgrip.

enemy, and it took careful discussions led by Alexeev's chief of staff, General Denikin, to create a joint position, which was articulated in January 1918. The two generals made clear that the Volunteer Army would defend south and southeastern Russia against armed invasion, be that by the Germans or the Bolsheviks. To ensure that the Cossacks remained supportive, Kornilov and Alexeev agreed that General Kaledin, the elected Cossack leader, would remain in control of all aspects of Cossack affairs. Alexeev would oversee administration of the Volunteer Army and relations with the Allies, while Kornilov would be responsible for commanding the army itself.

The Volunteer Army gained an early boost when the British Government decided that it would support it. The death of Alexeev from a heart attack and Kornilov's loss in action in April 1918 meant that Denikin assumed command of the White forces in South Russia. The initial success he enjoyed encouraged the Allies, particularly the British, who sent him a military mission to provide advice and to coordinate the provision of equipment. This mission arrived on 26 November 1918.

Thirteen days before, the British and French ended the coordination of their operations in North and South Russia. The British hoped to retain their bases at both Murmansk and Archangel, with the hope that they would remain until the Bolsheviks were overthrown. The French Government also held optimistic hopes for its position, aiming to create a border between Riga and Odessa over which the Bolsheviks would be unable to cross. French naval units were given orders to transport troops to Odessa, as a precursor to the arrival of two divisions of Greek troops. At a conference arranged by the French, pro-Allied Russian groups were informed that the Allies would restore order in Odessa and provide the volunteer Ukrainian Army with protection from Bolshevik attack while they trained in preparation for an offensive of their own. The pro-Allied groups agreed to support the French and British in restoring Russia to its pre-1914 borders (with the exception of territory in Poland). The conference also led to agreement that Denikin would command the White Russians, thus bringing a unified command structure to the anti-Bolshevik forces.

The plan suffered an immediate setback when Ukrainian nationalists staged a coup in Kiev on 17 November 1918, declaring independence. The French now faced the unpalatable prospect that their troops would land in Odessa, only to find it occupied by Ukrainian nationalist forces that would be less than eager to see them, given the French aspiration to recreate a Russian state that contained Ukraine. Negotiations between the French consul, Henno, and the Ukrainian leadership started immediately, and the French diplomat managed to secure agreement that the Ukrainians would not occupy Odessa and oppose the French, thus allowing the landing of French troops and subsequently their allies.

The French then found themselves facing further difficulties when the Peace Conference at Versailles failed to reach any agreement over a unified policy towards Bolshevik Russia. On 22 January 1919, a plan for military intervention by the Allies that had been drawn up by Marshal Foch was rejected. The end result ensured that there would be no coordinated Allied effort in Russia. The failure to agree over a policy created Anglo-French tension. By the time of Kolchak's assumption of power in Siberia, the French had grown to mistrust the British to the point where they assumed that the coup that had installed Kolchak had been arranged and supported by the Bolsheviks.

It was also quite clear that while there were a number of pro-Allied groups in Russia, the only common ground between many of the groupings was their shared enmity for the Bolsheviks. Rivalries between various groups were a clear obstacle to success, and the military capacity of many of the White Russian forces was limited.

To complicate matters further, the White Russians were not simply willing to sit back and be given direction by the Allies. After the landing in Odessa, the military governor of the town, General Grishin-Almazov, took the view that he was under the command of General Denikin, rather than the French.

ODESSA EVACUATED

The French were also more than capable of annoying their allies, since an agreement concluded between France and the Ukrainians in March 1919 allowing for an independent state completely compromised the plan for a united Russia. When Denikin protested, he was told that without the Ukrainians the French would have found the prospect of landing at Odessa impossible to achieve. This was perfectly true, since the French forces in Odessa were insufficient to defend against the Bolsheviks. By the end of March, the Bolshevik forces under Ataman Grigoriev were in a far stronger position than the French forces at Odessa. A battle at Berezovka at the end of March ended with Grigoriev's troops driving the French back and capturing two tanks. A mutiny within the French Black Sea Fleet proved the final straw; the French Government decided that there was little point in remaining in Odessa, since the Bolsheviks were in the ascendency. The French therefore evacuated Odessa at the start of April, and on 5 April 1919 Grigoriev's troops entered the city.

British officers arriving in South Russia are greeted by General Denikin, who had inherited command of the White Russian forces from Kornilov. The British supported Denikin until 1920, by which time it was obvious that the Whites were doomed to defeat.

While the French had departed, the British chose to remain, and continued to supply Denikin. By March 1920, equipment provided included over 1000 artillery pieces, 100 aircraft and 74 tanks, as well as millions of round of ammunition, engineering and medical equipment, motor transport and uniforms.

By November 1919, Denikin's forces were in trouble, despite the assistance given by the British, and Prime Minister Lloyd George informed parliament that he had serious doubts as to the viability of Denikin's aim of establishing a reunited Russia. Naturally, such expressions of doubt by the main source of external support did little for the morale of the White Russian forces. As the Whites finally succumbed, the British advisory units retreated, and it became absolutely clear that there was little point in prolonging the intervention any further.

THE ALLIES DEPART

At a meeting on 4 March 1919, the British cabinet decided that troops should be withdrawn from North Russia during the summer. There was little appetite

White Russian troops wearing French uniforms and manning a PM1910 machine gun pose for the camera. Late in 1918 (after the Armistice in the west), French troops were landed in Odessa as part of an Allied joint anti-Bolshevik strategy that failed to materialize.

within the British Government for further confrontation with the new communist regime, and justifying the continued presence of British troops in Russia was becoming increasingly difficult for the Lloyd George administration. To compound the problems for the British Government, by 1919 the intervention had expanded to beyond North Russia, and had become a far more complex political and military situation than had been envisaged. With the threat of the Germans removed, the only way in which the intervention could ever be successful was if the Bolsheviks were removed from power; however, the cost of achieving this seemed far too high, making withdrawal inevitable. As noted above, it took until 1920 before the last British troops left Russia and there were further painful moments before this was achieved. In September 1919, a battalion of Royal

Marine Light Infantry mutinied on the Murmansk front, ending with 93 court-martials. In Vladivostok, the withdrawal of the Middlesex Regiment in autumn 1919 meant that there were no troops left to guard the stores. It was ironic, given that one of the reasons for intervention was to protect military stores from the Germans, that the remaining British troops dealt with this problem by taking the supremely practical step of enlisting some of the remaining German and Austrian prisoners of war to fulfil this task. The ex-prisoners, still desperately awaiting passage home and short of food and warm clothing, gleefully accepted the offer of winter clothes and food in exchange for ensuring the security of the supplies. They finally returned home, along with the British, the Americans and the final members of the Czech Legion in 1920. The Japanese, determined to maintain influence in Siberia, remained, but by 1922, public opinion in Japan had turned against the presence of Japanese troops and they too were withdrawn.

Finally, in southern Russia, the reversal of fortune suffered by Denikin's troops meant that Britain, as the last of the intervening powers to remain, was faced with little option other than to withdraw. As the British withdrew through Odessa, Novorossiysk and, at the very end, from Sevastopol, vast amounts of war *matériel* were destroyed.

By mid-1920, the Allied interventions had all failed – although as the main aim of intervention had been achieved by November 1918, and given that supporting the White Russian forces was at best half-hearted, this is no surprise. With external powers gone (bar the Japanese in the far east), attention turned to the conclusion of the Civil War and the outbreak of conflict with the newly created state of Poland.

As the Allied intervention gradually disintegrated, troops of various nations were withdrawn through Russian ports and embarked for home. These French troops remain wary even though they are aboard ship; not all of the withdrawals were without incident.

CHAPTER 7

The Civil and Russo-Polish Wars

Following their seizure of power in the October Revolution of 1917, the new Bolshevik Government of Russia faced a number of internal and external threats. These included a number of disparate groups that opposed the Revolution and came to be known as the 'Whites', as well as the newly formed state of Poland that sought to lay claim to its historic territory in the west of Russia.

The first challenge facing the Bolsheviks in the aftermath of the Revolution was to re-establish an army from the disorganized rabble that much of the Russian forces had become in the last days of fighting on the Eastern Front. In January 1918, legislation allowing any Soviet citizen over 18 to volunteer for the Red Army was enacted and thousands of men volunteered, not least because being in the army offered food and pay. This represented only part of the solution, however, as the recruits could not be considered anything like an effective

The personnel of the Red Army came from many walks of life. Many were agricultural or industrial workers whose disaffection with their lot in life was sufficient to make them take up arms to change the social order. Some, ironically, came from an army wearied of conflict.

fighting force, since the training they received was minimal. This was not helped by the lack of competent officers. The policy of allowing units to elect their officers was ill suited to the demands of creating an effective army, since the officers were frequently chosen on the basis that they were unlikely to work their men hard. Many of the elected officers had little military experience and it was no surprise that many Red Army units lacked basic military skills. The Bolshevik leadership became increasingly concerned at the prospect of committing these troops into battle, particularly against disciplined opposition, an increasingly likely prospect as the Allies pondered intervening in the country to reopen the Eastern Front as a peace settlement between the Germans and the Bolsheviks became increasingly likely. Furthermore,

Leon Trotsky, founder and commander-in-chief of the Red Army, inspects his troops. The Red Army's system of elected officers was politically necessary, given the sentiments of the time. However, it was not conducive to an effective fighting force and many units were inefficient.

the Soviet Government was concerned at the prospect of the Germans going beyond the harsh terms of the Treaty of Brest-Litovsk and exploiting Russian territory to support their war effort. In such circumstances, it seemed essential to have an army to attempt to resist such attempts.

As a result of their concerns, after the signature of the Treaty of Brest-Litovsk, the Bolsheviks appointed Leon Trotsky as War Commissar. A particularly practical revolutionary, Trostksy did not allow high-minded revolutionary ideals to interfere with the process of creating an effective and efficient army. To reimpose discipline upon the Red Army the death penalty was reintroduced, while the matter of providing clear and effective leadership was addressed by the simple expedient of centralizing control of the Red Army and ending the power of local army committees made up of the soldiery. The election of officers was ended, but this created a new difficulty. Although it ensured that wildly unsuitable men were not appointed to command positions, it did nothing to

increase the leadership proficiency of the Red Army. Trotsky solved this problem by allowing officers from the Tsarist Army to rejoin the colours, and by conscripting others who had been dismissed or who had resigned in the aftermath of the Revolution. The conscripted officers were left in no doubt that if they attempted to desert their posts, retribution would be exacted upon their families. Many of the returning officers were simply content to be rejoining the army: they had joined the army to serve Russia rather than the Tsar and saw the change in government as being irrelevant to their doing this. By the time Trotsky's recruitment drive for officers was complete, over 50,000 Tsarist officers had taken up positions in the Red Army. Trotsky was well aware that drawing upon former Tsarist officers might be unpopular with the rank and file and his colleagues in government. The latter were relatively easily persuaded of the merits of calling upon the skills of trained officers, while the soldiers' councils were told that Trotsky was merely using the 'bricks of the old order' to help build the new socialist state. To ensure that the newly returned officers did nothing to undermine the Red Army, Trotsky created a cadre of political commissars who were to oversee their actions. The commissars possessed considerable political influence, and in some cases, some commissars began to believe that they knew better than the highly experienced senior commanders in whose headquarters they worked, creating problems as militarily sensible orders were rejected as being counter-revolutionary. The commissar system survived into World War II, and the attempts by militarily incompetent political officers to overrule generals would cause considerable difficulties in the early stages of the German invasion of the USSR. However, in 1918 the step appeared to be a sensible

Many career officers were entirely happy to join the Red Army as their loyalty was to the army, not the Tsar or any particular political system. Nevertheless the Bolsheviks formed a corps of political commissars to ensure the loyalty of the officer class.

means of ensuring that officers of suspect loyalty were watched and kept on a tight political leash.

The need for a more effective army was not the only challenge facing the Bolsheviks, since it appeared that there was a danger of a food crisis in the summer of 1918. Having gained much of their popularity with their pre-revolutionary promises of a greater supply of food for the population, the Bolshevik leaders were painfully aware of the possibility of a lack of food undermining their support and creating a situation that might be exploited by pro-Tsarist forces. As a result of these concerns, the Bolsheviks attempted to impose greater control over the countryside, with the appointment of so-called 'committees of poor peasants' who were tasked with requisitioning grain supplies from farmers. The farmers – the *kulaks* – were portrayed as enemies of the Revolution, determined to use their control of food to make huge profits at the

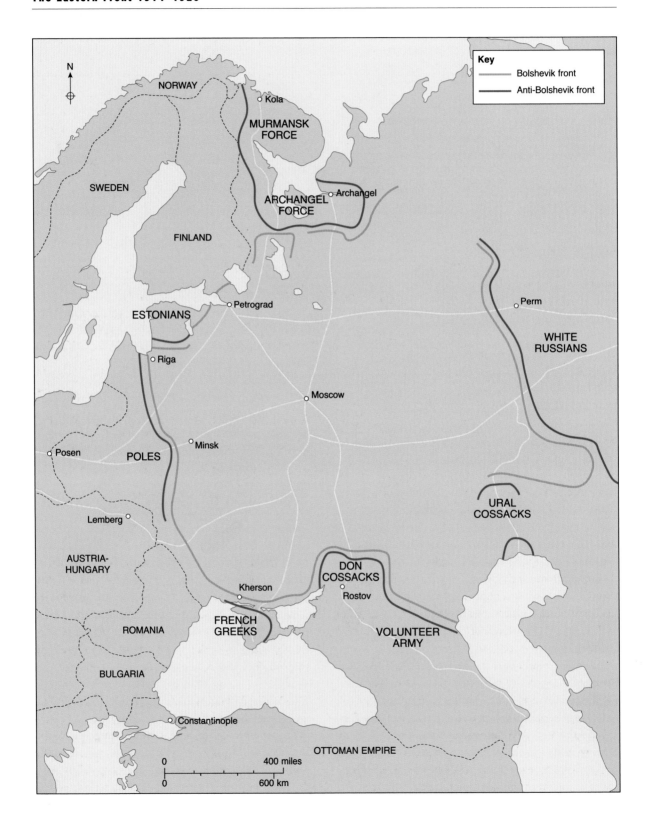

Key
- Bolshevik front
- Anti-Bolshevik front

NORWAY

Kola

MURMANSK
FORCE

SWEDEN

ARCHANGEL
FORCE

Archangel

FINLAND

Perm

Petrograd

WHITE
RUSSIANS

ESTONIANS

Riga

Moscow

Posen

Minsk

POLES

URAL
COSSACKS

Lemberg

AUSTRIA-
HUNGARY

DON
COSSACKS

Kherson

Rostov

ROMANIA

FRENCH
GREEKS

VOLUNTEER
ARMY

BULGARIA

Constantinople

OTTOMAN EMPIRE

| 0 | | 400 miles |
| 0 | | 600 km |

N

Although this map shows neat divisions of territory, with the Bolsheviks in control of the major cities and the Whites pushed back to distant areas of relatively low importance, nothing is ever so neat and tidy. True control over the country took years to establish and required harsh measures.

expense of the urban population and the poor peasants in the countryside. Unfortunately for the Bolshevik leadership, they over-estimated the level of inter-communal tensions in the countryside, where supposed class distinctions amongst the peasantry were unclear and there was little desire to seize food. The end result was the dispatch of parties of workers from the cities to seize food supplies. This did nothing to endear the Revolution to the peasants, many of whom were loyal to the Social Revolutionary Party with its pro-agriculture agenda. As a result of this ham-fisted approach to obtaining greater party control over food supplies, the Bolsheviks alienated the population of much of the countryside. The heavy-handed approach of the requisitioning parties sent from the cities led to such resentment that the peasants began to resist. In the late spring of 1918, risings against the Bolsheviks began, and increased considerably during the summer, to the point that the city of Tambov fell under peasant control until the Red Army restored order. In July, the Social Revolutionary delegates at the Communist Party Congress protested at the way in which the Bolsheviks had implemented their agricultural policy, claiming that the committees of poor peasants were filled with incompetent lazy and unpopular members of the local community who had joined the committees to have power over their neighbours, merely increasing the dislike of other villagers towards them.

The Social Revolutionaries became increasingly militant in their views, and shortly after the Party Congress, members of the radical Left Social Revolutionary faction assassinated the German ambassador, Count von Mirbach, in the hope of restarting the war between Germany and Russia. This led to the Social Revolutionaries being expelled from the soviets across the country, a move which simply drove them to even more violent acts. A series of abortive uprisings followed, most notably the seizure of the city of Yaroslavl, which held out against the Red Army for a fortnight. This uprising occurred at the same time as the revolt of the Czech Legion, described in the previous chapter, giving further cause in the eyes of the Bolsheviks to murder the Tsar and his family. The Social Revolutionaries' violent militancy reached its peak with an assassination attempt against Lenin, which came close to success. The assassination attempt led to the creation of an Extraordinary Commission for Struggle with Counterrevolution and

'An army cannot be built without reprisals. Masses of men cannot be led to death unless the army command has the death-penalty in its arsenal … Upon the ashes of the great war, the Bolsheviks created a new army … The strongest cement in the new army was the ideas of the October revolution, and the train supplied the front with this cement.'

Leon Trotsky, *My Life*, Chapter XXXVII

Sabotage, otherwise known as the Cheka, headed by Felix Dzerzhinsky. Dzerzhinsky was tasked with launching a 'Red Terror', in which the Bolsheviks unashamedly resorted to state terrorism to impose control upon the country, beginning a period of 'War Communism' as the government attempted to prosecute a civil war in a climate of increasing chaos.

THE WHITE RUSSIAN COUNTER-REVOLUTION
One of the primary difficulties facing the Bolsheviks in terms of establishing their power throughout Russia lay in the fact that they had not seized control as the result of a widespread popular uprising, but in a discrete *coup d'état* centred around the capital. This

left vast swathes of countryside that were, in effect, ungoverned as local soviets attempted to impose Bolshevik rule in the face of opposition from a variety of groups, who ranged from being at best ambivalent about the Bolshevik seizure of power to being implacably opposed and prepared to fight to overthrow the new regime.

Many Tsarist politicians gravitated towards the 'White' camp, but it was soon clear that any armed struggle against the Bolsheviks would have to rely upon the skills of the senior army officers who had not committed themselves to the Bolshevik cause. The Whites were united only in that they wished to see Lenin and his government removed from power at the earliest opportunity, and – perhaps to their detriment – had no clearly stated alternative policies to those laid down by the Bolsheviks. Although the Whites were, in general, in accord that Russia should be a republic ruled by a representative government, their leadership failed to articulate this with sufficient clarity, leading to suspicions that the movement was dedicated to the restoration of the Tsar. This provided the Bolsheviks with a useful propaganda tool on occasion, since they were able to present the choice as being between a government of the people (which, it soon became clear, they were not) or a royal government of the sort which had plunged Russia into the chaos in which the country now found itself.

BUILDING THE WHITE FORCES

The first military figure of note to be associated with the Whites was the former commander-in-chief of the Tsar's forces, General Kornilov. After the failure of his coup attempt in September, he had been placed under arrest and was in captivity along with a number of other generals. However, his guards were sympathetic, and allowed Kornilov and his subordinates to escape with ease. They headed to Rostov-on-Don to join the Cossack leader General Kaledin, who had successfully resisted all attempts by local Bolsheviks to impose a revolutionary government on the Cossack areas. The failure of the Bolsheviks to penetrate this area meant that the Whites had a convenient base that was relatively secure; all that was required was for the

General Mikhail Alexeev's career as an anti-Bolshevik leader was marred by his difficulties in cooperating with Kornilov. Alexeev had served as the Tsar's chief of staff, before performing the same role for the Provisional Government following the Tsar's abdication.

establishment of an agreement between the Whites and the Cossack leadership to ensure that the nascent anti-Bolshevik coalition did not collapse. Even before Kornilov arrived in the Rostov area, General Alexeev, the former chief of staff to Tsar Nicholas and commander-in-chief of the army at the beginning of the Provisional Government, set about establishing the forces necessary to both support the Allies by re-opening the Eastern Front and to resist the Bolsheviks. Alexeev's early attempts were reasonably successful in bringing together some fighting forces, but it took the arrival of Kornilov and the issuing of a general appeal for volunteers in early January 1918 for the Whites to begin recruiting in numbers. Even then there was a problem, since it was inevitable that many recruits would have to be drawn from the local peasantry – but relations between the Cossacks and the peasants were poor, and Kaledin was faced with the considerable task of attempting to win the peasants around.

Despite Kornilov's arrival increasing the number of volunteers for the Whites, it soon became apparent that there was a problem: out of the first 3000 men to sign up for the Volunteer Army, all but a dozen were officers. This created a situation in which the men who had previously commanded platoons, and sometimes even regiments, in the old Tsarist army found themselves fighting as ordinary soldiers with no leadership responsibilities, something with which they were most uncomfortable. Kornilov was anxious to ensure that his army was led by the most capable men, but this created difficulties when officers refused to serve under men who had been promoted above them on merit. Those officers who wished to see the restoration of a monarchical government could not be persuaded to serve under officers who were in favour of the creation of a constitutional monarchy, while others, finding that they could not serve with their previous rank and privileges, decided not to participate at all.

If this was not enough, the Whites were seriously hampered by a lack of cooperation between the generals. Alexeev had established himself as the commander in Rostov and was not prepared to subordinate himself entirely to Kornilov. The end result was a messy compromise in which Kornilov had command of the Volunteer Army, but Alexeev had control over all political matters and the business of financing the army. This division of command was ineffective, hampered by the fact that Kornilov and Alexeev spent much of their time arguing over what the Whites should do. The situation reached its nadir when the two men stopped talking to one another, bringing the Volunteer Army to a grinding administrative halt as contradictory orders and instructions were issued. Alexeev and other White generals regarded Kornilov with a mixture of disdain and distrust. They thought he was little more than a populist rabble-rouser, concerned more with cementing his own popularity and position; adding to their low opinion was the fact that he had risen to high

White recruits wearing British uniforms and serving an Austrian Schwarzlose machine gun (left). Many of the recruits to the Volunteer Army were officers, which meant that many had to accept the role of common soldiers, which did not please them at all.

rank quickly and was therefore younger than many of the senior officers he had overtaken on his way to the top. However, none of the distrustful generals could deny that Kornilov *was* highly popular, and this meant that he had to be tolerated, since he could command the respect of those who would be doing the fighting to a far greater degree than perhaps any of the other White generals in the Don region.

To make matters worse, relations between the Whites and the Cossacks were tense. The Cossacks were far from united in their views on the Revolution, and many of them were tired of fighting, having seen active service since the outset of World War I. A strong body of opinion existed in favour of seeking some sort of accommodation with Lenin and his followers, but

White Russian infantry in training. The two nearest the camera have rolled blankets slung across their bodies. A few personal items could be carried this way if a knapsack was not available, and the blanket theoretically offered a little protection from a cavalryman's sword stroke.

this was counterbalanced by views from Cossacks living in South Russia, who were concerned that the Bolsheviks would remove long-standing Cossack privileges over land so that it could be given to the peasants. Cossacks from the north resented the wealth of those living in the south, and were unhappy at the way in which Kaledin had given the impression that the Cossacks were united behind him. Many Cossacks living in the northern Don region sided with the Military Revolutionary Council led by Philip Mironov, who wished to see the creation of an independent socialist Cossack republic. To complicate matters further for the Whites, they discovered that most of the inhabitants of the Don cities were in favour of the Bolsheviks. As a result, factory workers staged a number of strikes, which the Whites unthinkingly put down with considerable vigour. The repressive response only confirmed the views of the workers, who moved from striking to killing anyone suspected of being a supporter of the White

Officer cadets of the Volunteer Army. As the support of the Cossacks faded away, Kornilov's Volunteer Army was shown to be inadequate to the task of keeping the Reds out of the Don region. Fear of failure deterred many potential recruits, further crippling Kornilov's army.

movement. The White response was even more brutal, and within a matter of weeks the Don region, at least in its urban areas, was on the brink of civil war.

This had a decidedly negative effect on the morale of many of the younger Cossacks, who became increasingly concerned that the presence of the Whites would simply lead to fighting between the Red Army and the Whites in their homeland. Furthermore, having been badly led at the front between 1914 and 1918, most of the younger Cossacks had little desire to fight on behalf of the Whites, who seemed to contain a large number of those who had so badly handled the fighting against the Central Powers. The end result was a division in the Cossack community, followed by the desertion of Cossacks from the Whites. The

defence of the Don region increasingly fell upon Kornilov's Volunteer Army, bolstered by a few remaining Cossacks. Alexeev's efforts to find funding for the Volunteer Army had borne little fruit, and by late January 1918, the local population, including members of the middle classes who might have been thought likely to support an anti-Bolshevik movement, were showing signs of hostility to the Whites. One of the reasons for this lack of local support may have been a growing appreciation amongst the locals that the Volunteer Army was most unlikely to be able to resist an attack by the Bolshevik forces, and that it was better to hope that the failure to find support would drive the Volunteers away.

DEFEAT IN THE SOUTH
On 2 February 1918, the workers in the city of Taganrog rebelled against the Whites. The Red Army moved in six days later, prompting the rapid retreat of the few remaining Volunteers in the city, who headed

Anton Ivanovich Denikin (1872–1947)

Denikin was born in December 1872, the son of a retired Russian officer and a Polish mother. He grew up in reduced circumstances, with his father's pension being barely adequate to sustain the family. Denikin followed in his father's footsteps, attending military college in 1890, and graduating as an officer two years later. He saw active service in the Russo-Japanese War, and rose through the ranks until, by the outbreak of World War I, he was a major-general commanding the Kiev military district. He then took over as deputy chief of staff of the Russian Eighth Army and was then given command of the 4th Rifle Brigade. In 1916, he was posted to command VIII Corps, and led his troops in Romania during the Brusilov Offensive. After the revolution, he supported the attempted coup by Kornilov and was imprisoned as a result. He escaped, along with Kornilov, and joined the White forces, taking command after Kornilov's death. He resigned from his post as the Whites in South Russia teetered on the brink of defeat, and went into exile along with many other senior White officers.

He lived in France from 1926 and, unlike Wrangel, played no part in attempting to agitate against the Soviet regime, although this did not prevent Stalin from ordering a failed attempt to abduct him from Paris and return him to Moscow for trial. After France fell to the Germans in 1940, he went into exile in the

Denikin helped form the Volunteer Army and commanded it after Kornilov was killed in April 1918. He led the last White offensive towards Moscow in 1919.

French countryside and refused all efforts by the Nazis to use him for anti-Soviet propaganda broadcasts; appalled by the Nazis he in fact gave support to his local resistance movement. At the end of the war, concerned at the prospect that the Russians might demand his return, Denikin left France and took up residence in New York. He died in the United States in August 1947 while on holiday. He was buried in Detroit, but in 2005, President Vladimir Putin gave permission for his remains to be re-interred in Russia. They now lie in the Donskoy Monastery in Moscow.

towards the much more important town of Rostov. It seemed pointless to allow the Bolsheviks to destroy the Volunteer Army around Taganrog, leaving the heartland of the Whites in the south at the mercy of the enemy. Kornilov hoped that the withdrawal of forces back to Rostov would be accompanied by an agreement with the Cossacks to stand against the Reds. This was optimistic; on the same day, Kaledin, feeling that the situation was hopeless, submitted his resignation as Cossack leader. Having laid down his office, he shot himself. The Whites in South Russia were now on the point of disintegration, as the Reds

advanced on Rostov and took it on 23 February. The capital of the Don region, Novocherkassk, fell two days later. Lenin claimed that the Civil War was over, since only a small pocket of resistance remained. In fact, he was being decidedly optimistic, since, in defeat, the Whites finally began to coalesce into a recognizable opposition. As the Red Army advanced on Rostov, Kornilov led the Volunteer Army out of the Don with the aim of making the Kuban. The resultant retreat became known as the 'Ice March', and served as a rallying point for the Whites. The Volunteer Army marched deep into the steppes, pillaging from peasant communities on the way, and committing a variety of atrocities against the peasantry simply on suspicion that the locals were likely to be Bolshevik supporters. Eventually, the Ice March reached the vicinity of Ekaterinodar, the capital of the North Caucasian Soviet Republic, and were joined by the Kuban Army of over 3000 Cossacks. The Kuban Army had not planned to meet with the Volunteers, but almost literally bumped into them as they retreated from Ekaterinodar. Kornilov decided that with 7000 men

under his command, he should attack the city. This was a ridiculous proposition, since his force was outnumbered by more than two to one, yet he persisted, even after the failure of the first assault on 10 April. It appeared to his subordinates that Kornilov

In the immediate aftermath of World War I, weaponry was not a problem for either side. Small arms in particular were very easy to come by but even artillery, like this 4.5in howitzer, was relatively simple to obtain. As a result both sides were able to field effective conventional forces.

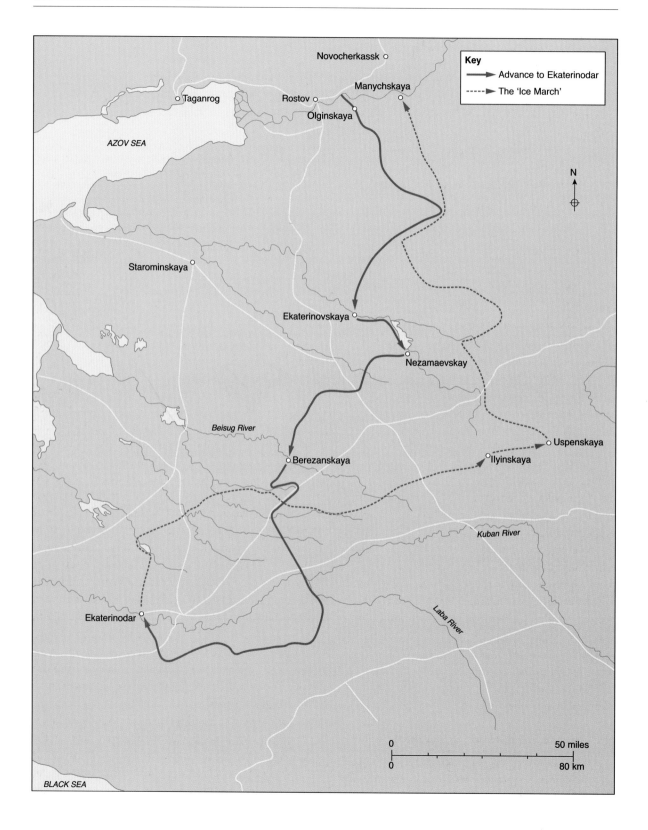

Novocherkassk

Taganrog

Manychskaya

Rostov

Olginskaya

AZOV SEA

Key
→ Advance to Ekaterinodar
⇢ The 'Ice March'

N

Starominskaya

Ekaterinovskaya

Nezamaevskay

Beisug River

Berezanskaya

Uspenskaya

Ilyinskaya

Kuban River

Ekaterinodar

Laba River

0   50 miles

0   80 km

BLACK SEA

was about to embark upon a course of action that would lead to the complete destruction of the Volunteer Army and the allied Kuban Army. Perhaps fortunately for the Whites, but distinctly unfortunately for Kornilov, the Red Army shelled his headquarters on the morning of 13 April, and he was killed by a direct hit on the building he was in.

DENIKIN TAKES OVER

Kornilov was replaced by General Anton Denikin, who ordered an immediate withdrawal. The Volunteers paused only to bury their fallen leader, and resumed the Ice March, heading back towards the Don. The Red Army chanced upon Kornilov's grave as they pursued the retreating Whites, and stopped for a macabre celebration in which they desecrated Kornilov's grave and defiled the corpse, a process that allowed the Volunteers to put enough distance between them and their pursuers to make it impossible for the Bolsheviks to catch them. Over the course of the 1120km (700-mile) retreat, the Volunteers suffered heavy losses to the cold, but this time found that their columns were joined by volunteers, many of whom had seen the full brutality of the 'Red Terror' and who decided that while the Whites were brutal, they were a preferable option to the Bolsheviks. When Denikin's force finally arrived on the Don, its ranks had been swelled considerably; more importantly, the rigours of the Ice March and the experience of battle against the Reds had fostered a fighting spirit that had been signally lacking when the Volunteer Army formed. Just as Lenin and the Bolsheviks thought that the war was over and the Whites in the south destroyed, the situation changed. Over the course of the next few months, the Bolsheviks managed to aid the Whites into turning into a truly credible force.

The reason for this lay in the way in which the Bolsheviks had behaved in the Don region. The Don

As the situation deteriorated and the local population turned against them, the Volunteer Army retreated southwards. Although Lenin thought that the Whites were finally beaten, in fact this period marked their emergence as a much more effective fighting force.

The British Webley-Fosbery revolver as used in Russia and elsewhere during World War I. Reloading a revolver was normally a fairly slow business. One solution was the fore-runner of the modern speedloader. This example refills all six chambers at once.

Soviet Republic behaved with incredible barbarity towards the local population. Food was requisitioned from the peasantry, priests were murdered and hundreds of hostages were taken and then shot. The area was inundated with Red Army troops as they withdrew from areas being occupied by the Germans under the provisions of Brest-Litovsk, with the end result that the locals in the Don were subjected to a wave of terror that drove them to open revolt. A series of Cossack risings followed, and within a month, there were at least 10,000 Cossack cavalrymen determined to fight the Bolsheviks under the leadership of the new Ataman, General Krasnov. In the first week of May 1918, Novocherkassk was taken, and within six weeks, Krasnov found himself at the head of an army 40,000 strong. Finding weapons and supplies for the army was easy, since the Germans were happy to provide rifles, ammunition and other military *matériel* in exchange for wheat.

However, Denikin seemed curiously eager to maintain the Whites' record of never missing the opportunity to miss an opportunity, and instead of allying with Krasnov's forces for a drive on Moscow, which might well have led to the collapse of the

Although a popular stereotype of the Cossack as a wild tribesman exists, most of those that served the Russian military wore uniform and served in trained cavalry units. Cossack units in White Russian service often included a mix of World War I veterans and new volunteers.

Bolsheviks, he led his army south to the Kuban steppe, intent on building up a large army of his own. In this regard, he was successful. As the Volunteer Army marched south, it attracted increasing numbers of recruits, many of whom were locals who had seen the brutality of the Bolsheviks at first hand and who were now implacably opposed to the Revolution. By August 1918, Denikin had a formidable army nearing 40,000 strong, which he used to capture Ekaterinodar, driving the Reds out of the Kuban region. By the winter, Denikin found himself in complete control of the White Army in the south, leading a battle-hardened force that controlled a substantial area of countryside. He was also undisputed leader of the Whites: Alexeev had died in October 1918, and this meant that the problem of divided command in the Volunteer Army was finally overcome. However, despite this unexpected upturn in the Whites' fortunes, there were

still fundamental problems that would, in the end, contribute to the final failure of their quest to remove Lenin from power. Denikin and his subordinates did not fully understand that the Whites were not just a military force, they needed to establish political structures that would enable them to govern the territory under their control. This lack of political awareness was to become an increasing problem in 1919, since relations between the Whites and the Cossacks deteriorated, not least because the Cossacks were most reluctant to move away from their homelands to fight the Bolsheviks. To make matters worse, the Cossacks continued to ignore the need to earn the support of the peasants; if anything, the behaviour of their troops in peasant villages did much to turn support away from the Whites as the long-suffering rural population struggled to decide which side was the lesser of two evils and decided that it was, perhaps, the Bolsheviks.

Despite this haemorrhaging of support thanks to the behaviour of the Cossacks, Denikin's forces began 1919 with a series of significant victories over the enemy. The Volunteer Army, now renamed the Armed

Forces of South Russia, began to enjoy some aid from the British, and was vastly increased in size compared to its parlous state just after the Revolution. In May and June 1919, the Whites in southern Russia met three Bolshevik armies and soundly defeated all of them, giving them control over a large area stretching from Kharkov in the Ukraine through to Tsaritsyn on the river Volga. At this point it seemed that the White forces under Admiral Kolchak in the east might be able to link up with Denikin, but the opportunity soon passed. Denikin abandoned ideas of forcing a link with them and instead ordered a march on Moscow. He planned an advance along three main axes: units under General Wrangel would advance along the Volga; General Mai-Maevsky would attack from Kharkov, taking Kiev as he went; while General Sidorin was to attack from the Whites' positions around Rostov.

By the end of August 1919, the offensive had enjoyed considerable success along its western flank, and a number of major towns and cities were under Denikin's control, including Odessa and Kiev. The Bolsheviks attempted a counter-offensive, but this was halted. The Whites took Kursk in September, followed by Voronezh and Chernigov in October, successes swiftly followed by the Bolsheviks losing Orel and lead elements of the Whites reaching Tula, the last major city before Moscow. Meanwhile, in the north, General Yudenich's Northwestern Army looked to be on the verge of seizing Petrograd. It seemed that the two major Russian cities might fall at any moment to the Whites; but the impression was illusory. Yudenich's forces were repulsed by Bolshevik units under Trotsky's command and by early November were back at their start line.

Denikin's forces, meanwhile, had reached their culminating point and were in no position to go on. Their supply lines were over extended, and the length of the front was such that forces were thinly spread. On 20 October, the Bolsheviks retook Orel, and Voronezh fell to Red Army forces under Marshal

In a civil war where the support of the general populace was of critical importance, the behaviour of Cossack troops towards the peasant population was counterproductive to the anti-Bolshevik cause.

Pyotr Nikolayevich Wrangel (1878–1928)

Wrangel was born into a Russian family of Germanic origins in 1878. After graduation from the Institute of Mining Engineering in 1901, he sought a commission in the Russian Army, joining the cavalry in 1902. He fought in the Russo-Japanese War of 1905, and participated in the punitive expedition in the Baltic during the following year. After staff college, he undertook a number of command appointments, culminating with the leadership of a cavalry corps during World War I.

After the Bolsheviks seized power, Wrangel went to the Crimea where he joined the Volunteer Army. He was given command of a cavalry division, before taking command of the Caucasus Army. His troops captured Tsaritsyn in summer 1919, and he became commander of the entire Armed Forces of South Russia in March 1920 after Denikin's resignation.

A series of defeats at the hands of the Red Army forced him to retreat to the Crimea, and he evacuated his army along with all the civilians who wished to accompany him. His status as the last White commander meant that he was perhaps the most prominent Russian exile of the 1920s. He died in 1928, with claims by some members of his family that a Soviet agent poisoned him.

Budenny. The central sector of the White front became increasingly disorganized as General Mai-Maevsky, already known for his excessive drinking, spent increasing amounts of time viewing the world through the bottom of a vodka glass instead of maintaining discipline amongst his troops, leading to his dismissal and replacement by Wrangel, who had the thankless task of restoring the fighting power of the forces in the centre. However, his arrival came too late to save the situation. The Bolsheviks exploited the failure of the Whites to win the support of the peasants, and, as the Red Army advanced, it created units of partisans drawn from the peasantry to attack the Whites in rear areas and disrupt what was turning into a retreat. In December, the Bolsheviks reoccupied the Ukraine, and the Whites were in danger of being overwhelmed. Finally, in January 1920, the Whites made their last stand around Rostov, but the position was hopeless. Falling back on the port of Novorossiysk, Allied ships helped to evacuate his forces into the Crimea, whereupon Denikin resigned his command in favour of General Wrangel in March. Wrangel set about rebuilding his forces. A capable leader, Wrangel won a few local victories against the Red Army to the extent that the French were moved sufficiently to recognize him as leader of South Russia. However, this moral support was not accompanied by any munitions or equipment, which left the Whites in an extremely difficult position.

There was one final hope for the southern Russian Whites, and this came thanks to the Russo-Polish War. While the Bolsheviks were distracted with the fighting against the Poles, Wrangel took the opportunity to launch a new offensive on 6 June 1920, breaking out of the Crimea. The Kuban was invaded in August, but Wrangel was forced to evacuate. The final blow came when news of the Russo-Polish armistice arrived. The Bolsheviks were now able to turn their full attention to dealing with the Whites in the south. On 28 October 1920, the final Bolshevik attack began, and the Whites were forced to fall back into southern Crimea. The position was now hopeless, and the Armed Forces of South Russia were evacuated to Constantinople, where it disbanded. The Bolsheviks were faced with the need to deal with a few remaining troubles in the east, and with a variety of separatist movements, but to all intents and purposes the Civil War was at an end.

THE WHITES UNDER KOLCHAK

The emergence of White forces in South Russia was soon followed by the creation of similar units in the east. This owed much to the Czech Legion's attempts

Neither side was sufficiently well organized to be able to deploy large, well coordinated forces in all areas. However, even a relatively small garrison, such as this Red Army force with its makeshift barricade, could hold a town against most opposition with a few well sited machine guns, freeing more men for operations elsewhere.

to return home, as described in the previous chapter. In the chaos caused by the fighting between the Czechs and the Bolsheviks, local leaders proclaimed Siberia to be an autonomous state. On 30 June 1918, a Siberian Government was created under the leadership of Pyotr Vologodsky. Vologodsky suppressed the local soviets and began the creation of an anti-communist army. This was not the only government, however, since the Social Revolutionaries established an administration of their own in Samara. The two administrations co-existed, but news of the Bolsheviks' retaking of Kazan in September 1918 led to a compromise agreement under which the Siberian Government and the Samaran 'Komuch' combined to form a supposedly 'national' government at Omsk, known as the Directory. The Directory was beset with political wrangling between moderate and conservative factions, but both sides agreed upon the appointment of the recently arrived Admiral Alexander Kolchak as war minister. Kolchak had been the commander of the

The activities of the Czech Legion in the east contributed to a separatist movement in Siberia and the formation of a government there. The Czechs' control of the Trans-Siberian railway was of great importance to this region, and their influence on local affairs was considerable.

Black Sea Fleet, and had gone to the Far East after the Revolution. He was on his way to join the Whites in South Russia when the invitation to be war minister for the Directory was issued. The conservative faction in Omsk launched a coup against the Social Revolutionary members of the Directory on 18 November and imprisoned them; they promptly offered Kolchak the position of Supreme Ruler and commander-in-chief of all Russia. Kolchak accepted, although the creation of the position was a source of some confusion, since the White forces in southern Russia were not minded to take orders from someone appointed without the slightest reference to them.

Kolchak's experience as a naval officer meant that he did not fully understand the dynamics of land warfare, and this created a number of problems when it came to planning campaigns. He was also an unskilled politician, and relations between Kolchak's forces and the Czechs began to deteriorate. To complicate matters further, the way in which Kolchak had assumed power had created dissent amongst the anti-Bolshevik forces; one month after his taking office, the local Social Revolutionaries staged a counter-coup attempt against him. This failed, but a number of the Social Revolutionaries abandoned him and changed sides. Kolchak determined that it was

Aleksandr Kolchak (1874–1920)

Kolchak was born in 1874 in St Petersburg, the son of a naval officer. From an early age it was clear that he was going to follow his father's career, and he attended naval college, graduating in 1894. He was posted to Vladivostok in 1895 and served there until 1899, when he was sent to Kronstadt. While there, he joined a Polar expedition in 1900 as the expedition's hydrologist. Kolchak returned to Kronstadt in 1902, but was to participate in three further Arctic expeditions.

Kolchak was sent to Port Arthur during the Russo-Japanese War, and commanded the destroyer *Serdityi*, which sank the Japanese cruiser *Takasago*. Wounded during the siege of the port, he was taken prisoner, but poor health meant that he was repatriated before the end of the conflict.

Kolchak was a leading figure in the rebuilding of the Russian Navy after the disaster of the Russo-Japanese War and by 1916 he had been promoted to the rank of vice-admiral, the youngest admiral in the Russian Navy. Kolchack was given command of the Black Sea Fleet, but although the fleet participated

with some success in operations against the Turks, it collapsed into revolutionary chaos in 1917. Kolchak was removed from command and sent to Japan as a military observer, and was still there when the October Revolution occurred. He was persuaded to join the White Russian forces, but while on his way to South Russia, he was persuaded to join the anti-revolutionary Directory Government at Omsk. Appointed to supreme command after the 18 November coup against the government, Kolchak instituted a military dictatorship and enjoyed some initial success against the Bolsheviks. However, it was not long before the tide turned, and the Whites in Siberia were forced into retreat. By the end of 1919, the Bolsheviks were on the verge of victory, and Kolchak left for Irkutsk. However, his poor relationship with the Czech Legion led to his being handed over to a new revolutionary government in Irkutsk in exchange for the Czechs being given uninterrupted passage to Vladivostok. Kolchak was arrested and the new government began interrogating him in preparation for trial; however, the process was circumvented when orders arrived from Moscow that Kolchak should be executed immediately. He was shot by firing squad in the early morning of 7 February 1920, and his body dumped in the river Ushakovka.

necessary to begin his military campaign against the Bolsheviks in a bid to distract from the political situation and, initially, these operations went well. The Siberian armies, commanded by the Czech General Gadja, took a number of towns and cities, and Kolchak hoped that it might be possible to link up with the White forces cooperating with the Allies at Archangel. To this end, Gadja pressed onwards, taking the town of Galzov by the end of April 1919. However, the Bolsheviks launched a counter-offensive under Mikhail Frunze, which swiftly drove the Whites back. The Bolshevik leadership decided that it would press on with the pursuit of Kolchak, and he was forced to retreat. This meant that Kolchak had to abandon plans to join with the other White forces in Russia. Driven back into Siberia, Kolchak dismissed the commander of his army, General Diederichs, when he suggested the evacuation of Omsk. On 14 November 1919, it proved necessary to follow Diederichs' advice anyway, and the city fell to the Bolsheviks. At this point, the Whites in the east had lost all confidence in Kolchak,

Jozef Pilsudski always believed that Poland's independence could only be won by force of arms. He formed what amounted to a private army, fighting on the side of the Central Powers. His forces later fought the Russians during the Russo-Polish War.

and he attempted to leave Siberia for Irkutsk, where his cabinet awaited him. They were overthrown by an Social Revolutionary-dominated group, and this prompted Kolchak to resign in favour of Denikin on 4 January 1920. Kolchak now attempted to reach Irkutsk, where he hoped to seek sanctuary with the British military mission. However, the Czechs, seeing the opportunity to gain safe passage from Siberia, handed him over to the administration in Irkutsk. The Irkutsk Government was replaced by a Bolshevik soviet on 21 January, and Kolchak was summarily executed by firing squad on orders from Moscow, without even a show trial. The Czech Legion finally left for home, and the resistance to the Bolsheviks in the east ended, leaving the Whites in the south to struggle on for a few more months until they, too,

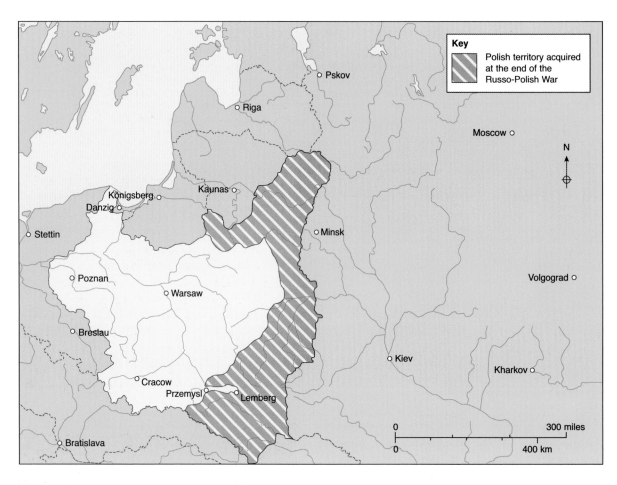

Key

Polish territory acquired at the end of the Russo-Polish War

were forced to abandon their efforts in October. The Bolsheviks successfully mopped up resistance from a variety of anti-communist groups and peasant councils, and by the end of 1921, the Civil War was over. Bolshevism had triumphed, and it could be said that at long last, the trauma of World War I was at an end for Russia.

THE RUSSO-POLISH WAR

The establishment of a Polish state in the aftermath of World War I represented the realization of a long-held set of aspirations of the Poles, particularly the social elite, which (in various forms) had been attempting to create an independent Poland for two centuries. In the eighteenth century, Poland had been partitioned between Russia, Germany and the Austro-Hungarian Empire, and the Poles had fought to re-establish their

The seeds of further trouble were sown when the Versailles conference gave Poland territory that had been part of Russia for a century. Russia was in chaos at the time and unable to do anything about the decision, but once the Civil War was over, the situation was very different.

nation ever since. World War I brought about their best opportunity for years. The principle laid out by the Allied powers that peoples should be granted self-determination meant that it was almost inevitable that the defeat of Germany and Austria-Hungary would lead to the establishment of a new Poland. The situation, however, was complicated by the fact that the Poles desired territory that had been part of Russia for over 100 years by the time that the Versailles peace settlement was signed. The utter confusion that existed after the Bolshevik Revolution meant that it was impossible to determine the border between

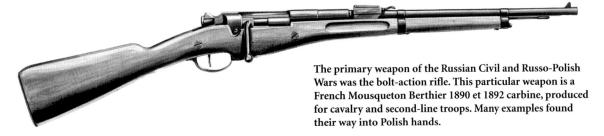

The primary weapon of the Russian Civil and Russo-Polish Wars was the bolt-action rifle. This particular weapon is a French Mousqueton Berthier 1890 et 1892 carbine, produced for cavalry and second-line troops. Many examples found their way into Polish hands.

Poland and Russia at the peace conference. This in turn meant that the Poles' perceived a window of opportunity that could be exploited to their advantage, both to regain historic Polish lands and ensure that the reformed Polish state enjoyed a level of security that it had not enjoyed in the eighteenth century.

Within the Polish political leadership there were two competing views as to what should be done with the eastern border region. The first point of view, articulated by Roman Dmowski, the leader of the National Democratic Party and founder of the Polish National Committee that had been established in Paris as a means of advocating Polish national self-determination, as well as chief Polish delegate to Versailles, held that Poland should include all the land that had been Polish territory in 1772, regardless of the nationality of those living in those areas in 1919. This perspective was difficult to argue in an atmosphere where the principle of self-determination drove most considerations regarding the redrawing of the map of Europe, but Dmowski was a forceful advocate of the case. However, he did not represent all of Polish opinion.

In contrast to Dmowski, the Polish head of state Jozef Pilsudski felt that it was only appropriate for the non-Polish nationalities living in the Russo-Polish border region to have independent states of their own. He also argued that it was the duty of Poland, as the strongest of the newly created states, to ensure that

Roman Dmowski made a strong argument at Versailles that Poland should be given all the land she had traditionally held (as defined by being Polish territory in 1772) rather than being allocated territory according to whether the population that lived there were Poles or not.

there was sufficient regional security to guarantee that all the nations in the area remained free, and would not succumb to attack by either a resurgent post-revolutionary Russia or a stronger Germany seeking to re-impose itself upon central and eastern Europe.

Pilsudski therefore proposed the creation of a Polish-led federation, which would provide the member nations with much greater security. The peace settlement had left East Prussia separate from the rest of Germany, linked only by the soon-to-be-infamous 'Polish Corridor', vulnerable to blockage by the government in Warsaw at any time. The Poles were well aware that a recovered Germany might regard this as an unacceptable situation and seek to reverse it by

Military operations in Poland made considerable use of armoured cars and motorized transport. The Red Army in particular developed a number of motorized artillery pieces such as the one shown here.

retaking the land removed from it by a peace treaty that was already being referred to as a 'diktat' by the Germans, unjust and unreasonably imposed upon the defeated nation.

By contrast, Lenin and the Bolshevik leadership saw Poland as a part of revolutionary theory. Poland represented the land over which the Revolution must cross if it was to be exported. If, for any reason, this proved impossible, it imperilled the Revolution as a whole, since communism would be trapped within the borders of a single nation, vulnerable to attack by capitalist, bourgeois nations anxious to crush Marxism at the earliest possible opportunity. However, the Bolshevik position was not as clear cut as it might seem, since the leadership had given clear statements that it supported Polish independence. However, while supporting the nation's freedom from external rule, Lenin and his fellow communists were simultaneously supporting Polish communists who were anxious to bring about the collapse of the newly formed nation. Pilsudski and many others thought that the Bolsheviks felt that the independence of Poland should be limited, preferring to see the country as part of a wider communist federation that would be dominated by Moscow. The Poles were particularly suspicious of Lenin's intentions in the light of the manner in which the supposedly independent Ukrainian Republic, declared in January 1919, seemed to be completely in thrall to the dictates of the government in Moscow. In addition to this mistrust, the fact that Poland and Russia were historic opponents, with the enmity stretching back to the early years of the seventeenth century, was likely to be a source of tension between the two powers. Thus, by early 1919, the grounds for there being considerable tension between the Poles and Russians were fairly extensive. It would not be long before the tension spilled over into all-out war.

THE SPARK FOR WAR

As the German Army withdrew its positions in Eastern and Central Europe as mandated by the terms of the peace treaty, the Poles moved forces into the borderlands. This was accompanied by the formation of a number of Polish self-defence units in areas such as Western Belarus and Lithuania, as ethnic Poles sought to create organizations through which they might support the move eastwards by Polish regular forces and defend their communities against the possibility of the Bolsheviks taking over. From early January 1919, there were a series of skirmishes between the Polish groups and bands of pro-Bolshevik troops, and from February the situation began to resemble the preparations for war.

The Poles were fortunate in that they had many men who were trained soldiers who could be transformed into an established regular army, but there were some major problems that needed to be addressed. The first was that the Polish Army was made up of a variety of units from several different armies, and there was no real command structure. The cohesion of the Polish Army, at least initially, was based around loyalty to the new nation and to Pilsudski himself. The Polish parliament was faced with the need to bring in legislation to regularize the new army, a task made imperative when Polish units advancing eastwards came into contact with Bolsheviks at Mosty on 14 February. Although the Russian troops withdrew, the two sides took up positions so that a nascent front line was in place. On 15 and 16 February 1919, the Poles and the Bolsheviks experienced the first clash of what was to develop into a fully fledged war around the Belarussian towns of Biazroza and Manievwicze. Realizing that the need to establish the Polish Army on a proper footing was now vital, Polish parliamentarians set about creating the legal framework for the new force, and managed to complete the process with the Army Law of 26 February 1919.

At this point, the Poles had some 110,000 men under arms. The nucleus of the new army came from units that had been raised by the Germans in 1917 as they sought more manpower, and which had come under Pilsudski's control in November 1918 with the cessation of hostilities. There were only 9000 men in

Mikhail Frunze (1885–1925)

Frunze was born in Bishkek, the son of a Romanian peasant (originally from Bessarabia). He was an able child, and gained a place at the Polytechnic Institute at St Petersburg. While a student, he joined the Social Democratic Party and became a supporter of the Bolshevik faction. His political activities attracted the attention of the authorities, and in November 1904 he was arrested after a demonstration and expelled from St Petersburg. This did not deter him, and in the 1905 Revolution, he led striking textile workers at Shuya and Ivanovo. He was arrested and tried for his involvement in the uprising and sentenced to death. The sentence was commuted to life imprisonment with hard labour, and he was sent to Siberia to serve his sentence. After ten years, Frunze managed to escape to an area where the Tsarist regime had little control, and became the editor of a Bolshevik newspaper. During the February Revolution in 1917, Frunze led the Minsk militia, and was then elected president of the Byelorussian Soviet. He moved on to Moscow, and commanded a workers' militia unit during the October Revolution that brought the Bolsheviks to power.

Frunze was appointed military commissar of Voznesensk Province, and quickly became embroiled in the Civil War. Following his defeat of Admiral Kolchak, he was given command of the entire Eastern Front, and oversaw the final defeat of the Whites in this area. He retook the Crimea in 1920, ending the war in the south, and destroyed the anarchist movement in Ukraine when it refused to amalgamate with the Red Army.

Frunze's success led to his election to the Central Committee of the Bolshevik Party, and in January 1925 he was appointed chairman of the revolutionary military council. Frunze's time in prison had not aided his health, and he suffered from a weak heart and stomach ulcers. His doctors debated whether or not they should operate on his ulcers, but concluded that this would be too dangerous, since they feared that their patient would not survive the anaesthetic. They were overruled by the Central Committee, and the operation went ahead. Just as the doctors had suspected, the anaesthetic was too much for him, and he died on the operating table on 31 October 1925.

Frunze was buried in the Kremlin wall, and he was recognized with the renaming of his birthplace in his honour (it reverted to its original name in 1991), and the most prominent military academy in Russia bears his name to this day.

the ex-German forces, but their numbers received a considerable boost when many of the former members of the Austro-Hungarian Polish Legion (which had been commanded by Pilsudski until its disbandment in 1917) joined the services. Within a matter of months, the Polish Army had increased in strength and was in a position to wage war with the Bolsheviks on a reasonably equal footing. By the end of 1919, a clear front line had developed between the Russians and the Poles, and a series of border skirmishes developed into full-scale warfare as the Poles moved ever further eastwards, faced by an enemy which was hard pressed, dealing not only with the Polish attack but with the efforts of the White Russian forces in north, south and eastern Russia.

The turning point in the Russo-Polish conflict came when Pilsudski's troops began Operation Kiev in April 1920. The Poles hoped that an invasion of Ukraine would allow the creation of an independent Ukrainian state, which would then become part of the

> 'Had the Battle of Warsaw ended in the Bolshevik victory it would have become a turning point in the history of Europe, and it is beyond any doubt that with the fall of Warsaw Central Europe would have opened for communist propaganda and a Soviet invasion.'
>
> Lord Edgar Vincent D'Abernon,
> head of the British Military Mission in Poland

planned anti-Soviet federation. Early clashes with the Red Army went the way of the Poles and by 7 May 1920 a combined force of Poles and an anti-communist Ukrainian army had taken Kiev. The Poles began to plan for the next phase of the operation, but were soon met by a fierce counterattack by the Red Army. Polish positions near Ulla were attacked on 15 May by the Russian Fifteenth Army, while the neighbouring Russian Sixteenth Army crossed the

Armoured trains were deployed by both sides in the Russo-Polish War as a means of protecting their rail network and bringing firepower to bear quickly when and where it was needed. This example was operated by the Red Army.

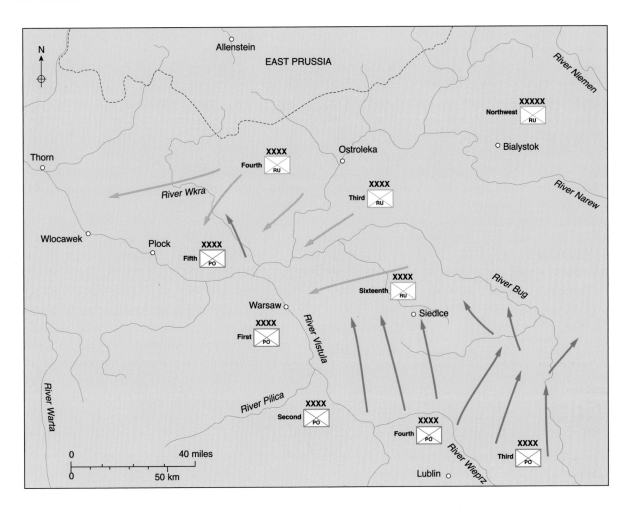

Once the thin Polish defensive line was broken, a desperate scramble to halt the Bolshevik advance ensued culminating in the Battle of Warsaw. The 'miracle of the Vistula' saw the Polish forces manage to hold up the Russian advance and then split their armies, forcing them to withdraw.

Berezina River. Although the Poles were able to throw the attack back, they had to abandon their plans for a further advance. To the north, the Russian counterattack had defeated the Polish First Army, which was forced to retreat. Although the Poles launched a counterattack of their own, they were unable to do anything more than slow down the Russian advance. By the end of May, after fierce fighting, the front had stabilized near the river Auta. Repeated attacks by General Budenny's Cossack cavalry broke the Polish-Ukrainian front on 5 June,

and Russian cavalry units poured into the Polish rear areas, causing havoc. The Poles were forced into full retreat, and Kiev had to be evacuated to prevent the forces there from being completely surrounded by the Russians. The Poles stabilized their position in June and attempted a series of counterattacks of their own during the rest of the month and in July, but none of them were successful. However, it appeared that the Bolsheviks had at least been stopped – an optimistic assessment as it transpired.

THE MIRACLE OF THE VISTULA

The Russian Northwest Front, under the command of General Mikhail Tukhachevski, launched an offensive on 4 July 1920, attacking along the line Smolensk–Brest-Litovsk. Although the Poles put up a fierce resistance, they were outnumbered four to one and the Russian numerical advantage told. Within three days, the Poles were in full retreat along the entire front and, by the middle of the month, they had been forced back across the Niemen River. The Russians followed, and it was not long before the retreat resumed once more, with the Russian armies moving at a rate of approximately 32km (20 miles) a day. When the Poles were driven out of Grodno in Belarus, Tukhachevski gave orders that Warsaw was to be seized by 12 August. It seemed that this was perfectly possible when, on 1 August, Brest-Litovsk fell into Russian hands and the last river barriers before the river Vistula and the Polish capital were crossed. By the following day, Russian forces were only 97km (60 miles) away from Warsaw, and it seemed likely that the

city would fall to the Russians within a matter of days, a viewpoint given further credibility when Russian Cossack units crossed the Vistula on 10 August, with the aim of driving into Warsaw from the west. Polish resistance meant that Tukhachevski had to modify his planned date for the capture of the city by 24 hours, but was confident of success. However, the initial Russian attack on 13 August 1920 failed. Tukhachevski was unmoved, confident that his superiority in numbers would tell in the end, but his confidence was misplaced.

On 14 August, the Polish Fifth Army, under the command of General Vladislav Sikorski, launched an attack from around the Modlin fortress area. Bitter fighting ensued for a day, but at the end of the battle, the Russians had been halted. Furthermore, they had lost momentum to the point where the Poles were able to seize the initiative and turn the tables decisively upon their opponents. Sikorski drove his army on, and the exhausted Russians were forced to fall back. On 16 August, Pilsudski launched a counter-offensive of his

Soldiers of the Red Army on campaign in Poland. During the drive on Warsaw the Reds became over extended and outran their supplies. Their weariness and disorganization allowed the Polish Army to push the Russians back a considerable distance before a ceasefire was agreed.

Russian troops, the officers with swords drawn, headed towards the Polish front. The Red Army was forced to fight on several fronts, with major White Russian field forces still in being as well as unrest and insurrection in supposedly cleared territory.

own, and the Poles were able to exploit a gap between the Russian fronts. The Polish advance continued, wrapping up the flanks of the Russian forces, so that, by 18 August, the majority of Tukhachevski's rear areas were on the brink of encirclement. When Tukhachevski realized what was happening, he gave orders for a withdrawal, but his instructions appear not to have reached many units, which were routed during the course of the next two days. The Russian forces broke down into chaos, and by the end of the month, the prospect of Warsaw falling into Russia hands had passed. The so-called 'miracle of the Vistula' raised Polish morale, as did the failure of the

Russians to take Lvov. Budenny's army broke off the siege on 31 August 1920, but as he withdrew, his forces were engaged by Polish cavalry in what was possibly the last great cavalry engagement on European soil.

The Polish advance continued, with the Russians suffering further defeats at the Battle of the Niemen River between 15 and 25 September. By the middle of October, the Poles had reached the line Tarnopol–Dubno–Minsk–Drisa, but they were exhausted. The Bolsheviks were desperate to end the war, to allow them to finish dealing with the threat presented by the Whites, and the Poles could go no further. In addition, the Poles were facing considerable pressure from other nations to bring the war to an end, so the Russian offer of peace was accepted, with a ceasefire coming into effect on 18 October 1920. The war was brought to a formal conclusion with the Treaty of Riga on 18 March 1921.

FURTHER READING

Brusilov, A., *A Soldier's Notebook* (Wesport, Greenwood Press, 1930)

Bullock, D., *The Russian Civil War 1918–21* (Oxford, Osprey Publishing Ltd, 2008)

Davies, N., *White Eagle, Red Star: The Polish-Soviet War, 1919–20* (London, Pimlico Books, 2003)

Dobson, C. and J. Miller, *The Day We Almost Bombed Moscow* (London, Hodder & Stoughton, 1986)

Dowling, T., *The Brusilov Offensive* (Bloomington, Indiana University Press, 2008)

Figes, O., *A People's Tragedy: the Russian Revolution 1891–1924* (London, Pimlico Books, 1997)

Hasek, J., *The Good Soldier Svejk* (New York, Penguin Modern Classics, 1985)

Herwig, H., *The First World War: Germany and Austria-Hungary* (London, Edward Arnold, 1997)

Jackson, R., *Battle of the Baltic* (Barnsley, Pen and Sword, 2007)

Kinvig, C., *Churchill's Crusade: the British Invasion of Russia 1918–1920* (London, Hambledon Continuum, 2006)

Lincoln, W.B., *Passage Through Armageddon: the Russians in War and Revolution* (New York, Simon and Schuster, 1986)

Moore, J.R., H.H. Mead and L.E. Jahns, *The History of the American Expedition Fighting the Bolsheviks* (Nashville, The Battery Press, 2003)

Rothenberg, G., *The Army of Francis Joseph* (West Lafayette, Purdue University Press, 1999)

Showalter, D., 'The Eastern Front and German Military Planning, 1871–1914: Some Observations', *Eastern European Quarterly* 15:2 (June 1981)
—— *Tannenberg: Clash of Empires* (Dulles, Potomac Books, 2003)

Stone, N., *The Eastern Front, 1914–1917* (London, Penguin Books, 1975)

Strachan, H., *The First World War, vol. 1, To Arms* (Oxford, Oxford University Press, 2001)

Swain, G., *The Origins of the Russian Civil War* (London, Longman, 1995)
—— *Russia's Civil War* (Stroud, Tempus, 2000)

Tunstall, G.A., *Planning for War against Russia and Serbia* (New York, Columbia University Press, 1993).

Zamoyski, A., *Warsaw 1920: Lenin's Failed Conquest of Europe* (London, HarperPress, 2008)

INDEX

PICTURE CREDITS